Heartfelt Moments in
Australian Rules Football

HEARTFELT MOMENTS IN AUSTRALIAN RULES FOOTBALL

ROSS FITZGERALD, PHILLIPA POWER, BRIAN DIXON, KEN SPILLMAN, DICK WHITAKER, BARRY DICKINS, PETER LYONS, JAMES GILCHRIST, FRANK DIMATTINA, PHIL TAGELL, MATT ZURBO, JEFF KENNETT, BILL HAY, SUSAN ALBERTI, CHRIS BOWEN, CARDINAL GEORGE PELL, LES EVERETT, PAUL SANTAMARIA, JOHN BIRT, PEGGY O'NEAL, ROBERT PASCOE, RICHARD ALLSOP, AMANDA VANSTONE, CHRIS KENNY, GABRIELLE TRAINOR, SALLY MURPHY, MICHAEL GORDON, JULIE BISHOP, CHRIS GRIFFITH, GERALDINE DOOGUE, GERARD HENDERSON, JOHN ELLIOTT, JOSH FRYDENBERG, ANTHONY CAPPELLO, ANDREW IRELAND, MICHAEL O'LOUGHLIN, WEATHERMAN DICK

EDITED BY ROSS FITZGERALD

connorcourt
PUBLISHING

Published in 2016 by Connor Court Publishing Pty Ltd

Copyright © Ross Fitzgerald

All rights reserved. No part of this book may be reproduced or transmitted in any form or by any means, electronic or mechanical, including photocopying, recording or by any information storage and retrieval system, without prior permission in writing from the publisher.

CONNOR COURT PUBLISHING PTY LTD
PO BOX 7257
REDLAND BAY, QLD, 4165
sales@connorcourt.com
www.connorcourt.com

ISBN: 978-1-925138-94-8

Front cover photos:
Darren Millane, Collingwood, photo courtesy of News Ltd. Gary Ablett makes sure Robert DiPierdomenico pays the price in the 1989 Grand Final. The other Hawk is Andy Collins, picture Sebastian Costanzo, courtesy of *The Age*. Simon Black the first player in AFL/VFL history to win a Brownlow Medal, a Norm Smith Medal, a Premiership Medal and play 300 games, photo: News Limited, used with permission. Adam Goodes, Sydney, courtesy News Ltd.

Cover design by Ian James.

Printed in Australia

For Dick ("The Weatherman") Whitaker

Table of Contents

1. Introduction	*Ross Fitzgerald*	*9*
2. The Death and Life of Darren Millane	*Ross Fitzgerald*	*13*
3. Blood Lines	*Phillipa Power*	*19*
4. Playing For Melbourne	*Brian Dixon*	*25*
5. Falling to Earth	*Ken Spillman*	*31*
6. Black Magic	*Dick Whitaker*	*37*
7. Fitzroy Football Club 1954	*Barry Dickins*	*45*
8. Yabby's Dilemma	*Peter Lyons*	*51*
9. Rose to Walsh – on Football and Fatherhood	*James Gilchrist*	*57*
10. Three Brownlow Votes: First Game	*Frank DiMattina*	*63*
11. The Kennedy Curse	*Phil Tagell*	*69*
12. Some Players Are Tough	*Matt Zurbo*	*73*
13. Teams Deliver Individuals Don't	*Jeff Kennett*	*77*
14. Up On Windy Hill	*Bill Hay*	*85*
15. Love of the Dogs	*Susan Alberti*	*93*
16. When the Giants Shook Down the Thunder From the Sky	*Chris Bowen*	*97*
17. Aussie Rules	*George Pell*	*101*
18. Fitzroy's last game 1996	*Les Everett*	*109*
19. The 1970 Grand Final	*Paul Santamaria*	*115*
20. An extraordinary era of Grand finals and Premierships	*John Birt*	*123*
21. 9 games	*Peggy O'Neal*	*131*
22. Robbie Flower	*Robert Pascoe*	*137*
23. Heartfelt Hawthorn moments	*Richard Allsop*	*141*

24. The Port and the Passion	*Amanda Vanstone*	*147*
25. Born to be Rivals	*Chris Kenny*	*153*
26. A Thousand Giant Reasons	*Gabrielle Trainor*	*163*
27. Freo Dockers: Purple, Pain and Possibilities	*Sally Murphy*	*169*
28. Heartfelt Moments	*Michael Gordon*	*175*
29. Home and Away – Australian Football Rules!	*Julie Bishop*	*181*
30. The Brisbane Three-Peat	*Chris Griffith*	*191*
31. The End of the Affair? Reflections on a Grand Final	*Geraldine Doogue*	*197*
32. John Coleman and the Ghosts of Princes Park	*Gerard Henderson*	*205*
33. We Are the Navy Blues	*John Elliott*	*213*
34. Carlton: Much More Than a Football Club	*Josh Frydenberg*	*225*
35. "Give me a child until he is 7" – the 1989 Grand Final: Geelong vs Hawthorn	*Anthony Cappello*	*231*
36. The Drawn VFL Grand Final of 1977	*Andrew Ireland*	*235*
37. An Inspirational Journey with No. 37	*Michael O'Loughlin*	*243*
Epilogue: The Highs and Lows of Aussie Rules Football Weather	*Weatherman Dick*	*247*

1

Introduction

As these thirty seven contributions about the most heartfelt moments in VFL/AFL demonstrate, Aussie Rules football cuts across all divides.

Hence this book of original essays includes contributions by and about football players, supporters and administrators who are vastly different in religion, class, income, ethnicity, gender, race and sexual preference.

The contributors within range from Christians such as Cardinal George Pell, Geraldine Doogue, and John Birt to atheists like myself, Dick Whitaker and Barry Dickins.

Indeed unbelievers and clerics of all persuasions often highlight Aussie Rules.

Hence the retired Roman Catholic Archbishop of Perth, Barry Hickey, regularly told this story:

> An AFL umpire died and found himself at the Pearly Gates. When he related what he had done on Earth, the Saint replied: 'Well we can skip Purgatory, you've done enough as a football umpire, but is there anything weighing on your conscience that you need to admit before we consider letting you in?' And the umpire said: 'There was this match, Collingwood versus St Kilda, Magpies ahead by three points, and the St Kilda full-forward went for a mark right in front of goal. The sun was in my eyes and I couldn't be sure whether he made it or not, but I gave him the mark and he scored and St Kilda won.' 'Think nothing of it, my son, come right in'. 'Oh thank you, thank you Saint Peter' said the umpire. 'I'm not Saint Peter' replied the saint, 'I'm Saint Kilda'.

As far as I know, it was the only joke Archbishop Hickey ever told! Talking of the Mighty Magpies, my late father Bill ("Long Tom")

Fitzgerald who played over 100 games for Collingwood Seconds, but never for the firsts, would regularly recount on my birthday, Christmas Day, a story about the Richmond great, Jack Dyer. Dad explained that Dyer, who was commonly known as "Captain Blood", often said: "Whenever I have a nightmare it's never in colour – it's always black and white. Collingwood!"

On a more earthy note, one of my favourite footballing tales concerns a lad from the country who was to play his first senior game. When the coach took him aside and said, "I might have to pull you off at three quarter time", the lad responded, "Golly, where I come from we usually are only given oranges!"

Contributors to this collection of fine writing about heartfelt moments in Aussie Rules football also include current and former federal parliamentarians from both sides of the political divide – including Labor's shadow treasurer Chris Bowen; Liberal Minister for resources, energy and northern Australia, Josh Frydenberg; Liberal Foreign Minister Julie Bishop; ex Liberal federal minister Amanda Vanstone and ex Victorian premier, Jeff Kennett. Contributors also hail from many Australian states and territories and range in age from the young to the very old.

Following Collingwood for a lifetime has taught me that Aussie Rules football is a metaphor for life and that, to take one crucial example, the game is never lost until it's lost.

Being, and remaining, a dyed in the wool barracker is a sign and test of character, just as switching teams seems to me a symbol of a loss of loyalty, faith and heart.

Changing clubs for which to barrack merely because of a team's consistently poor performance is something that no true supporter would ever entertain – not even for a second.

Indeed it is a sign of true fandom never to let any number of losses interfere with or dilute a passionate and unrelenting support for a person's chosen (or in my case inherited) team or club.

The fact is that because it is Aussie Rules football we are dealing with in this book, a number of contributors explore, directly or indirectly, what it means to be an Australian and/or what are key Australian characteristics and personally traits. Also a number of contributors uncover how, over the decades, our great game has developed, often for the good, but sometimes not, in terms of its treatment of indigenous players and its dealings with women.

Being a lifelong supporter of a club, any club (in my case of the Mighty Magpies) involves a lot of downs and ups.

At the very least, to be a true supporter means never giving up or relinquishing one's team. Indeed it means even more than that.

Ultimately it is the downs that enable supporters to show their true colours and the depth of their personal attachment and commitment to each club. Thus, as Roger Kahn wrote, in his case about The Brooklyn Dodgers: "You may glory in a team triumphant, but you fall in love with a team in defeat."

How true is that?

Ross Fitzgerald

Emeritus Professor of History and Politics at Griffith University, Ross Fitzgerald AM has published 38 books, spanning fiction and non-fiction. These include his influential memoir *My Name is Ross: An Alcoholic's Journey*, published by NewSouth Books, Sydney – which is available as an e-Book and a Talking Book with Vision Australia.

Professor Fitzgerald is also author of five Grafton Everest adventures, most recently *Going Out Backwards*, co-authored with Ian McFadyen and published by Hybrid in Melbourne.

A regular columnist for 'The Weekend Australian', Professor Fitzgerald writes widely on Australian Rules football. As well as authoring *The Footy Club* in 1996, Professor Fitzgerald was contributing editor, with his Western Australian friend Ken Spillman who is also a contributor to this book, of two collections of fine writings about Aussie Rules – *The Greatest Game*, published in 1988 and *Australia's Game*, published in 2013.

A life-long Collingwood supporter, Professor Ross Fitzgerald now lives in Redfern in Sydney with his wife Lyndal Moor Fitzgerald.

Darren Millane, Collingwood
Photo courtesy of News Ltd.

2

The Death and Life of Darren Millane

Ross Fitzgerald

One of my favourite Collingwood Football Club players of all time is the deeply talented wearer of the 42 guernsey, Darren Millane.

A year and a day after starring in Collingwood's 1990 Grand Final triumph – the Magpies first premiership in 32 years and our 14th overall – Millane, a strongly built, daringly courageous wingman who played 147 games for Collingwood, was killed in a car crash.

Early in the morning on 7 October 1991, driving on Queens Road, near Albert Park Lake on his way to his home in the working-class southeast Melbourne suburb of Noble Park, Millane clipped a semi-trailer and rolled his car. Aged only 26, he was killed instantly. The autopsy revealed Millane's blood alcohol content was 0.322 – almost six-and-a-half times the then Victorian legal driving limit of 0.05.

Later that day he had planned to join the nineteen other members of the 1990 premiership side. Instead of attending the reunion, Collingwood players, officials and scores of faithful fans gathered at the Magpies iconic home ground, Victoria Park, to mourn Millane's tragic and untimely death.

It was only confirmed at the morgue that the body was indeed Millane when, accompanied by Collingwood's Football Manager Graeme ("Gubby") Allan, the then Collingwood president Allan McAlister asked the attendant to briefly lift the sheet. When they observed a magpie tattoo on Darren's hip, they both knew for certain that it was him. Fittingly, to commemorate the 1990 premiership victory, Millane had been tattooed with Collingwood's much-loved symbol, the Australian magpie.

Over 5000 people attended Millane's funeral, which was held at the Dandenong Town Hall. An even larger crowd outside listened to the service on a loudspeaker. In a funeral featuring the John Lennon song, 'Working Class Hero', Millane's No 42 guernsey was laid on the coffin, while Collingwood's 1990 premiership flag hung in the background at half-mast. In the Melbourne 'Age', Peter McFarline wrote that Millane's death "affected part of this nation more acutely than any since (Prime Minister) Harold Holt drowned in 1967."

Born on 9 August 1965 and nicknamed "Pants", Millane had played through the 1990 finals series with a broken thumb. This painful injury had occurred in round 21 – in Collingwood's massive win against Fitzroy at Victoria Park.

Under the guidance of coach Leigh Matthews – an ex Hawthorn premiership star – Millane was only able to continue to play during the 1990 finals campaign with the liberal aid of painkillers, often by injection.

In Collingwood's 48-point Grand Final victory against Essendon, in front of a crowd of 98,994, Millane had 28 possessions and was one of our finest performers; perhaps second only to captain Tony Shaw who won the Norm Smith medal for best on ground in the Grand Final. As the siren sounded at 5:11 pm on 6 October 1990 Millane had hold of the ball – which, arms raised in triumph, he tossed into the air. He then tucked the Sherrin under his arm and thereafter refused to relinquish it.

In this premiership drought-breaking year for the Magpies, Millane was at his peak. Indeed many experts thought that he had the potential to captain Collingwood. One of the Mighty Woodsmen's favourite sons, in 1990 Millane won the AFL Players Association MVP Award, now known as the Leigh Matthews Trophy; was selected in the AFL Team of the Year; and came second to captain Tony Shaw in Collingwood's best and fairest. And, to cap off the 1990 premiership season, Millane won the J.F. ("Jock") McHale Trophy for Collingwood's most courageous player.

Although 1991 was a disappointing year for himself and for the club, Millane – who was troubled throughout the season with a severe thigh injury – still averaged 22 touches in his final year as a player.

But it was his skillful and courageous performance during the 1990 finals campaign, and also for his sadly premature death, for which Millane is now most recognized and best remembered.

As a 19 year old with an infectious grin, Millane (who had previously starred for Dandenong in the Victorian Football Association) began playing for Collingwood firsts half way through the 1984 season. Even though Millane only played eight games that year, he won the club's best first-year player award. His footballing abilities further blossomed under the guidance of Magpie great Bob Rose who in 1985 had briefly returned to Victoria Park for a second stint as coach of Collingwood. Millane's form and fitness improved when early into the 1986 season Rose was replaced by recently recruited assistant coach, and strict disciplinarian, Leigh Matthews. In 1987, aged 22, Millane won Collingwood's best and fairest award – the highly prestigious Copeland Trophy.

Millane gained his nickname "PANTS", because he had appeared at his first training session at Victoria Park in 1984 wearing brightly coloured check pants. And also because he often attended Collingwood functions wearing white trousers with black noughts and crosses that his mother Denise had made. At the same time, Millane didn't deny that he was also a well-known "pants man" – in the sense of being somewhat of a sexual athlete who had considerable pulling power with young women.

During his footballing career with the Mighty Magpies, Millane was actually suspended only four times – including being rubbed out for three matches for striking Steve Da Rui of Carlton in round 2 of the 1990 season. Thankfully, "Pants" was cleared of another striking charge just before the 1990 finals.

As well as being extremely tough as a player, Millane was no stranger to trouble with the law. In 1989 he appeared in court for his part in a brawl in November 1988 involving his father, Robert ('Bob') Millane and a barman at the Boundary Hotel in the Melbourne suburb of East Bentleigh. This fracas resulted in a court appearance for both father and son. A year later, Millane was convicted on another charge of intentionally causing injury.

In fact, "Pants" stayed out of trouble until the end of the 1991 season in which he and the Magpies had performed poorly, not even making what was then the final six.

But at the time of his death Millane and his close friend and teammate Denis Banks were facing charges involving taking control of a Brisbane-bound McCafferty's bus early in the morning of 1st September 1991. This occurred while they were severely intoxicated the morning after the Magpies last game for the season – at Kardinia Park, the home ground of Geelong, who had walloped Collingwood conclusively. Some time after 3am Millane and Banks had stumbled out of their regular Melbourne haunt, The Tunnel nightclub on Little Bourke Street, and headed for Spencer Street train and country bus station. Failing to find a taxi, the inebriated pair jumped into the front seat of an interstate bus bound for Brisbane.

Not surprisingly, the metropolitan media in particular had a field day. The Melbourne 'Herald-Sun' ran a huge headline "Bus Hijack!" Blazoned on the papers' advertising banner was the phrase PIES STEAL BUS.

Banks (who had just played his last game for Collingwood and who had climbed into the drivers seat first) and Millane – whose favourite drink was ouzo and coke and who insisted that they were both simply skylarking – were charged with a serious offence, in Millane's case the theft of a bus. Sadly, the bus incident had a devastating effect on Darren, especially as he felt that it might well have destroyed his chances of succeeding Tony Shaw as captain of the Magpies.

The trial was due to take place on 8 November 1991 – a month after Darren Millane's premature and tragic death. As it happened, the grieving Banks was let off with a fine.

Collingwood's fitness guru Ray Giles, who was Millane's close friend, mentor, and trainer who often oversaw the strapping of his injuries, rightly remarked that Millane's courage was remarkable: "How he got through the 1990 final series with that broken thumb will become one of the greatest legends in football history."

Giles once described "Pants" as "an angel with a dirty face."

Perhaps this lyrical description of the many-faceted Millane, who lived at home until he died and who was voted a member of Collingwood's Team of the Century, is more than justified. This is in part because, as Darren's mother Denise confided, as a lad he wrote a lot of poetry. Moreover when playing for the Mighty Magpies, Millane was well-known as an amateur magician who sometimes performed party tricks at a number of Melbourne nightclubs which he often frequented. Many who knew him remark on the fact that, quite often – on his own accord – "Pants" went to visit sick children. He especially spent time with leukemia patients at the Royal Children's Hospital.

Throughout his tragically truncated career with the Magpies, Millane was also extremely helpful to the disabled. Indeed he played a significant role in getting a ramp installed at Victoria Park so that supporters and other people in wheelchairs could better access the grandstand near the Collingwood clubrooms.

All Collingwood players and officials at the time stress Millane's courage and his loyalty to the Club. Hence, each season, the player judged Best Clubman receives the Darren Millane Trophy.

In March 2015 Denise Millane presented to the Collingwood Football Club the Sherrin football Darren Millane held proudly aloft at the end of the 1990 grand final and which, after his death in October 1991, she had kept wrapped in tissue paper in a wardrobe at the family home in Noble Park. It is in near mint condition.

Recently, the Melbourne-based writer, and Fitzroy fanatic, Barry Dickins told me how, a week before Millane's fatal car crash, he met the Collingwood star in the office of 'The Melbourne Times' in Lygon Street, Carlton. With his handsome torso and jet-black rippled hair, Millane "looked like the son of God." When Dickins said: "I'm a great fan of your brilliance on the field", Millane – with a twinkle in his eyes – responded: "That's very nice of you to say so, old bean!"

After his death, Darren Millane, who is buried at the Springvale Cemetery, became the only player in Collingwood history to have his guernsey number (42) retired indefinitely by the club.

Let's hope that this continues forever!

Toasting Dad and our Swans at Mum's, Grand Final night 2005, from left Pete, Mum, Damien and me (Phillipa Power).
Photo courtesy of Phillipa Power.

3

Blood Lines

Phillipa Power

Framed in gilt, a gift from my Mother, Paula, is a cherished possession. It's a print of a painting by Paul Crompton depicting the 'Lakeside Oval', South Melbourne, circa 1960. That year, I was 9 and had been going to the Oval for six years with my family supporting the local Aussie Rules team, the South Melbourne Swans. Mum was originally from Sydney, loved the creative and performing arts and knew little about footy. She met Dad, Phil Power, when he returned from service at the end of WW2. She fell in love with him, then his Swans; to both she remained fiercely loyal. This is my family footy tale, just one of many of unconditional love for the Swans and hope in a Flag for the 72 years of thick and much thin, to 2005.

Dad was born in 1917 in Middle Park, where he lived with his large family until the outbreak of War in 1939. As part of the local community they supported the Swans, known then as 'South' and the 'Bloods'. He was at South's 1933 winning Grand Final, where he saw Laurie Nash (his "best ever" footballer) play. Dad's attendance at the infamous 'Bloodbath', the 1945 grand final between South and Carlton, imbued his children, 'the troops' as Dad called us, with what loyalty meant in action. The game was played at Princes Park because US military occupied the MCG. Dad hadn't seen his family since 1939 having been transferred from the Australian to the Royal Navy.

Following the separate deaths of two brothers, both airmen, Dad was brought closer to home, to PNG. In 1945 he was evacuating POWS from the infamous camp at Ambon. His beloved South in another grand final was a rare ray of sunshine; his journey to Melbourne for the game, another ordeal, in the bomb bay of an American Liberator. At Princes Park, he met his father, an editor at *The Age* and his old friend JJ Listen. Together they watched the game; as if they had not enough of bloodbaths. At the end of the carnage Dad said goodbye to his father, returning to PNG. He died in 1993 without seeing the Swans in another Premiership. Throughout the vagaries of the intervening years and the Club's move to Sydney in 1982, Dad was steadfast in his support for the Swans.

Mirth and hope sustained us in the long drought to 2005.

When the Swans moved from South, for live footy, Mum and Dad attended the 'Match of the Day' at the MCG with old South friends sharing the day's roast in the Long Room. Two were elegant sisters; one, Glad, was also at the 'Bloodbath'. She was 19 and had a spot on the boundary. When the Carlton enforcer, Bob Chitty, pummelled little Billy Williams nearby, Glad jumped the fence and belted Chitty with her umbrella, was arrested, then released on good behaviour. Legend has it Billy said Glad saved his life and in deference to her youthful gallantry, she acquired a pair of Bobby Skilton's shorts following his retirement. After a Swans win at Waverley, Mum recounted, Glad flashed open her stylish coat revealing she was wearing the Skilton shorts [to the taunts of her sister who told her to "stop skiting"]. Mum observed not only were the shorts in remarkably good condition, but Glad had a very good pair of 'pins' for her age.

One afternoon at the Lakeside Oval, Max Oaten kicked the ball from the pocket in front of the Cricket stand where Mum sat with "the troops". The ball went off the side of Max's boot, over the crowd, then disappeared into an unroofed ladies loo. A hush fell over the crowd, as all wondered what had become of the footy. Miraculously, the ball careered out of the loo, back over the crowd and landed on the Ground; it was a magnificent kick! An old member who religiously sat in the same seat for as long as we could remember [perhaps awaiting a 'sign'] pulled himself to his feet and yelled out 'Sign her up'.

After winning games, "the troops" tore the footy record [pocket newspaper size then] into confetti which we threw in the air on the final siren. After losses, we consoled ourselves with jam doughnuts from the caravan outside the ground. The boys kicked the footy as the mist and seagulls descended on the Oval, Mum and I watching patiently while Dad and Alwyn [Dad's childhood friend] enjoyed an analytical beer in the bar. For away games, Dad, Alwyn and the older troops stood near the goals at the Visitors' end. Damien and I made red and white papier mache streamers stuck to lengths of dowel. When it rained, the red ran into the white and on to us. Mum called us her 'little Blood Stained Angels' as she welcomed us home at the front door, wafts of Spaghetti Bolognese behind her. 'Sweet dreams', she said as she later tucked us into our warm beds. For the troops, winning a premiership was a distant dream.

The long Geelong game trips in the Ford Prefect filled our developing neurons with Dad and Alwyn's game analysis, supplemented by the Saturday night replay and commentary from Lou, Jack and our 'hair' favourites, Chicken Smallhorn with his pre-war hair central part and Harry Beitzel with his miraculous pre 'Warnie' regrowth. We learnt perseverance. During one win, against North during the couple of years they played at Coburg, it poured all afternoon. Mum later had to throw out my waterlogged [and only] boots. We had to stay to cheer the team at the final siren; we were all in the battle together. The example of Bobby Skilton and many players in defeat, taught us as much about fortitude and bravery, as football skills. It was unthinkable to change teams, so the move to Sydney was just another life test.

From 1980 I lived in Queensland. Media coverage of Swans games was limited. I travelled to many games. Mum kept me informed in between. She sent me a small bear with red and white ribbons, a counterpart to the one she had in Melbourne and phoned me between quarters with a comprehensive breakdown of play. One memorable report was during a Swans v Eagles game played in the West. When she finished her half time report [we weren't doing well], she said 'We have another problem, Philly love; our coach has been reported for using a four letter word 150 times'.

1996 replenished our hope. At half time in the Grand Final v North we were looking promising. Mum disappeared, returning with an enormous beer. She drank every drop saying 'This is for your Father'. At a subdued family dinner that night, the unspoken fear was we wouldn't see a Swans Flag during our lifetimes. The Finals loss to the Lions in 2003 reinforced that fear, but we hung on.

2005 started badly with several losses, then Mum's cancer diagnosis, gruelling surgery and treatment. Mid Season while staying at her home, I noticed a parcel under my bed. Mum said she was going to give it to me at the end of the season. It's another treasured possession, a white plate she bought with 'Swans SFC 2005 Sydney Swans Premiers' plus all the player names from the actual game and Paul Roos' name as Coach painted on. Mum had a history of dreaming Melbourne Cup winners, so I took this sign seriously, reinforced months later by the miracle of the SCG, the Davis four goals.

Grand Final day 2005 was a further test. Damien and Peter queued on our parents' old beach seats for spots in the Members. Peter found a $1200 per ticket package, which we bought just for the seats – the only way we could get two seats together for me and Mum. We didn't know they were up on the incomplete top level in the area being redeveloped. It was bitterly cold; I went to look for a hot drink. Mum was distressed when I came back, her hands shaking like a frightened bird. A couple had accused her of sitting in their seats and demanded she hand them her ticket, then they swapped the tickets around and gave her one of their tickets [for seats that didn't exist].

They were nasty and aggressive [don't ask me what the pre game entertainment was and we missed the famous Two Cities, One Team, sharing the Dream banner]. Eventually, an usher moved us to the lowest level in the last row. We were in front of a standing room area where a very old man leant on a stick. He wore an old coat and an older red and white, plain stitch, home-knit beanie in which the red had run into the white, just like our childhood homemade streamers. In my heart, I prayed we would all make it through the game. Mum sat patiently throughout, with little comment other than after Barry Hall's final quarter 'Captain's Goal'. We couldn't see Leo's Leap, but a man and his son from Sydney next to us said 'don't worry ladies, it's a Swans mark'. On the final siren, together people from the Two Cities who shared the Dream repeatedly sang 'The Song'. As the final notes drifted away, the old man's grizzled face was awash with tears; he whispered gently to me and Mum 'play it again Sam'. That night the family celebrated at Mum's with Spaghetti Bolognese. It was her last game. As she drifted away, I whispered in her ear 'remember Leo Barry's mark'. A smile spread across her pale face and she breathed , in her finest Richie Benaud impression, 'marvellous'.

In 2012, I was the Swans number one ticket holder. A Swans hallmark is inclusiveness so our Club rotates this honour annually. I went to all the games, saw many heroic performances on field, complemented by many equally brave supporters off field. My heart has a nook for Launceston on the occasion of Adam Goodes' 300th game and 37 point win over the Hawks. I noticed a young couple sitting quietly nearby, the man wearing black arm bands on each arm. At post match drinks they told me of their aspirations. When asked who they were honouring with the armbands, softly they said one was for their daughter, who died a few weeks prior and the second for his father, who died that morning. 'Dad would have wanted us to be here', the young man said, his teary partner nodding.

To the 2012 Grand Final my sister and I wore Mum's jewellery, our brothers, some of Dad's war medals. As the second ball off Nick Malceski's boot glided between the big posts, I thought of the people of Sydney. It was 30 years ago they embraced the baton for us all in a gruelling endurance race to 2005. As the final siren rang, Damien emailed each of the troops a surprise; a photo of red and white flowers he had quietly placed on our parents' graves the day before. Our Coach, John Longmire, said this win was the sum of many 'one-percenters'. That Season, around Australia, I was enriched by many 'one-percenters', people in the Bloods' spirit of my parents. The local footy community of my childhood had evolved into a unique fusion of people in many cities, all sharing a Sweet Dream.

Philippa Mary Power

Philippa Power is a lawyer who practised as a barrister in Victoria and solicitor in Queensland. She has many interests including the arts, politics, artificial intelligence and spirituality, but especially Aussie Rules and cricket.'

Brian Dixon 1969 Scanlens Footy Card
Private Collection, used with permission from the collector

4

Playing For Melbourne

Brian Dixon

Without doubt, my most heartfelt moment playing for Melbourne was seeing Neil Crompton kick a goal in the 1964 Grand Final which ultimately won the game and won the Premiership for Melbourne, defeating Collingwood by 4 points. Previous to Crompton's kick, Ray Gabelich had kicked a wonderful goal after a seventy metre run bouncing the ball somewhat erratically, then kicked a goal to put the Magpies in front.

Then Hassa Mann took a mark and kicked a point. Bob Rose sent his runner out to the Collingwood fullback – "don't kick it to Dixon's wing" were his instructions. Unfortunately for Collingwood, the message was never delivered and the ball was kicked out to Dixon's wing, where he marked the ball.

Dixon sent the ball back to the full forward line, where the ball bounced off the hands of the pack to Neil Crompton, who kicked a magnificent goal straight through the middle. Melbourne hung on to win the Premiership by 4 points. The fact that Crompton had followed the Collingwood rover to the forward line, against Norm Smith's instructions, was understandably overlooked.

Another fact which was overlooked was an incident which took place in the Melbourne team's bathroom after the Thursday night's training before the Grand Final. Norm Smith had finished training early and was taking a shower, Frank Davis – up from the under 19's was taking a bath as was Frank Adams, one of Brian Dixon's best mates.

The custom at Melbourne was to share the large baths with two players. As Smith showered, I (Dixon) entered the bathroom and had to decide whether to bathe with Bluey Adams or Frank Davis. Having spent 10 years as a mate of Blueys, I (Dixon) chose to bathe with him. Norm was not amused and reported the matter to the match committee. Dixon should have chosen Davis to bathe with and not his friend Adams. Davis would have liked the encouragement, Smith said. Norm Smith then suggested to the match committee that Adams and Dixon should be omitted from the Grand Final team for not bathing with Frank Davis. Fortunately, the match committee did not agree and all three players took the field and played well.

Of course Melbourne was fortunate to finish on the top of the ladder after the home and away fixtures were completed with Hassa Mann kicking a miraculous goal from an almost impossible angle which gave Melbourne a 4 point victory over Hawthorn at Hawthorn and second top place on the Premiership ladder.

I was fortunate to play with Melbourne from 1954 to 1968. I had wanted to play for St Kilda, as my family barracked for St Kilda and 2 of my uncles played for St Kilda Reserves, between the two world wars. Dick Piesse and Lindsay Thompson – football coaches at Melbourne High School arranged for me to try out for St Kilda and I remember meeting my hero Neil Roberts. Fortunately St Kilda was unimpressed with me and my offer to live with my grandmother to be residentially bound to St Kilda. Lindsay Thompson spoke with Jim Cardwell and arranged for me to train with Melbourne. After 4 practice games, 2 on prize recruit Laurie Mithen, I made the Melbourne list.

My most heartfelt disappointment was not being chosen to play in the 1955 Premiership Team, being replaced by Geoff Case, despite having played 16 of the 18 home–and–away matches.

Throughout 1955 I had been captain/coach of the Commerce and Economics Faculty in the inter faculty Premiership series at Melbourne University. The 1955 University Premiership was being decided between Commerce and Dentistry, whose captain and coach was Allen Aylett.

Allen Aylett was a famous North Melbourne rover at the time, a wonderful captain of North Melbourne and subsequently President of the Club and President of the VFL/AFL.

Norm Smith decided I should not play in that game as I might get injured and not be available to play for Melbourne in the 1955 Finals Series. I took this instruction seriously and turned up for the team meeting without my boots, so I could not play, as I had left my boots at home in Nunawading where I lived. My university team mates were devastated, saying "we would be beaten by an Aylett led 'Dentist' Team".

Rex Thompson was one of the few people in those university days who owned a car. He offered to drive me to Nunawading and pick up my boots if I would play. I consented. The pressure from my university mates was too much and they did not want to be denied a Premiership. I was wrong and paid the price. After the Commerce Premiership win, the Age newspaper reported Dixon had been best on the field. Norm Smith was most unimpressed I had disobeyed his instruction.

I was not considered for selection for what was ultimately the VFL Premiership team of 1955. However I did play in the University Premiership Team of 1955, which does not rank publicly with Melbourne's first premiership of the fifties.

When I look back at my time with Melbourne and think about my most heartfelt moments, what happened off the field comes to my mind and it was a very important factor in our success – eleven times in the four and six premierships.

The most precious moments in terms of football were the stirring addresses by Norm Smith. Norm did his homework well and every match was preceded by an immaculate address outlining our opponents strengths and weaknesses, how to take advantage of them or nullify them. Equally, Norm's addresses at quarter time, half time and three quarter time were clinically correct and most helpful to the team to enable it to win, which we did on a record number of occasions.

While not directly related to the football match of the day, our off field involvements were critical in terms of team bonding and ultimately team success on the field.

Every home game, at the conclusion of the game was a gathering with our opposing team lasting about one and a half hours. About 6:30 the Melbourne players and staff would make our way to a small room on the ground floor of the MCC stand. There would be a dinner. The

Chairman of the dinner was always preselected and he was entitled to run the dinner as he saw fit. "The fines are on" was the speech most feared as the players could be fined by the Chairman for real or unreal events and the fine could usually be avoided by singing a song. The evening was always punctuated by numerous verses of the Grand Old Flag and the Collingwood theme song to the carefully constructed Demons' words. Any money raised went to the player's end of season trip fund.

After the dinner followed a barn dance, compered usually by either Mike Williamson or Tony Charlton and the Dennis Farrington Band. The Club would pay for taxi's to bring wives, girlfriends and partners to the dance which followed the dinner. The most popular dance was the barn dance which involved everybody and usually lasted one hour. Afterwards there was usually another party terminated by the thought of Sunday morning training and medical examinations.

After the 1964 Premiership dinner and dance all the team and officials came to the Dixon's home in Moorabbin and there the grand final was relived with numerous verses of the Grand Old Flag and Good Old Collingwood Forever to the Melbourne Club words.

Many of my most heartfelt moments were against skilled opponents like Reg Burgess, Greg Sewell, Barry Capuano and Jack Clarke of Essendon, Thorold Merrett and Brian Gray of Collingwood, Brendan Edwards and Colin Youren of Hawthorn, Laurie Dwyer of North Melbourne, Ian Aston of Fitzroy and Dennis Marshall of Geelong. I was inspired by Polly Farmer with his magnificent palming of the ball and long hand passing. Of course my favourite players were Ron Barassi and Frank Adams of Melbourne and anyone who represented the Demons.

Finally, I was inspired by our end of season trips to New Zealand and the USA. We visited New Zealand in 1961 and the USA in 1963. In 1963 Jim Cardwell and Les Millis arranged for us to replay Geelong in Honolulu and San Francisco. We won both games as Norm Smith was determined to enact revenge against Geelong for winning the 1963 VFL Premiership. The trips also gave me the insight to understand Australian football could be a truly international sport. I subsequently persuaded the AFL to spend funds on promoting AFL internationally and I was delighted to be Chairman of AFL South Africa. I wish to dedicate a whole part of the rest of my life to seeing AFL become a recognised sport and played at Championship level in many countries including Asian, American and European countries.

Brian Dixon

Brian Dixon played 252 games for Melbourne between 1954 and 1968, becoming one of the VFL greats for the era. He was best and fairest for the club in 1960 and played 11 games for Victoria, winning the Tassie medal for the best player in the 1961 interstate Carnival series. He was later inducted into the Melbourne Football Club Hall of Fame. After leaving football he became a distinguished Member of Parliament for Victoria from 1964-1982 and a strong advocate for the international playing of Australian football.

Barry Cable 1966 Scanlens Footy Card
Private Collection, used with permission from the collector

5

Falling to Earth

Ken Spillman

He was dead. Craning to watch the action through a thicket of heads, I had seen the hit clearly; I might even have heard it as well.

"E 'asn't moved,' intoned the man who was letting me stand on the edge of his upturned milk crate. He reeked of tobacco and was lighting one Peter Stuyvesant from the butt of another. "E was out before 'e even 'it the ground.'

Moments earlier, a hairy cube of gristle had lined up Barry Cable on the opposite flank of Subiaco Oval. Cable's eyes were on the ball – as ever – and mine were on him. The cube had an elbow and it was lifted to the plane of Cable's blond curls. This was JFK in Dallas. Cable's head jolted and I was witness to his assassination.

'Matthews, you bloody mongrel basta...!' The man beside me bellowed. It was all he could manage before coughing violently into his jacket.

I had just turned twelve. It was the afternoon of Saturday, 17 July 1971, and the future had suddenly been drained of its appeal. If I'd been five years older, I might have thought of Hamlet:

> How weary, stale, flat, and unprofitable
> Seem to me all the uses of this world!
> Fie on 't! ah fie! 'Tis an unweeded garden
> That grows to seed. Things rank and gross in nature
> Possess it merely.

As my milk crate proprietor had identified, the cube was Leigh Matthews. He was wearing the Big V in a team coached by Tommy Hafey, and Victoria had led Western Australia by 22 points at half time.

With Cable lying prone on the grass, there was no hope of a comeback, no hope of anything.

'E's moved,' offered my most proximate commentator, restoring at least one hope.

I saw Cable move too. Soon trainers were helping him to his feet. His head was hanging from his shoulders like a tennis ball in panty hose. He staggered, that famous balance a thing of the past, as extinct as the Arabian gazelle.

Although Cable didn't remember anything after the blow, he managed to stay upright in a forward pocket until three-quarter time. He didn't get another kick. Victoria piled on the goals, eventually cruising to a 38-point win. The *Sunday Times* described the Big V as 'machine-like'. Matthews was booed by 39,000 voices every time he touched the ball. Peter McKenna bagged six, John Murphy roved well and kicked 3.2, and a lean, blond schoolboy named Peter Knights soared above packs in a manner I might have found exhilarating if my thoughts weren't fixed on the fate of that other blond, who had disappeared down the players' race after the interval.

Where was Cable now? Was his brain bleeding silently into – what? Itself? Would he ever play again?

Over the next few days, I followed the story as closely as I'd followed the Apollo 11 space mission exactly two years earlier. According to the newspapers, officials from Cable's WAFL club, Perth, had rushed to the change rooms just after the siren that announced the start of the last quarter. Cable was showering but appeared completely disoriented. 'What happened?' he asked. 'Are we winning? Was I playing well?' They drove him home, where a doctor instructed him to stay in bed for forty-eight hours.

When Cable was able to view replays of the incident, he said he was 'annoyed' he wasn't taken immediately from the ground. 'I remember getting four or five kicks at the start of the third quarter – the next thing I knew I was having a shower… I must have been out on my feet for about twenty minutes.'

Leigh Matthews was asked about the incident not long after the game. He put it this way: 'The ball was between Barry and myself and it was a straight contest... I'm sorry that it happened but it's part of the game.' Cable, however, didn't seem altogether convinced that the clash was 'a straight contest' and 'part of the game'. He said:

> Getting knocked about is part of football – just as long as it's fair... But using an elbow or a forearm is dangerous stuff... it can injure a person. From the television replay I'd say I was hit with a forearm.

That Monday, the *Daily News* ran pictures of a pyjama-clad Cable talking to well-wishers on the phone and looking through match reports with his wife and sons. Another photograph showed him with Allen Aylett, the president of the North Melbourne Football Club, at his bedside.

Aylett, of course, was worried about more than Cable's health: he had flown west for the weekend desperately hoping to entice the star rover back to Victoria. Cable had spent the 1970 season immersed in VFL action, taking with him a reputation that was arguably even greater than that which accompanied Polly Farmer to Geelong in 1962. By the end of 1969, Cable had played in three premiership teams with Perth and won two Sandover Medals, as well as five club champion awards. Steadfastly resisting overtures from Carlton and Hawthorn, he had also been selected in two All-Australian teams. At the Australian National Football Championship held in Hobart in 1966, indeed, Cable won the Tassie Medal as the carnival's outstanding player ahead of such fellow All-Australians as Darrel Baldock, John Nicholls, Ian Stewart, Kevin Murray and Peter Hudson.

That Cable's season in Victoria had seen him win North Melbourne's best and fairest award was scarcely unexpected – in fact, the only surprise to most Western Australians was that he finished as low as fourth in the Brownlow Medal count behind Peter Bedford, Gary Dempsey and Alex Jesaulenko. That Cable had returned to Perth in 1971 was no great sensation either. He had nothing to prove to anyone, and could rejoin a WAFL that was full of vim and vigour, affording him decent surfaces for the launch of unerring stab passes and long dropkicks. But Aylett and North wanted Cable back. Like Leigh Matthews, they wanted him bad and got their man – albeit not until 1974, by which time Ron Barassi had started assembling an all-star team and Cable had won his third

Sandover Medal.

Clearly, Cable had suffered no permanent damage on the afternoon of 17 July 1971 – and he didn't hold a grudge. In 2012, speaking at an AFL Hall of Fame function that belatedly bestowed 'Legend' status on him, he said of the Matthews encounter: 'He accidentally put his elbow out, I just ran into it.'

For me, however, the Matthews hit had left an ineffaceable impression, as if it had rattled not Cable's brain but my own. My idol seemed a shadow of his former self even as he starred for North and helped them to two premierships. He remained a champion but would never again seem transcendent. The winged, luminescent hero who had inscribed a message on one full page of my autograph book in 1968 had fallen permanently to earth on that shocking 1971 afternoon.

Leigh Matthews, of course, was then in the early years of a stellar career with Hawthorn. The man I had seen as no more than a cube of cold calculation was a champion by every measure and himself became a legend, though as John Devaney wrote:

> [T]here was nothing delicate or fancy about the style of Hawthorn champion Leigh Matthews… Australian football scores do not derive in any directly assessable way from perceived aesthetic merit. Efficiency and expediency are paramount in Australian football, and Leigh Matthews possessed both in abundance.

I went through my teens and into my twenties watching that career unfold, abundant in its efficiency and all the more remarkable for Matthews' feat of colliding with a behind post and rendering it truncated. Yet, for all his achievements, I was never able to forgive Matthews for what he had done to Cable.

In 1985, the football world expressed dismay when the much older Matthews king-hit Geelong's Neville Bruns, whose jaw was broken while the ball was in dispute more than twenty metres away. The circumstances were very different from those of the Subiaco Oval hit in 1971 – weren't they? In my eyes, the motive was the same, and it revealed an ugly side to the man and our game. In the simplest of terms, both actions were unnecessary. In 2008, Matthews summed up the Bruns incident at Princes Park with disarming candour: 'It was an ugly game and when the game turned ugly, I turned ugliest.'

Felling Bruns resulted in a month-long cancellation of Matthews' playing permit by the VFL, as well as a police charge and a $1000 fine for assault – later reduced to a 12-month good behaviour bond. A volume titled *100 Years Of Australian Football*, published in 1996, notes that the police investigation 'ended the polite fiction that football assaults are somehow legal'. This 'polite fiction', of course, was part of what had so deeply disturbed me in July 1971.

It disturbed me again in July 1972, when dashing Collingwood youngster John Greening was left fighting for his life after an off-the-ball incident involving St Kilda's Jim O'Dea. A few matches short of his hundredth game, Greening had already made his mark on the game. He was best afield when the Magpies defeated North on the day I watched Cable go down, and teammates Peter McKenna and Barry Price reckoned long afterward that Greening was the most exciting athlete they played with. Their coach, Bob Rose, believed Greening was on his way to establishing himself as one of the greatest players of all time. That afternoon in 1972, the course of a young life changed.

As Greening recalled: 'I was only twenty-one, not even at my peak… suddenly you wake up in hospital with someone thumping on your chest, saying you nearly died.' The blow from O'Dea cut oxygen to Greening's brain and he lay in a coma for more than two days; there was no certainty that he would ever come out of it. In the Melbourne suburb of Broadmeadows, a seven-year old named Eddie McGuire spent 'the best part of a week praying'. McGuire was not, by any means, the only one.

Collingwood sought police intervention and Greening's wife filed a Supreme Court writ alleging assault, which she only dropped after St Kilda and Collingwood set up an appeal for Greening and his young family. For the time being, polite fiction had won the day. The matter was adjudicated by the VFL tribunal, with O'Dea suspended for ten matches. Greening, meanwhile, spent nearly six months in hospital and rehabilitation clinics. Remarkably, he finished only 11 votes behind teammate Len Thompson in the 1972 Brownlow Medal.

Why did these two incidents in the early 1970s have such a profound impact on me? I was callow, but at twelve and thirteen I could not have been so naive as to think that thuggery didn't exist in football. After all, Malcolm Brown was captain-coach of East Perth, while Cable's own coach in Perth's hat-trick of premierships was another renowned hard man, Mal Atwell. Somehow, though, I had deceived myself into thinking that thugs went toe to toe with their targets. They looked them in the eye. The rough roughed up the tough. The tough gave as good as they got.

The playing field I had known changed forever on that dark day when Matthews took out the fairest of them all. If dull-brained malevolence could iron out Cable, it could iron out rectitude. It could cripple grace. Never again would I imagine a world in which right had the right to triumph, where true heroes were immortal. Out there – on Subiaco Oval, on any other oval and way beyond their boundaries – dwelt brutishness.

Ken Spillman
The author of 60 books and the editor of many others. More than 40 of his books are for children or young adults, and this writing has appeared in more than 15 countries and in many translations. Ken is probably best known in Australia for his *Jake* series for early readers and his acclaimed YA novel *Love is a UFO*. He is a popular speaker on writing and creativity, and is WA ambassador for The Footpath Library, which enriches the lives of many homeless people through the provision of quality books.

6

Black Magic

Dick Whitaker

"Get out of the road you black bastard!" roared the fearsome Jack Dyer, Richmond hard-man, as he burst through a pack and was confronted by his diminutive Aboriginal Fitzroy opponent, Doug Nichols in the mid 1930's.

Dyer was not consciously racist but merely the product of his time – a time when it was quite permissible to racially abuse an Aboriginal if it would help put him off his game. As Dyer said later in his biography *"Captain Blood"*:

> I've no colour hatred, in fact two of the nicest blokes and best footballers I have seen were aboriginals. Norm McDonald of Essendon and Pastor Doug Nichols of Fitzroy. Still their colour was a weapon I thought I could use against them on the field. All's fair in war and football.

Some two years later Dyer and Nichols were on an interstate trip together, playing for Victoria, when Dyer realised that Nichols was quietly hostile towards him. Asked why, Nichols told him he resented the way he had been insulted in that previous match against Richmond. The puzzled Dyer offered an apology – that was graciously accepted by the quiet and self-effacing Nichols.

Aboriginal players of the 1930's and 40's were subject to continuous racial abuse both on and off the field and even from within their own teams. Nichols left his first VFL Club, Carlton, when his team mates objected to having an Aboriginal in the side. He went across to Fitzroy in 1932, and expecting the same treatment, sat by himself in the change room before his first training session. But this time he was welcomed to the club and befriended by the great Hayden Bunton, the Brownlow Medal winner that year.

Nichols rewarded Fitzroy by quickly becoming a great and valuable player for his side. He came third in the Brownlow Medal in 1934, and in 1935 made history when he became the first Aboriginal footballer to play for Victoria.

His extraordinary athletic career also extended across into footracing and boxing and his strengths in these areas, as with football, stemmed from his speed rather than his size. He stood only 158 cm (5' 2") tall but was extremely fast on his feet and proved to be a top class sprinter. In 1928 he won two major professional footraces, the Warracknabeal and Nyah Gifts, earning "a sash and a cash prize of £100" for each win.

He also became a well-known performer in the Jimmy Sharman boxing troupe, usually fighting much larger opponents and despite this handicap, always performed well.

Nichols became a baptised Christian soon after his mother's death and an aboriginal community leader in the late 1930's. He enlisted in the Army in 1941, but was discharged on compassionate grounds the next year and became an ordained Pastor in the Churches of Christ in 1945.

As Pastor Doug Nichols he performed sterling work for Aboriginal people over the next thirty years, receiving many honours and awards along the way. He was knighted in 1972, and as Sir Douglas Nichols was appointed Governor of South Australia in 1976. He died in 1988, aged 81 and was given a state funeral.

Doug Nichols was one of the first, if not the very first, of the elite Aboriginal athletes to make a stand against racism, firstly in sport and then across many other areas of Australian society. His "heartfelt moment" was the refusal to accept Jack Dyer's racist insult, and then to demonstrate the ignorance of racism through his stellar achievements in sport, religion, politics and community affairs.

These achievements were remarkable in themselves, but when placed in the context of his journey through discrimination, poverty and hardship, were exemplary for all Australians.

Fast forward to round 4 of the 1993 season. Nicky Winmar is playing for St. Kilda against Collingwood at Victoria Park – the home ground of the Magpies. Winmar, and his mate Gilbert McAdam, both top-flight Aboriginal footballers, had been copping plenty of racial abuse all day from the then notorious Collingwood crowd and had reacted by playing superlatively and helping St. Kilda across the line for an unexpected win. It was later revealed that McAdam and Winmar had been voted two of the best three on the ground by the field umpire.

Walking off the oval, they were abused further and Winmar responded in what was one of the most memorable moments in Australian sporting history. Raising his arms over his head before lifting his St Kilda guernsey, he pointed to his bare skin and declared: "I'm black - and I'm proud to be black!" This was his heartfelt moment and brought the injustice of racial vilification onto the front page of Australian conscience.

Neil Elvis "Nicky" Winmar was born into humble circumstances in Pingelly, about 160 kilometres to the southeast of Perth in 1965. Showing early athletic talent he began his football career with South Fremantle when he was only 17. His ability soon attracted the attention of the VFL and he was picked up by St. Kilda in 1978.

Winmar then played with the Saints for the next 12 years.

He was involved in several racial abuse incidents, including a celebrated on-field brawl with Hawthorn's Dermot Brereton in 1990. Brereton admitted later that he had deliberately taunted Winmar with racial insults to put him off his game – and that policy was also used by his Hawthorn team members against Chris Lewis – the great indigenous player for the West Coast Eagles.

Winmar attacked Brereton and was subsequently suspended for 11 weeks. Brereton said later "I'm ashamed of what I did back then to provoke Nicky. But, with education, I have learnt from the error".

Winmar's illustrious playing career was one of the finest of any footballer of the 1980's and 1990's. Some of his highlights included St. Kilda's Best and Fairest in both 1989 and 1995, twice a member of the All Australian team, the Aboriginal Sportsperson of the Year 1999 and named in the Indigenous Team of the Century in 2005. But of all his deeds on the field, he is best remembered from his symbolic stand against racism in Australian Football – at Victoria Park in 1993.

Running parallel with Nicky Winmar, but across town at the Essendon Football Club, was another Indigenous great – Michael Long – a man born in Darwin but who, from the 1989 season onwards, spent all of his AFL playing career in the black and red of Essendon.

Right from the start Long was a champion, playing many sensational games, with his signature style being what modern commentators call "run and carry". In this manoeuvre Long would take possession of the ball and play on, lighting up the turf with sheer speed and having the uncanny ability of being able to cut and swerve through the swarming defence of opposition players at top pace, at the same time bouncing the ball.

He employed this technique in bucket loads during the 1993 Grand Final between Essendon and Carlton. Long's game on this day was nothing short of incredible and he was justifiably awarded the Norm Smith medal – best on the ground in a Grand Final.

But an equally memorable match, for a host of different reasons, followed during the ANZAC Day fixture against Collingwood in 1995. The match was an absolute cracker from start to finish and ended with a heart-stopping draw that most believed was a just result for a superlative game.

But the aftermath was even more sensational. Michael Long claimed he had been racially abused by Magpie ruckman Damien Monkhorst during the game – and demanded an apology, as well as further action by the Australian Football League.

A mediation meeting was arranged between Long and Monkhorst at which a public apology was given, but of far more significance was the fact that it triggered a seachange within the League. Just two months later the AFL had hammered out and implemented a racial and religious vilification policy – the first of its type in Australia and later used as an international model across many other types of sport.

This policy was designed to put an end to the racial sledging that had been part of Australian Football for more than 100 years, as practiced by Jack Dyer, Dermott Brereton, Damian Monkhorst and many others – that was designed to unsettle their Indigenous opponents but in the worst possible way.

Michael Long went on to reach great heights in the AFL. He was twice a member of the all-Australian team (1988 and 1995) and played in two winning Essendon Premiership sides (1993 and 2000). He was also inducted into the Australian Football Hall of Fame in 2007 and during the John Howard era became a noted spokesman for Indigenous Australians.

The year that Nicky Winmar was declared Aboriginal Sportsperson of the Year – 1999 – was the same year that another Indigenous footballer made his debut in the Swans first grade team.

His initial season was so impressive that he won the Leagues Rising Star award for that year. His name was Adam Goodes and like Doug Nichols, Nicky Winmar and Michael Long he was to have a major impact on the game, both through his superlative playing skills and his promoting the rights of Indigenous Australians.

Born in South Australia in 1980, Adam Goodes played representative high school football in the mid 1990's after his family moved to Horsham. His talent was recognised by the Swans, and as the cliche goes, the rest is football history.

Goodes' AFL career was star-studded from its early days. He became a dual Brownlow medallist and dual Premiership player, an all - Australian four times, and a member of the Indigenous Team of the century. The crowning glory came in 2014 when he was named Australian of the Year for his work with Indigenous peoples and his advocacy against racism in Australian society.

It was this work that brought Goodes even more sharply into focus – both as a player and community leader - when he took a stand at being called "an ape" by outing a young Collingwood supporter in a match against the Magpies in 2013. Amid great controversy the teenager was ejected from the ground.

During 2014 and 2015, Goodes was repeatedly booed by opposition fans during matches, with the issue coming to a head in May 2015 when he celebrated a goal by performing an Indigenous war dance, culminating in the throwing of an imaginary spear at the Carlton cheer squad.

The attention this event generated, combined with the persistent booing that followed, distressed Goodes to such an extent that he made himself unavailable for selection at the August 1st 2015 match against Adelaide.

The motivation for the booing was the subject of great debate – was it racism, resentment of his perceived denigration of European settlement during some of his Australian of the Year public appearances, or just "the tall poppy syndrome"? Or perhaps all of the above?

But in a heartfelt response in favour of Goodes, many clubs, players and opposition fans came out solidly in his corner, with senior political figures also condemning the booing campaign. The match he missed, at the SCG, attracted a near capacity crowd that gave him rousing cheers, as his images were flashed on the giant screen overlooking the ground

Indeed, to honour and support Goodes whose number was 37, at the 7 minute mark of the third quarter, almost all of those present at the game stood and provided him a continuous one-minute standing ovation in what many interpreted as a resounding "No!" to racism.

Although Adam Goodes retired at the end of the 2015 season, his experiences of racism still lingered and had the capacity to blight his stellar career.

The long football journey, from Pastor Doug Nichols, to Nicky Winmar, to Michael Long and then through to Adam Goodes has shown that although some racism still exists in football, it is no longer accepted by the great majority of players, clubs or fans.

Apart from their Indigenous ancestry, these four players have something else in common. The fact is that their achievements, on and off the field, are far above those of their denigrators, which surely is the best possible response to racism in all its forms.

Pastor Doug Nichols' contribution to the game was formally recognised by the AFL Commission in 2016 when it named the Indigenous Round 10, the highlight of which is the night match between Essendon and Richmond, after Sir Doug Nicholls.

In announcing the honour, the AFL Chief Executive Gil McLachlan remarked that "Sir Doug Nicholls is the great untold story of Australian football and he represented both the values of our game and epitomised the spirit of reconciliation."

Sir Doug Nicholls is the only VFL/AFL player to be knighted.

Richard (Dick) Whitaker

Dick Whitaker is a meteorologist, author, television and radio presenter and football fan – being a member of the Sydney Swans since 1996. He has been married for over 40 years, has two children and four grandchildren.

Once a Royboy, always a Royboy.
Sketch courtesy of Barry Dickins.

7

Fitzroy Football Club 1954

Barry Dickins

It is in the mud, ferocious yet quagmire, black molasses popular with our half-back-line, our ruck is Butch Gale who also captained Victoria one year because he felt like it. It is Fitzroy Football Club at Saint Georges Road and my short but fearless father Len is wearing a gaberdine overcoat buttoned up to the almost over-shaved neck and has Brylcreem in his jet-black-short back and sides. He is immaculately working-class and you can just about see your copy of 'Footy Record' in his shoes as he shouts me a ticket to get in. 'One and a child thanks'.

We enter the Elysium of Old Royboys where Dad points out very politely Chicken Smallhorn and I thank him for he is a great hero of The Lions and that is a very great privilege to glimpse him.

'There's a spot over there we might crack it for a seat if we're in luck!'

We squirm through a mayhem of great grandchildren of convicts. There are red-faced men shrieking about frankfurter sausages and you can smell the burst things being grasped by spoon-tong-things and furious fanatics paying and belching as the siren sounds to commence proceedings. It's an amplified car horn.

Lots of people all pretty much insane and identical in their way, some swearing incoherently and others standing on jagged broken beer bottles to get up a bit higher to view the match, others have kids on their staunch shoulders and even infants blaspheme I was surprised to see and hear.

The language I can hear and I am just five years of age is the shock of truth. Collingwood run on and look just like what we call them; which is a word you never hear at our place, i tell you that for nothing. Dad is opening his army issue leather kit-bag and unscrewing a piping-hot thermos of tea and he uses its screw-on-end as a cup. 'Any good!'

The noise is so great it creates in my mind a colossal almost migraine which is orgiastic in its new intensity, the clamor and glamour interspersed with the rock-jawed Collingwood men all bounding about with magnificent glossy haircuts with razor-sharp sideboards, the panting and the gasping, especially the gasping is supercharged because we are a goal up a minute into the first quarter.

My cool and collected father is licking the lead on his H.B black lead pencil and writing the names of Fitzroy players who've scored a behind. He tells me a behind is the same as a point although I don't know what he's on about.

The furious Collingwood players are so close to the fence where I sit on my dad's crook knee I can see their teeth fillings deep inside their mouths and I can even see their tortured adenoids I'm so near. My dad lends me his great big heavy black binoculars and I can see Harry Beitzel's nostril hairs, the umpire that is. He is forever blowing into a tin whistle and is scarlet in his jowls. The irritable spectators screech and boo him and one chap threw a beer bottle at him filled with wet cement. It just missed him by a cigarette paper that's all. It would've knocked him rotten no doubt.

By quarter time the crowd have sort of settled but not really for some of them have now set fire to three or four oil drums used to collect rubbish such as spat out pies and vomited mince and shattered beer bottles and I can see these hooligans war-dancing around their impromptu incinerators and the exhausted frankfurter chap remonstrating with them, for they have succeeded in trampling his stall over; and yet he is still calling out his steaming wares with the call that goes 'Hot Frank Free!' I don't know why he called his sausages by that name but he did sixty one years ago.

The quietude that creeps over the crowd is rather excellent in my view and my dreamy father is pointing out the lucky owners of Victorian Terrace Houses of Freeman Street, at right-angles to the old Brunswick Oval. 'You can see them on their wrought-iron-balconies', he says with an ironic smile, shielding his blue eyes from a fluke of early afternoon sunshine. Maybe he is thinking about how lucky they are to live right near the home of The Mighty Royboys.

The stadium behind looks nice but is so overcrowded and raucous I wouldn't want to watch from there, from where Dad and I are it appears grandiose and more for people with posh cars and posh properties but the fans up there are shouting loudly now as the second quarter is starting up in a second. The amplified car horn blasts again and I whirl around in order to see where that incredible blast comes from and I just saw the man sound the horn in it and other people screaming and laughing at nothing. The football is opera.

My hero Butch Gale gallantly rots on with big barrel chest out and lots of people reaching over the concrete race to pat him on the back, he is glossy with Deep Heat Muscle Ointment which I forever associate with courage and determination and agonizing ligaments; his rover trots on next who is wearing the very first example of the famous Flat Top Hair Cut and he is Wally Clark; and Fitzroy fans yell out excitedly on viewing him 'Good on yer Wal!' And 'You're a white man, Wal!'

Butch and Wal are made of sterner stuff

Although all of this is a long time back in the Deep Heat ointment past I only have to stroll by the old gates where the football club was and a billion memories boomerang back like a playful hit over the head. The roaring sounds resurrect and the anguished countenances re-moan. I can see in my memory's eye the old weather-beaten peanut gentleman who hauled stale nuts around in a gunny sack he held over his burly shoulders and he cried out 'Getcha fresh nuts!' But he in fact duped all who were innocent enough to trust him as each nut was stale and husky and probably poisonous. His mortal ghost is still on the flog.

The violence of the second quarter is alarming as I have never seen the art of eye-gouging before and there are many men holding vastly bloodied eyes and hooting in pain, there is testicle biting in the pack that is lying down on top of each other at the moment and I can clearly see Lou Richards from Collingwood engaged in the profane deed of munching Wally Clark's testicles with tremendous savagery and interest in the outcome. Thankfully Russell Crow our Centre Player wanders over and kicks him hard. The grim boundary umpire balls it in and he laughs and the crowd surges and sighs for justice, the one thing there isn't.

My father isn't fazed by the violence because he served in New Guinea and has seen everything in six years of service for he served an extra year on Bougainville Island with peace keeping duties, guarding hundreds of Japanese Prisoners Of War and once said to us all at the tea table 'Those Japs could have beaten us off with bamboo sticks there were that many of them'.

Now he is heading over to a bright jubilant pie boy and comes back to our pozzie with a couple of hot 'Four 'N Twenty pies' with a discreet blob of tomato sauce on them and he carefully hands me one. 'Gee thanks a lot dad!'

He is a real toff my father and so unlike the boring drunks who cry out the identical swear word over and over and are ignored by their stoical wives, of course; my father isn't afraid of anything above or below the surface of the earth and people instinctively seem to know it. He doesn't provoke people but he isn't scared of anything they'll do to him or try it on.

Now Butch Gale has kicked a goal from point blank range and Wally Clark is rushing across to hug him but the next second there's a big stoush.

I have excellent infantile eyesight better than an eagle maybe and through the fence railing on the jade green grass and lovely brown baby snails and stones I can easily see a footballer's gumguard spat out because it was probably belted out with a great big fist or something similar.

I've never seen a gumguard before or a jock strap and there's one of those there too to accompany it. I am now looking at Russell Crow being hit so hard in the stomach by a running Collingwood man that his white shorts came off and he has to keep his great big hands over his private parts as they are called. The crowd thought this was hilarious.

The hitting and bumping and groaning and biting and the aerial skills are like minced meat married to ballet, it is crude, it is angelic, it is boring, it is unlike anything else in the world when it's good and today is good. At half time it is even at six goals sixteen points each right on the dot.

The crowd applaud the rooted warriors as they groan off.

I examine my very first piping-hot Four 'N Twenty pie and see it is excellent and a miracle of baked mince and thumb-holes; my dad eats his most delicately and hands me a lovely clean handkerchief to put under the still-hot feast on my knee, resting neatly on my own copy of today's 'Footy Record' which is read as if it's the gospel by the fans educated enough to get past the ads for Violet Crumbles and Repco Spark Plugs. it was sixpence back then and it included a drawing of the oval with the places underlined where each particular player was to play.

In fact the religious and emotional impact The Footy Record had on you meant that you were really surprised when you observed a player somewhere else on the oval.

He should really have been where he was typeset.

I forget who won that day but my dad certainly loved me and looked after me that first experience of proper fair dinkum Australian Rules Football. Years later I was certainly shocked when the Chairman of our club informed me that thousands upon thousands of dollars, hard-fought-for-dollars had from ordinary battlers donating to try to save Fitzroy Football Club from oblivion has been stolen from the coffers of The Social Club and in many instances metamorphosed into cream brick four bedroom homes in the Eastern suburbs or posh European sports cars.

He told me in 1996 that it was such a burden to him that people who swore by the club and raised money around the clock to save us from disappearing from the league had rorted.

He wept in the bar in Fitzroy where my mates used to have a drink after the game, he cried into his double vodka someone shouted him after a half-hearted game of pool where he dropped his cue.

All through the solemn year 1996 we had striven to tip enough money into Fitzroy to somehow keep it alive, there was can rattling in just about every street in Melbourne and fiery debates on radio and television over the moral dilemma posed by a football club in millions of dollars of debt and whether it was right to keep bailing them out or propping them up with more floats that simply couldn't be paid back.

I wrote lots of passionate articles published in 'The Age' and 'The

Melbourne Times' where I was a Fitzroy columnist of twenty years standing and when our steadfast chairman Leon Weigard cried as he shared with me the names of those within Fitzroy deemed loyal but who rorted, then I wept hard with him in that pub, The Lincoln it is.

In the end Fitzroy were got rid of and called The Brisbane Lions, what a joke!

I was pressured by some of the old push to write supportive newspaper articles promoting the new amalgam but my heart wasn't in it and it still isn't. It made me want to vomit about fifteen years ago when some old mates put on a movie night at a pub where you stared at the old team's heroes playing Essendon in the 1960s or something. Time out of mind.

They were getting boozed watching this bullshit and crying out the dead club's song and their eyes were crowned with overwhelming and dangerous nostalgia, the whole lot of them crying over someone's Super Eight home movie of Fitzroy Football Club; now dead as a doornail.

Barry Dickins

Barry Dickins is an atheist and patriot aged god knows what. He was deliberately born in Reservoir which has been an unforgivable oversight on his mother's behalf. He has watched Fitzroy lose since the first home game he viewed with his father Len.

He is the poet in residence at All Hallows Girl's School in Balwyn in Victoria to the Year 9's and the father of his son Louis who plays pool with him once a week at The Red Triangle Pool Room in Fitzroy; the closest he can get to his old stamping ground and urge on The Mighty Roys!

He won The Premiers' Award For Drama in 1995 with his play 'Remember Ronald Ryan', which looked into the politics behind Australia's last execution, apart from Fitzroy Football Club that is.

8

Yabby's Dilemma

Peter Lyons

The late and great Richmond coach, Jack "Captain Blood" Dyer had no hesitation in naming former Premiership captain, Darrel Baldock, as the best he had seen.

Writing in his weekly Melbourne Truth column, "Dyer 'Ere" Dyer said: "Mr Magic, that's what the fans have dubbed him. The most freakish footballer I have seen.

"Yet he lacks everything that makes a champion. He lacks height, pace, marking ability for a key position and a vicious streak.

"What he has is an unbelievable quantity of courage, absolute dedication and a ball control I have never seen equalled.

"Don't let anyone tell you that Les Foote, Haydn Bunton senior or Laurie Nash had his magical touch. He threads his way through packs backwards and forwards with the ball seemingly out of reach, yet really always under his control".

So spare a thought for Alan Yabby Jeans, the only coach to lead St Kilda to a Premiership. It was 1966 and the Saints, sitting in second spot on the ladder, were to face a danger game against Hawthorn in the final home-and-away match. and without their captain and regular match-winner, Darrel Baldock.

Doc, as he was generally known, had ruled himself out, which was a most unusual occurrence as he repeatedly said he was OK, when, in fact, he carried injuries that would have sidelined many others.

Realising what a devastating effect his absence would have on the rest of the team, Yabby was determined that Doc should play.

Nor did it help matters when Yabby sought the assistance of Victoria's leading orthopedic surgeon at the time, Owen Deacon, only to be told if "Doc" took the field it would all be on his – Yabby's – shoulders.

"He, Owen, would take no responsibility for the aftermath".

But Yabby – and Doc – were determined the captain would come on at some stage.

In this Yabby had gone against the advice of an astute Melbourne coach, the late Len Smith who stressed that in finals one only fielded the fittest players.

Doc and wife Margaret and anyone else who knew of the plan were sworn to secrecy. In fact the Baldocks even went to Sandown where the first horse that they owned was running in the first race.

Doc got back to the ground at about 1pm, but when he sat in front of the stands in his dressing gown the game was up. He was a reserve and would play. Doc and Yabby decided that he would come on "at some stage".

Yabby admitted later he was desperate, particularly when Hawthorn was leading by 19 points mid-way through the third quarter.

As Hawthorn wingman, Des Meagher, said later: "I heard the greatest noise I'd heard on a football field. I could not understand it as St Kilda had not kicked a goal.

"But I soon realised what it was. Baldock had taken the field and had won a kick".

From then on Doc took control and goalled from his first kick. Then he passed to Kevin Neale in the goal square for another goal.

Between them, Baldock and Neale kicked five of the remaining six goals and St Kilda was the winner by 10 points.

But worse – far worse – was to follow.

St Kilda had won their way to the grand final and was to play Collingwood.

On the Thursday before the match it seemed all the Saints fans, booked for the grand final, had come to see the team strut its stuff for the last time before the grand final.

Then it happened.

"I remembered that we went through training drills for about 40 minutes then Jeans decided to put the players in their positions and conduct a mock match with no opponents. The diehard St Kilda fans were rapt."

"But it didn't last long. Ross Smith got the ball in the centre and passed it to me. I was a "smart arse" and jumped in the air. As I landed my legs crossed and I felt my knee 'go'.

"The knee would remain sore for only about three minutes, but I did not want to limp and upset the supporters.

"I immediately told Yabby and, without missing a beat, he told the boys it was the end of training and we all walked off in a group".

The club doctor then gave the skipper a cortisone needle, telling him it would take up to 20 hours to take effect.

So "Doc", leaving nothing to chance, had a run around the streets at 9pm on the eve of the grand final, before deciding he would be fit enough to play.

However, he knew he was not fully fit and would be lucky to see out the game.

But within three minutes of the bounce of the ball "Doc" had been given a free kick about 50 yards out from goal. He was looking to pass it to someone closer in when Ian Stewart ran passed and said: "You can kick it Doc".

So Doc had a shot, goalled, and in the process, damaged his knee – again!

The pain, as expected, lasted perhaps three minutes but Doc did not have the influence over the game he would normally have had.

Nevertheless, having since watched replays of that grand final Doc has noted he did not stretch out, nor bend down as he would normally have done, and was obviously subconsciously concerned whether his injured knee would flare up again.

It was a point picked up by former champion Melbourne wingman, Brian Dixon. Writing his usual press column, Dixon thought Collingwood centre half back, Ted Potter, had beaten Doc on the day 'partly because of Baldock's reluctance to battle into the packs with his normal bullocking, balance and strength.'

The game had been close all day, with only a handful of points separating the teams at the end of each term.

And, with four minutes to play, a Collingwood goal narrowed the gap yet again.

At three quarter time, the Saints were four points up. But Daryl Griffiths ran into an open goal to give St Kilda a 10 points margin.

Full forward, Kevin "Cowboy" Neale missed with a snap to edge his side a further point in front. Not long after he took a great mark on an angle but missed the lot.

Half forward flanker, later named best on ground, flashed in but his left foot shot was wide but it gave the Saints a two goal break – and they could almost taste the Premiership.

The Magpies got back into the game with a goal to edge closer.

Doc, sensing the Premiership was slipping away, took himself upfield to bolster the defence and the Saints lifted.

Later, when asked why he did it, he suggested the coach had made the move. But Yabby was adamant. The skipper had made the move on his own – which was part of their special relationship between the captain and the coach.

With a couple of minutes on the clock, Collingwood captain, Des Tuddenham, who had been well held by fellow Tasmanian, John Bingley, raced clear in the centre of the ground. He would have continued on down forward, but elected to kick with Collingwood scrambling a point to level the scores.

At this point, Doc shot the ball to Stewart, who kicked it forward.

With the scores level, Barry Breen had a shot, which rolled through for a behind to give the Saints back the lead.

Collingwood was able to scramble the ball forward for a last ditch attempt to snatch victory, but full back, Bob Murray, took what turned out to be a match-saving mark in defence.

As he claimed the mark, Murray thought what to do. He kicked to the outer half back flank, where he knew Alan Morrow and Doc were waiting

He reasoned that no Collingwood player was a realistic chance to mark it – and if Alan didn't, Doc would pick it up.

In the event, the final siren sounded with the Saints winning their first – and only, to this point – Premiership.

If Doc had been somewhat disappointed about his role in that famous grand final, he need not have been.

Looking back to the day, back pocket player, Rodger Head, summed it all up when he said: "Doc's leadership, both on and off the field, was the reason we won that 1966 grand final. He would carry injuries that most players could not and his example inspired all those players who played with him".

Yabby Jeans, although disappointed that St Kilda had not won more premierships during those golden years, later went on to coach Hawthorn to the 1988, 1989 and 1991 premierships becoming a legend of his second club.

Peter Lyons

Peter Lyons is a professional journalist of some 60 years standing, writing for such Tasmanian newspapers as the *Burnie Advocate, The Examiner,* and the *Devonport Times.* He was also the Sports Editor for the *Canberra Times* for a seven-year period.

Peter comes with a very high Australian pedigree – he is the son of Joseph Lyons, Australian Prime Minister 1932-39, and Dame Enid Lyons, Australia's first woman MHR and Cabinet Minister.

9

Rose to Walsh – on Football and Fatherhood

James Gilchrist

"Are you okay? He said. The boy nodded. Then they set out along the blacktop in the gun-metal light, shuffling through the ash, each the other's world entire."

The Road: A novel by American writer Cormac McCarthy

On July 3, 2015, I had kick to kick with my eight-year-old son wearing, as always, his Collingwood jumper with 'Grundy 4' on the back. He'd decided Brodie was his man based on the logic that they were both born in April. It made sense to him in much the same way the reasons for my early adulation of Peter Moore and the number 30 once made sense to me. We were in Cowes Park on holiday. It was freezing. My two daughters were playing nearby and normally, like most Dads, the simple metronome quality of kicking and marking the ball with one's son is a soothing Aussie benediction, the familiar backyard ritual where we ease our sons (and daughters) through rite of passage, preparing them for the oval, the park, the school yard.

This was just one of many cold mornings and evenings spent with my son from back in the time of his first, tentative Auskick outings as a five-year-old which had to be abandoned because he was more interested in staring at clouds or playing hide and seek in the scoreboard. Through to the days spent boundary-side watching in tentative frustration as he failed to get to the fall of the ball because he was … yet again staring at clouds, playing chasey, having wrestling matches or making friends with his opponent in the backline over some point of mutual interest.

Meanwhile, in the wings I calmly resisted the urge to deliver my comprehensive post-game Power Point with rafts of detailed bullet points on ways that he could improve his performance, realising that the best thing a father can do to sustain a love of the game is distil the Power Point to the simple message 'Gee I love watching you play footy' while learning to let go and leave some things to the 'cosmos'; and then having that one, perfect, unexpected moment on another frost-filled, mid-winter morning when it somehow magically came together and he won the coaches' medal for best on ground: the joys and tribulations of fatherhood.

Kick to kick with my son will always be an act of love as meaningful as teaching him to read or tie his shoelaces. But on that day in Cowes I did so beneath the dark shadow of the news of the death of Adelaide coach Phil Walsh. On that morning there were shockwaves of disbelief around the nation as people on the airwaves, in newsprint and in cafes and kitchens awoke to the news and tried to make sense of how a lively, quirky and dedicated father figure and leader of young men, loved and respected by so many, could be killed by the hand of his own son?

Football and fatherhood go together. Or in the right circumstances, should. When I wrote the story of the St. Pat's First XVIII coach Howard Clark in 2009 in *Wednesday Warriors* I was inspired by the strength and breadth of the love this man seemed to possess for all those in his charge; broad enough to encompass the many boys within his football program, with plenty left over for his sons at the end of the day. Although the most successful school football coach in the state and possibly the country, guiding St. Pat's to a record six successive Herald-Sun Shields and a record twenty-three past students into the AFL system (by 2015), when asked at the time what he hoped to achieve, Clark said very little about football itself:

> I want to produce outstanding citizens, men with a sense of justice for others, a sense of service to others, good males, good partners to their wives, role models for their own children – that's why I let them see me interact with my sons, kiss them. They need to experience that gentle side of being male.

Recent decades in AFL football have seen the rise of a 'relational' coach who is becoming more aware of the 'connection' between the on-field performance and external or off-field 'character' of young men and then the need in some way to try to connect the two, encouraging stable, sensible, perhaps even admirable modes of behaviour outside the football club. Such coaches seem mindful of their own conduct, perhaps aware of their role as models to young men as well as simply coaches. The ironic tragedy of Phil Walsh's death appears to be, at least on the surface, that he was not able to have the kind of fatherly relationship that he shared with Adelaide Captain Taylor Walker, with his own son. There is something in this that touches other fathers on a slightly primal level, perhaps explaining why Nathan Buckley's response upon hearing the news of Walsh's death was to bring his young sons into bed for a protective hug.

In my lifetime of being a Collingwood Tragic, I can recall three images of fatherhood that have stuck with me. The first relates to that loveable, yet wayward icon Darren Millane. Like most of us I can recall what I was doing upon hearing the news of his death in a terrible car accident in 1991. A twenty-one-year-old uni student living my carefree existence at Don Bosco Hostel in Brunswick I awoke that morning to find a fellow resident, both a mate and an avid Carlton supporter, had left a paper message under my door – "I'm sorry to tell you this James but Darren Millane died last night." I thought it was a bad joke and took some time to come to terms with the reality of the news. Such a towering figure in life, Millane made his team mates walk taller. He was a player once described by *Herald* writer Trevor Grant as the ultimate team man: "His mates say they could not find a better friend than Darren Millane, on or off the field."

Millane's biography *Pants* provides little clue to the relationship he shared with his father and what has been gleaned of his early life seems primarily seen through the eyes of his mother Denise. A superficial Google search displays only that Millane was mixed up in a "wild brawl involving his father" at the Boundary Hotel in the early 90s, a venue where Collingwood players of that era often mixed with some of Melbourne's more 'colourful' identities. The *Herald-Sun*'s death notice from the players in 1991 (which I kept) offers a moving tribute to a player who seemed to exercise an almost fatherly role towards his team mates who so often looked up to him because of his power and confidence and personality.

Whatever the nature of Darren's relationship with his own father, what stuck with many of us at the close of his all too brief life was that funeral procession and the endless repetition of his favourite song, Cat Stevens' "Father to Son", a beautiful and timeless reflection by a father, offering advice for the future before his imminent death. At the time it seemed to capture all that sadness we felt about a life short-lived and the evocative space Millane seemed to fill in our Collingwood hearts as bus-stealing poster boy, larrikin, flawed hero, brother-in-arms.

When I was, for a time, a Collingwood Social Club member during the mid-90s I remember seeing the great Bob Rose enter the Club for an after-match function pushing a guy in a wheelchair. At the time I was struck by the event, knowing nothing of Rose's personal story. It seemed to me Bobby Rose was performing some act of 'charity' for a disabled fan. It wasn't until some years later when reading the moving tribute *Rose Boys* by poet and author Peter Rose, son of the aforementioned Collingwood legend, that it dawned on me that the person I had seen in the wheelchair was Bobby's other son Robert, the subject of the book. *Rose Boys* provides a glowing testament to human courage in the face of adversity. Robert is looking very much destined to step into his father's footsteps as a gifted footballer and cricketer, perhaps even on the way to greatness in one of those sports, when tragedy strikes in the form of a terrible car accident on the Western Highway near Ballarat, leaving Robert a quadriplegic for the rest of his life.

Bob Rose, the face of epic, enduring tragedy at Collingwood, who was denied victory so cruelly, so often as a coach, defined 'legend' in a different kind of way. Although a member of the 1953 Collingwood Premiership side as a player, he 'failed' as a coach, most terribly in the dramatic 1970 Grand Final, where he endured the greatest comeback in Grand Final history from the detested arch-rival Carlton. Rose was always graceful and composed through all these football heartaches. It seems so unfair and improbable that behind all of that he had to cope with a far more grave and personal heartbreak, the breaking in body of his own son. As Peter observes without bitterness, the talented one, the physically capable sports star bound for greatness.

If there is anything epic or legendary about Bob Rose, to me it was his Promethean fatherhood, his (and wife Elsie's) boundless love for their son and constant proximity in his life through all the incalculable trials and hardships of being caught in that lifetime 'limbo' of quadriplegia: the image of father and son I was so ignorant of that night but which has remained with me ever since. In addition to emphasising the fortitude of Robert in his writing, Peter Rose also notes in his brother's funeral oration:

> Bob and Elsie's devotion to Robert was unqualified from day one and remained passionate and limitless, and always so intelligent and considerate of his physical and emotional needs. Robert returned that love in full ... For this son, it has been an extraordinary education to observe this tacit and everlasting pact. Putting aside blood ties for a moment, I am left with a sense of awe and good fortune at having known these three people.

More recently I was able to experience a footy 'life cycle' with the debut of the son of my childhood hero when Darcy, son of Peter Moore, arrived at the only club he could ever really play for. I took joy in describing his father to my own son and showed him You Tube highlights of Peter Moore, re-living my own childhood as my boy entered that exciting phase of life where footballers seem like titans striding the great amphitheatre of football.

One of the marvellous features of our unique game and one yet to be extinguished by the AFL is the Father-Son rule which provides many rich traditions within our game. People are well-versed in the folklore surrounding these relationships. Steve Silvagni will remain forever 'SOS', (Son of Serge) and his son upon playing for Carlton in the future may yet be SOSOS. Fans can debate whether Gary Ablett senior or junior is the greater footballing master. Collingwood fans are already scanning social media for updates on the sons of the legendary Peter Daicos. The joys and tribulations of fatherhood are woven intricately into the fabric of our game.

People got to see the pained expression on news reporter Tim Watson's face last year when reporting for Channel Seven News on the Essendon supplements saga where his own son was under siege as Captain and reigning Brownlow medallist. On the flip side, they were able to witness the unadulterated joy of former Hawthorn great Chris Langford embracing his son Will after a sterling performance in Hawthorn's Grand Final victory. The great life-cycle plays out before us as we recall our own youth and look at the renewal that occurs through our children. Just as I enjoy kicking the ball to my son and watching him play Tackers, I likewise enjoy watching Peter Moore embracing his son Darcy as he is presented with his number 30 jumper in the Collingwood huddle before taking the field against Hawthorn on the night following Phil Walsh's death.

In the heat of battle during a Friday night blockbuster when people wonder for a second how football could go on, Darcy Moore and Will Langford take the field on a night with no banners, theme songs or ceremony. A young and emerging Collingwood team are to test themselves and ultimately fall just short of the two-time reigning Premiership Hawks, the competition's benchmark. Langford is simply superb and his bullocking within contests one of several reasons Hawthorn secures the win. Moore looks lost in this baptism of fire but gives his all. He will be seen talking closely with his father post game.

Three weeks later he will return to the Collingwood forward line and kick five goals confirming his status as a future star of the game. And these two will join in that extraordinary circle of players at the end of the game, a mixture of black and white, brown and gold that I watched through glistening eyes. It was a gesture of grace and solidarity between young men from opposing teams, orchestrated by Alistair Clarkson that for a moment made football shine out, a moment that elevated the game beyond mere competition and gave us hope of something better in an often darkened world.

James Gilchrist

James Gilchrist grew up in Creswick in Central Victoria before becoming a teacher, tennis coach, traveller, writer, husband and father of three. His writings include the Fringe Festival Comedy Caution Teachers Crossing (2001) and books *Wednesday Warriors* – the story of the St. Pat's First XVIII (2009) and *Tortured Tales of a Collingwood Tragic* (2010) in addition to being a regular contributor to The Footy Almanac. James teaches English and History in Kew, residing in Melbourne's north with wife Gillian and children Amelie, Charlie and Imogen. He lives for road trips, bike rides beach holidays, country air, reading, music and bringing up the next generation of Collingwood tragics.

10

Three Brownlow Votes: First Game

Frank DiMattina

My life in VFL/AFL started on an unbelievable high. The reason for this is that I was a very early developer being a fairly well built young man who was lucky enough to be a particularly fast runner. I was a schoolboy champion athlete and had won many sprint championships at under age level.

I had been recruited to Richmond FC as I was in their designated zone. At that time in the early 1960's, Melbourne was divided into zones in which each club had a specific area. This was before the draft system came into operation. Such was the publicity and hype about me that if there had've been a draft system I would have been a top 1, 2 or 3 draft selection.

In my last year at school at De La Salle College Malvern, I had a very successful year and kicked many goals. Richmond FC had kept a close eye on me as in the previous year I played a few games in their under 19's. Richmond FC kept wanting me to play but the Brothers at school refused to let me play outside the school competition. After the school football finished, Graeme Richmond, the great Richmond football administrator, persuaded the Brothers to let me play. I was rushed straight into the Richmond senior side to play South Melbourne at Punt Rd oval in 1964, I was a 17yo at the time.

The game was played in abysmal conditions, the ground was covered in mud and it rained most of the day. With Neville Crowe dominating in the ruck and the fact I was playing on the great Bobby Skilton, who ended up being a triple Brownlow Medalist, I received much plaudits picking up lots of possessions and kicking a goal. Richmond won the game, but it was not until the end of the season when I received 3

Brownlow Medal votes, that the magnitude of that day really escalated

Back in those days we didn't know which games were allotted for Brownlow Medal votes, but as I was named in the best players in this game and Richmond won, it is 99% certain this is the game I received those votes. We only played another 4 games that year of which Richmond only won another one, and in that game I wasn't named in the best. Statistics show over the many years of the Brownlow Medal, a player in the winning side usually gets the 3 votes.

Therefore I think I can look back on something that will probably never be achieved again, a 17yo playing his first game in the senior team at top level picking up 3 Brownlow Medal votes.

My following years '65 and '66 were good years in which I was a top performer for the Richmond FC and kicked 41 goals.

The turning point of my career came in late 1966 when playing against the great Collingwood FC in front of a massive home and away crowd of over 80,000 people. I was knocked unconscious and carried off the ground in the first ten minutes of the game crushed by my own team mate, the colossus of Richmond the big Irishman, Paddy Guinane.

This was to be the beginning of an unbelievable legend. The nineteenth man that day sitting on the bench was to become the greatest rover to ever play for the Richmond FC and one of the all time greats of the game, Kevin Bartlett. Kevin quickly established himself in my position as first rover, and with my confidence diminished from the big collision and subsequent injuries including a broken leg and many hamstring problems, I struggled to regain my former great form.

These years I was fortunate to play with many Richmond FC greats of the game some of whom remain close friends even to this day. These included Roger Dean, Neville Crowe, Barry Richardson, Dick Clay, Francis Burke, Kevin Bartlett, Michael Green, Allan 'the bull' Richardson, Rex Hunt, Barry Cameron, Wayne Walsh and many others. This was to become a great era of the Richmond FC including the 1967 Grand Final victory. It was somewhat sad for me because I was not truly involved and missed playing in that premiership team.

After the collision I never seemed to regain my initial brilliance, flair and confidence to play the game at the outstanding level I had started my career on.

There were many clubs keen to recruit me as I was still a very young player who had played very well at the top level. Collingwood FC was at the forefront of these but Richmond FC had refused to clear me to the perceived number one enemy.

Consequently I made my way to North Melbourne FC where I immediately had a great friendship with the highly talented and flamboyant Sam Kekovich. I managed to play some good football for Nth Melbourne FC and I started to regain some of my old form. Then Nth Melbourne coach Keith McKenzie whom I had a good relationship with was replaced by former Melbourne FC great and politician Brian Dixon. Unfortunately Brian and myself didn't seem to get along well together. One early morning training session at Olympic Park he had us training under the great Ron Clarke, he was our running and fitness coach.

This particular morning we were doing 400m time trials, after 4 or 5 of these Brian accused me of not trying. I said to him, I will race against Ron Clarke to prove that he was wrong. Brian immediately bet me £20 that I couldn't beat Ron over 400m and a match race was hastily organised. Ron went out on the banks of the Yarra to do his warm up while I happily waited, getting my strength and wind back from our earlier runs. Brian was probably right, I was holding a little bit back. The match race had caused quite a stir and lots of interest from the boys, some backed Ron to win but most had their money on me.

The race started, I thought Ron would go full pelt all the way, but instead he decided to sit on me. I started at a frantic pace but then eased slightly hoping Ron would stay sitting on me rather than go straight past me and make me chase him. Luckily for me he sat and when I reached the 200m mark in front, I knew he would not be able to out sprint me. So to the cheers of the morning crowd I shot away opening up a break and beat him. It made the training morning a little bit different and exciting, but unfortunately it didn't help my relationship with Brian.

That year Brian caused quite a mass walkout from the club. Nth Melbourne FC were determined to secure a very promising player from Brunswick FC called Keith Greig. The only player Brunswick wanted from Nth Melbourne in exchange was me. So that was the reason I was pushed and so ended my VFL career while still a young 24yo.

If I had known Ron Barassi was coming the following year, I would have loved to have tried out because I felt I was still capable of playing at the top level. That ended a career that started on a great high and finished with disappointment and regrets.

There was to come another stint of the highs and lows of VFL/AFL football with three of my sons being drafted to AFL teams. My oldest son Paul who was a talented footballer, battled hard with many setbacks before he was finally drafted to the Footscray/Western Bulldogs FC. Paul then had a good career amassing over 130 games.

He too suffered great disappointment when Footscray were eliminated by Adelaide FC in the 1997 preliminary final. Paul who missed this game through suspension, had been told by the coach if they were to make the Grand Final he would be in the team such was his good form prior to the finals. Footscray after leading most of the day and being deprived of what everybody believed was a goal by Tony Liberatore, tragically lost by three points. Thereupon Paul's opportunity to possibly win a Grand Final was lost.

My second son Andrew also battled hard to get drafted. After playing a winning reserve Grand Final with Essendon FC, he was finally drafted by the Collingwood FC. He worked hard with Collingwood and finally made the senior side in 2000 playing one stellar season where he was used by Mick Malthouse as a tagger and played on many of the top onballers.

My third son Frankie was also drafted by Collingwood FC and was showing a lot of promise before being cut down by constant injury. As a result he never played in the Collingwood Senior side.

The rigours of VFL/AFL put much stress and punishment to the body and many past players are now counting the cost with knee, hip replacements, ankle problems and many with some form of brain damage due to concussions they suffered while playing.

Frank DiMattina

Francis (Frank) Xavier DiMattina was born in 1946, the son of Salvatore Francesco DiMattina and Angelina Santamaria, the 5th child of 6 children. Frank was schooled at De La Salle College, Malvern and St. Patrick's College Ballarat.

He had a distinguished career in the VFL, playing football at the Richmond Football Club from 1964-1968, followed by North Melbourne from 1969-1970. He then played with the Brunswick Football Club 1971-1973 and completed his football as captain/coach of Sorrento Football Club 1974.

After football Frank embarked on a successful career in the hospitality industry, and today DiMattina's Restaurant is a well-known Melbourne venue. He married Angela Pititto in 1973 and produced 5 children, Paul 40 Andrew 37, Frankie 36, Carla 32, and Nicholas 28.

Frank DiMattina 1966 Scanlens footy card
Private Collection, used with collectors permission

11

The Kennedy Curse

Phil Tagell

In the early 1960s, Des Kennedy, a young, rangy forward/follower emerged as a bit of a star at VFA club Sandringham, and won their B&F at the age of 19 in 1963 after having played a significant role in their premiership the season before. As it turned out, young Des kicked the winning goal in that final encounter to seal victory for the Zebras in the dying moments of the game. He was invited to St Kilda to train and made their list for season 1965. He would enjoy a sound debut and would go onto to play 20 games for the season culminating in their Grand Final loss to Essendon that was disappointing given their warm favouritism for the flag.

He would back up with a patchy season in 1966 and would play in the Second Semi-final for the Saints against Collingwood but in that game, sustained a knee injury early which would rule him out for the rest of the finals. He would have been a near-certain inclusion as a back-up ruckman as their regular star ruck, Carl Ditterich, had gotten himself suspended before the finals and could not be selected. The Saints then fronted up for the Preliminary Final with Brian Mynott as sole ruckman, which they won. The following Grand Final that they also won, was again against Collingwood in the thriller which went down to the wire. The Barry Breen shank that went through for the winning behind is now the stuff of legend but Des was denied his place in Saints history as was Ross Oakley who was also injured in the Second Semi. It was a bitter pill for them to swallow but such is the luck of football. Travis Payze who came in for Kennedy and Jim Read for Oakley will be forever grateful to the footy gods for their place in Saints folklore. History records that the 1966 flag is the only one the Saints have won in their long and troubled history since being a formation club of the then VFL in 1897. Significantly, Ross Oakley went on to have a profound effect on the game as VFL then AFL CEO during the expansion years for the competition in the late '80s. Des battled on with the Saints until the end of 1970 after which he returned to the Zebras for another 4 seasons winning their B&F again in 1973. His contribution to the Zebras was recognised by him being declared a Life Member of the club in 1977.

Business opportunity took Des and his family to the Gold Coast of Queensland in the early '80s and his son, Matthew, played junior footy with their local club, the Surfers Paradise Demons. Young Matt impressed and joined the dominant local senior club, then in the QAFL, Southport and made his mark as a serious contender for selection in the big league. After playing in the Sharks' premiership side of 1989, Matt, now known as Maxy, joined the fledgling Brisbane Bears in the then AFL for season 1990. The Bears were based at Carrara on the coast and their chequered history there made development hard for all concerned as the club was rocked by regular upheavals as coaches were sacked, the club's owner Christopher Skase disappeared leaving a mountain of dept behind him and the team struggled to survive let alone win games.

Despite the challenges that beset the club, Maxy developed as a player and played in the club's first effort to get some silverware when Rodney Eade coached the Bears Reserves to a premiership at Waverley in 1991. Maxy was at Centre-Half-Back and was a member of that side from which many future Brisbane players would emerge and was part of the shift to Brisbane for season 1993. He became a regular contributor to the team as it gained football credibility under coach Robert Walls in the years 1991 to 1995 and was part of the merged entity with the remnants of Fitzroy when they became the Brisbane Lions in 1997. Walls held him in high regard due his dedication to training and preparation and he invited Maxy to take the lead in an ill-advised effort to deal out some discipline to wayward player, Shane Strempel in 1991. Walls had just taken over and was said to have been horrified at the attitude displayed by some of the players, Strempel in particular. Kennedy was a tough boxer and solid trainer and facing him in the ring was said to be a daunting experience indeed.

Maxy's first years with the Lions were solid with him moving from his traditional key defence role at CHB to the wing. He had a standout year in 1998, coincidentally a wooden-spoon year, when he finished third with 62 votes in the merged club's B & F, the Merrett – Murray Medal. Under new coach, Leigh Matthews, Maxy exhibited consistent form in '99 but injuries early into the new century meant that opportunities were becoming very limited for him. By 2001, the emergence of younger, faster wingers meant that at 191cm and nearly 100kgs, 31 year old Maxy's days were numbered and by late that season, he and the club had agreed that this was to be it for this stalwart of the club.

He announced his retirement during the finals in 2001, with his team heading almost inexorably to finals glory and he was given an emotional send-off during the warm-up to the Second Qualifying Final against Port Adelaide at the 'Gabba on Saturday evening, the 8th of September. Serendipitously, the game was a fiery affair and amongst other incidents, Alastair Lynch lashed out at his bete noir, Darryl Wakelin and got reported for his efforts. The tribunal ruled that a one week penalty was appropriate so there was a space for a key position player for the Preliminary Final, also at the Gabba, against Richmond in 2 weeks time. Maxy was the logical choice so his retirement was immediately placed on hold and he was selected for the game against the Tigers.

I was there for what, barring injury to another key, would be Maxy's last game for the Lions. He did not star but he was very determined to keep the Richmond forwards honest and he did so with passion. Late in the game, with a Grand Final spot in the bag, he attacked Matthew Richardson with so much vigour that I thought Richo would never get back up. He finally did so but Maxy had well and truly taken the sting out of the big Tiger's tail. His departure from the field after the game was more muted due to the euphoria felt by the fans about their long-suffering team's accession to the Big One. It was easy during that tumultuous week to forget the efforts of blokes like Kennedy who had seen the club through their darkest days at Carrara, sackings, 3 wooden spoons, a record score against at the hands of Geelong in 1992, near financial death and relocation to the 'Gabba. All these disasters and embarrassments of the past were distant nightmares during that week which culminated in a charter jet to Melbourne due to the collapse of Ansett, the league's airline of choice.

Maxy was invited to join his colleagues for the journey and the experience, but not in the side to play. He watched that historic first premiership with other 'emergencies' but was inconsolable after the game. It must have been a wretched experience having been so close yet denied glory after 188 games with the club. He attended the after-parties and travelled home with the team. I watched him in pride of place share the lead car in the team's Grand Final Parade down through the Queen Street Mall the following Wednesday but saw little but sadness in his eyes.

Life after that has been most fruitful for Maxy, he studied and completed a Masters of Sports Coaching at Griffith University and now holds the position of High Performance Manager for the Gold Coast Suns, back at Carrara where his league career started. He is highly regarded and his time as assistant coach of the Queensland Under 18 State Team is remembered fondly by the young men over whom he had a very positive influence. My son Rhys knows as he was one of his charges in the state team in 2010.

He is a fine role-model for young sportsmen but will, for me, ever be the one who missed out on deserved glory in September. That he followed his dad Des in similar circumstances is one of those eerie foibles of sport.

Phil Tagell

Phil Tagell is a Collingwood supporter who moved from Melbourne to Queensland in 1982 for work in architecture and now runs his own project management consultancy. His work has taken him to the furthest corners of the state and he has been influential on some of Brisbane's most significant projects.

He has been involved in local Brisbane footy as a volunteer with considerable success as he watched his 3 sons all play junior footy and at AFLQ level, one still does. Phil has written a book *Footy Tragic* about his controversial time in community footy and hopes to have it published later this year.

12

Some Players Are Tough

Matt Zurbo

I spoke to over 170 legends of the game for my footy book, bouncing between wood-cutting in the Tasmanian bush to pay for it all and interviews all over the country. A few of them said things that stuck.

One, he'd achieved it all. Universally loved, universally admired for his courage. Five flags. All-Australian Team of the Century. Many awards. Francis Bourke was a hero of mine.

I went to see him at his nice, big home in Melbourne's eastern suburbs. It was a good house. Neat. Almost disciplined. He was still at work, so his wife Kerry let me in. She was a charmer. Friendly to the hilt. They had been together their whole lives. We talked a bit about him and them and his career and where the lines blurred, while, outside, neighbours slapped around tennis balls and mowed lawns.

When Francis Bourke came in his wife gave us room. We talked for five hours, It was no interview, rather a simple love of football. You can't preach that, it has to be shared. Two players from different worlds, the hack and the legend, speaking the one language.

Every hour we talked, I knew, would add another day of work, transcribing, editing, putting it all in chronological order. Another day away from the bush. I didn't care. He was my hero, but suddenly he was also a human being.

We talked about the mud and blood and glory. The mightiness! Ambition, despair, heartache, teammates, friends and politics. We grinded through gears that most people don't see. We covered five decades, from the 50s until now.

He told me of his fifth and last flag. How he was no longer a key player, how many had wanted him to go. He told me about the glory days, the great occasions, players and teams. I asked him, of all the things he achieved, what was the greatest moment of them all?

He paused. Thought. Said, "No, sorry, I couldn't pick one."

By the time we were done, it was past 9pm, neither of us had eaten. He insisted on giving me a lift all the way back to where I was staying, north of the city. Would not take no for an answer.

As we drove, we talked a bit and didn't, in a good way. Sharing silences with him felt every bit as special as did noise. More. Then, with a block to go, Francis blurted, out-of-the-blue, "My greatest moment was my wife greeting me on the fence after the last Grand Final's siren."

"Whu…?" I said.

"Everyone had written me off, Kerry was there. She was always there."

I said, "Why one earth wouldn't you want that in the book? It's a beautiful moment."

He just shrugged, this proud man. Would not be budged. Maybe he was just that bit too old school to let it out in public - love, in a moment that's meant to be all gristle and war cries. Who knows?

It's funny. You outgrow so much, yet cling to it like habits, as if there was nothing to replace it with. You still eat lollies but they just aren't as sweet, or as much of a reward. Neither is going to the movies, or even barracking for an AFL team. You still hero worship, but the brilliance of their light no longer blinds you. It can all be a bit hollow.

Yet, there he was, just a person in the driver's seat, a hero to me all over again. Because he was more than a legend. He was a good man.

I wondered if Francis Bourke had ever told his wife that part. Not that it matters. Just being around them, I'm sure she knows.

We parked and stepped out onto the busy street. Framed by neon and passing cars, some stranger took our photo, we shook hands well, and were gone.

Matt Zurbo

Matt Zurbo alternates working in the bush and writing about Aussie Rules. He has played 33 years, so far, of senior footy in various country leagues, in three states, from mountains to coast, as well as in cities. After further requests, Francis Bourke agreed this story could go on record.

Francis Bourke Scanlens footy card, 1975.
Private collection, used with permission

13

Teams Deliver Individuals Don't

Jeff Kennett

In mid 2005 I was approached to join the Board of the Hawthorn Football Club.

It was public knowledge that I had been a committed Hawks supporter since childhood, a member for many years, and that during my time as Premier of Victoria I had been active in hosting events for the Club.

My most important involvement before 2005 was encouraging the two property developers short-listed to develop the Waverley Football Ground and its surrounds that this should include a public or community ingredient, which would be part of the Hawthorn Football Club.

The result was that Hawthorn got access to a large oval and leading edge administrative and training facilities including an indoor pool.

This asset became the facility from which the Hawthorn Football Club built its football prowess, under the newly appointed Coach Alastair Clarkson.

In fact, Alastair was appointed against the wishes of the then President Ian Dicker and also Dermott Brereton who was at that time a Board member. They argued for an ex Hawthorn player in the person of Gary Ayres.

It was Jason Dunstall who was acting CEO, and a Board member, who convinced the rest of the Board to appoint Clarkson. A former player himself, who was enjoying an assistant coaching role at Port Adelaide, Clarkson was by profession a teacher. He was also a great student of the game, and of coaching methods generally across many sports.

Importantly Clarkson was hungry for the opportunity to put his learning ideas into practice. The Hawthorn Football Club will be forever indebted to Jason Dunstall for his advocacy and promotion of Clarkson.

In November 2005, I assumed the Presidency of Hawthorn. Sadly the Board had become dysfunctional and at least one Board member leaked to the media. So in 2005 we had a relatively new Coach in Alastair Clarkson, having been appointed at the end of 2004, a new CEO in Ian Robson who also was appointed late 2004 and a new President – myself!

The first task was to get the Board working as a team. That happened very quickly. The only Board member with direct Hawthorn Football experience was Jason Dunstall. He was the Board's conduit to the football department but also acted as a mentor to Alastair Clarkson. Jason served on the Board until 2012.

The other Board members led by Geoff Harris, Bruce Growcott, Martin Ralston and Andrew Newbold quickly came together and started working as a team and delivering a standard of governance that had not been practiced for some time. Importantly there were no leaks from the Board to the media or other parties.

Apart from supporting the football department, the Board had to build morale through all aspects of the club, lift our membership base and give our members some value for their membership. We had to rebuild our sponsor base, and significantly improve the Clubs financial position.

One of the first changes we made was to change the Clubs constitution so that no President could serve longer than 2 terms of 3 years i.e. 6 years as President of the Club. No Director could serve longer than 3 terms of 3 years i.e. 9 years unless they went on to become President as did my successor Andrew Newbold.

This put some discipline into the leadership group and allowed for renewal at the top.

The Board developed its Vision for the Club, simply expressed as

5-2-50 – 5 years being the 5 years remaining of my Presidency, 2 being winning 2 premierships within the 5 years, and 50 being the lifting our membership from 28,000 in 2004 to 50,000 by 2011.

When this vision was publicly released it was met with a high degree of skepticism by the media. However staff, players, members and supporters quickly understood the concept of 5-2-50. Over the time frame we delivered one Premiership, and hit 50,000 members. Indeed by the end of season 2011 we had 62,000 members.

The second transformational arrangement was the partnership entered into between the HFC and the Government of Tasmania. Up to this point both Hawthorn and St Kilda played 2 home and away games at Aurora Stadium in Launceston. When the St Kilda Football Club indicated they no longer wished to play in Tassie, we at Hawthorn jumped at the opportunity to add St Kilda's 2 games to the two that Hawthorn already played in Tasmania.

The deal was struck over a game of golf when I played with Tasmanian Premier Paul Lennon. Paul saw the economic benefit to Tasmania – particularly northern Tassie as Hawthorn bought planeloads of supporters to each game. We at Hawthorn saw the opportunity to grow our membership among an AFL loving Tasmanian community, the opportunity of having a real home ground advantage, and building a lasting relationship with the Tasmanian community. On every point the partnership has proved an outstanding success, but importantly for Tasmania it delivers over $30m of economic value annually. The original 5-year contract has just been extended for a third term. Indeed there is no more successful sponsorship in Australian sport, where the benefits against costs can be so accurately measured. So the Club now had a new level of good governance, the development of a Vision for the Club, and an exciting partnership with Tasmania.

At seasons end in 2006 Captain Ritchie Vandenberg retired. The players group and coaches recommended to the Board that Sam Mitchell and Luke Hodge should be appointed joint Captains.

The Board rejected this proposal as it muddied the lines of leadership and Sam Mitchell was appointed Captain. This was important in as much as it established a clear sense of discipline and authority that was driven by the Board.

On the football field the Club was slowly improving having won 5 games in 2005, 8 games in 2006 and 11 games in 2007.

2008 proved to be a Premiership year. Many thought Hawthorn secured its Premiership ahead of expectation. But by then Coach Alastair Clarkson had melded a very impressive and focused football support group and player list. The football department was well managed by Mark "Duggy" Evans, and with the close involvement of Jason Dunstall all the stars were in alignment. At a Board meeting towards the end of the year, after the Coach had made his presentation, he was asked by the Board, "Is there anything you need to complete the season?" He replied no.

In other words, since the end of 2005 the Club had been rebuilt, investing in first class people and resources. There was nothing else the Club could have provided the Coach in his pursuit of the Premiership. Hawthorn therefore was in a very sound position and had laid the base for its future.

The 2008 Premiership victory for players, employees of the Club, and our supporters after a drought of 14 years, was sweet.

As I stood in the stand, hearing the final siren that signalled victory, my feeling was not one of jubilation so much as that of the realisation of a job done, that those of us in positions of leadership had delivered on our Vision. I did not go onto the field to join the immediate celebrations, but waited until the players left the field and entered the changing rooms.

The Boards appointment of Stuart Fox as the Clubs CEO in November 2009 bought a very well experienced football administrator who was 2IC at the Geelong Football Club, and like Clarkson an individual desperately looking for the opportunity to prove himself, but also a person of very good personal values.

One issue and two moments stood out for me during my period of President of Hawthorn.

One was the intransigence of the AFL administration over their 3-strike drug rule. This in my opinion was terribly wrong in the interests of an individual, a club and the good name of the code.

It was clear the AFL held their line because they simply wanted to satisfy and protect the errant player who abused the rules of the game. That was not leadership by the AFL but a weakness borne out of the Alfa A boys club that existed at the time.

Sadly we latter found out that the AFL actually had in place a confidential self-reporting opportunity for players that carried no penalty. So the published rules were an absolute farce. Regardless of the number of times I raised the issue at AFL Commission/Presidents meetings I was almost treated with contempt by the top table. It was as though I was the delinquent child in the room!

I will never forget one of my fellow Presidents saying at one such meeting "I just do not want to know of any player who was taking drugs" This was a total failure of leadership.

The other two moments cut me to the quick.

Max Bailey a young player, had his career curtailed by serious injury. Having had two ACL injuries, each which required a yearlong rehabilitation period, he returned to play in round 21 in 2009 and the next week, 5 minutes into the game, landed awkwardly and suffered another season ending ACL injury. Watching Max lying crippled on the ground then being helped from the field ground it was the only time I have cried at a football game. Max Bailey is a superb individual. He never complained about his lot, he was cheerful during his periods of rehabilitations and was able to play in Hawthorns Premiership team in 2013, and immediately retired from the game. If any young player entering the game wanted a role model on persistence, of character then one needs go no further than Max Bailey.

The second heartfelt incident concerned Jordan Lewis in 2010, when he received a very heavy knock in a collision with an opposing player. He was cleared by the medical staff to return to the field later in the match.

He was clearly concussed and I was ropeable. I called the coaching and medical staff to a Board meeting to justify their position. The medical staff argued justifying their decision, the coaching staff hid behind the medical staff. It was a failure of duty of care to a player, which I found unacceptable. Lewis was cleared to play the following week but he now recounts it took him several weeks to recover from the incident.

Subsequently the AFL has introduced rules to protect players from head-high contact and rules governing when a player can return to play when concussed.

Football is a game. It is on the scale of other organisations a small business, but one where emotions run high. Football is more important for the supporters of the game than the players. For many supporters it is the only distraction from the two things that cause them stress and anxiety, their families and their work. It helps them get a balance in their lives. To discuss football at work and play, is an easy distraction from the struggles so many face.

To me personally while executing a vision and a strategy, that included winning a premiership, the greatest satisfaction came from building a strong team from top to bottom.

I have always believed that leadership is about delivering good governance but secondly the welfare of the team you lead is the next priority

Individuals do not deliver, teams do. At Hawthorn we have built a strong team, and a culture of governance, that continues to drive the club today.

While performance on the field may vary from year to year, a team has no chance of saluting unless it is strong from top to bottom.

More important to me than Premierships is the culture and values of an organisation. It is the people who make the whole. And Hawthorn has selected good people, with good values that have enabled them to deliver for their members.

I feel honoured to have been part of the Hawthorn Football Club for a few key moments of its history.

The Hon Jeffrey Kennett AC

Jeff Kennett AC is the founding Chairman of beyondblue: the national depression initiative and has been Chairman since 2000. A longtime Victorian Liberal MP, he was Premier of the State from 1992-1999. Prior to that he was Leader of the Opposition from 1982-1989 and during 1991-1992.

Mr. Kennett was president of the Hawthorn Football Club from 2005-2011. In 2005 he was awarded the Companion of the Order of Australia. Mr. Kennett was awarded an Honorary Doctorate in Business (honoris causa) by Ballarat University in 2000 and he was awarded an Honorary Doctorate of Laws (honoris causa) by Deakin University in 2014.

"After The Final Siren", Bill Hay drew this sketch that grew out of a peculiar vision that saw men in a boisterously cheering football crowd having an uncanny resemblance to mid-loin lamp chops.

Sketch courtesy of Bill Hay, used with permission

14

Up On Windy Hill

Bill Hay

Paul Van Der Haar sank eighteen luscious frothy topped pots of beer the Friday night before a Saturday afternoon game then took the field the very next day to leave no one in any doubt that he was indeed the very best on ground.

In fact better than best, he was miraculous. In the air, on the ground, anywhere you like, taking pack marks of astonishing courage, grace and charm, mixed with a carefree nonchalance and the alluring threat of self-harm.

Tim Watson, in what was for him a rare tagging role, tried valiantly to keep up with "Vander's" pre-game intake and then went on to play, by his own reckoning, one of the worst games of his brilliantly inventive 307 appearances.

At a time when the "Bombers" have felt the sword of Damocles dangling by a single thread above their troubled brows, this old story from the late 70s means both everything and nothing. Did "Vander" play better for his night on the turps; or Watson, with his red and black veins full of the same frothy potion, did he under-perform for having had that skin-full?

Notwithstanding the results of the enquiries by ASADA, WADA and the media's insistent Blah-De-Blah-Blah-Da, the supplementary injections appear not to have done the "Dons" all that much good these past few years. Yet Essendon, had they known it, possessed one long standing performance enhancing option dating back to the days when they were known as "The Same Old", and to other sepia tinted times when ringers and rouseabouts in far away shearing sheds dubbed them the "Blood and Tars".

"Go, You Same Old! Go, You Blood And Tars!"

But sadly the "Bombers" relinquished this assistance at the end of the 1991 season. The performance enhancer, the supplement of supplements was the Essendon Recreation Reserve, Windy Hill itself, … and no matter where the "Dons" stood on the ladder in any given year, you always gave them a chance if they were playing a home game at Windy Hill.

The Hill, that windy old hill would shimmer, in all its muddy, boot-studdy, mist and drizzle while exquisitely sharp, sparkling drops of Autumn and Winter rain peppered the cheering cheeks of the Essendon footy faithful.

During these chillier seasons Windy Hill produced its own mysterious and unearthly light, particularly where it pierced the stands at the Napier Street end of the ground. Late in a game everything glowed, both outwardly and inwardly, if such a thing is possible.

The Dick Reynolds and Allan Hird Stands colluded with the Showers Pavilion during many a thrilling final quarter to create something akin to a magnetic attraction for any "Bomber" booted ball.

In these tense moments the footy seemed magically drawn through the big sticks for another "You Beaut, Sausage Roll". Although strangely, when the other mob, whoever the other mob might be, were booting towards the Napier Street end, the great stands cunningly connived to create winds of cyclonic strength accompanied by a blinding and confusing winter light … or was it just the collective will and roar erupting from the Member's Stand?

This wind tunnel and the searing light could be understood and anticipated by the initiated "Bombers", while simultaneously creating moments of wobbly uncertainty in many opposition minds. To understand the vagaries of these Windy Hill elements took more than mere local knowledge as there was always something elusively unclassifiable about it.

One who understood it was our "Bomber" supporting comrade on the hill, the late and much lamented poet, Robert (Bob) Harris, who felt the power of place deeply and who also had at his command not only the words to express himself but also an ability to educate and explain the mysteries to we poor fools on The Hill.

I remember a half-time story he told me as we watched the little league game evolving from our weather worn position in the shade of the tattered windsock on the breeziest of Windy Hill's gradients.

Bob explained that all the old VFL grounds, (except of course Waverley, which was apparently devised by a cabal of embittered and sadistic town clerks), were formed from the footprints of Old Man Kangaroo as he bounded through the south-eastern corner of the Australian continental mass. Eleven times he landed amongst the creeks and tributaries of the Yarra and Maribyrnong Rivers before landing with a tail-thumping thud down at Kardinia Park in Geelong.

These ovals were in fact Corroboree Grounds, which is borne out by the canoe tree in Yarra Park, next to the M.C.G. and the Corroboree Tree still standing as a stoic sentinel, right beside the Junction Oval.

Bob's story also prophesised that if we were to lose the suburban ovals, we would lose more than mere footy grounds; we risked losing ancient and irreplaceable heritage as well.

A sense and an understanding of the power of place is a very potent thing, and for me one of those powerful places was always Windy Hill.

My Windy Hill initiation was at a training session, wearing a memorably itchy woollen Essendon jumper with Jack Clarke's No:1 stitched right in the middle of the back. I watched as larger than life players took the field, freed as they were from our black and white tellies and the Scanlen's bubble-gum cards, the sites of their previous existence. The players were already known, glorified, perhaps even deified, but the ground was fresh and immediately absorbed into the blotting paper mind of my childhood. There was the look, then the feel, then the smell; it was only a football ground, but my senses were taken by storm.

Standing at the fence, I watched the sun strike the Showers Pavilion standing off to the right on the Grammar School wing, and for me at that moment, this Art Deco grandstand was akin to a temple, a place of worship.

Absorbing all, as perhaps only a child can do, I received the ground's windy wisdom. There was John Coleman, once the genius full-forward, now the celebrated coach ... the history of this place was tangible and undeniable.

Early on I took up a position in the dry area on the Grammar School or Bowling Club wing, but in time it was necessary to venture out and understand the intricacies of the oval and find my own home ground position.

The goals at the Primary School end were a natural attraction, but it was always the most physical and volatile section, filled full of mad eyed men and fearless boys attempting to take kidney-crunching screamers each time the ball sailed through the sticks.

It was hard to hold your ground in this seething mixed up mass of human frailty and although from time to time I returned to this beautiful bedlam behind the goals, my search continued for a long-term vantage point.

There was a snug little spot on the Croquet Club flank, a small parcel of seats and standing room, but it was hard to get into, as the regulars who "owned" it would arrive before the first bounce of the Reserve's game. These habituates knew all that could be humanly known about every Essendon player who ever was, or even those who only might have been.

As a newcomer, I felt the intimidation in the blunt and forthright manner in which it was intended, as not one soul moved up to let the small boy squeeze in. Like the Rats of Tobruk, these Rats of Croquet Corner held their ground with a granite-like fixity.

Up behind these stoics was a line of peppercorn trees populated by the strange fruit of street-wise ex-pie and footy record purveyors, who having tired of warbling "Hot Pies, Get Your Hot Pies." or "Drinks, Lollies, Chocolates, Potato-Chips", had climbed the gnarly branches to spy the game through a curtain of green fronds and pink peppercorns.

To the tartan garbed mothers sitting below these trees, warmed as they were by tartan blankets and even more thoroughly tartaned thermos flasks, these boys were nothing but cheeky little darlings, whilst to other's of us they appeared to be more like the children of a Moonee Ponds Mephistopheles.

I blame the television show "Shintaro" for inspiring these diabolists to drop from the tree branches in the manner of Japanese "ninjas", landing on the unsuspecting heads of other young supporters. The "ninjas" would then make financial demands of their prey with very believable, if somewhat unsophisticated menace. I was only able to make an escape after convincing my assailants that it would be far more profitable to mug Hawthorn supporters.

It was not long after this that I found my place in standing room, up on the wind-sock hill, with a view overlooking the flank and the pocket. I loved to be standing there amongst those rough and raucous followers, who in their own gruff way could be caring and thoughtful about our strange shared Saturday afternoon space.

In the days when the mob could take unlimited quantities of their own booze to the footy, these mad "Bomber" fans would eagerly drain the steely strong lager cans to provide empties for me to stand on. Usually four cans was enough to provide the younger me with enough elevation for a decent view, but often the generosity of those around me meant I could build quite a respectable platform.

Being at Windy Hill was always as much about the crowd as it was about the game and there was nothing quite like being just one of that mob, united in the shifting, surging mass, screaming for another Simon Madden mark, a Garry Foulds run or the full blown Ronnie Andrews or Roger Merrett whack of the pack.

From earlier days, I remember in the late afternoon shadows of the stands the untamed Cheer Squad intoning their songs of love for Gerlach, Fordham, Fraser, McKenzie, Noonan and Blew. These weavers of player race run-throughs, the weekly Bomber Bayeux Tapestries, also invented chants of true devotion for their team, while for the opposition, there were mockingly scornful taunts unleashed with the full venom.

The Cheer Squad's chant of chants honoured a much loved "Bomber" of the 1960s, "What's his number, What's his name, Number seven, Charlie Payne." The crowd would belt out this homespun poetry with adoration as Charlie took yet another game saving grab on the back-line.

It was during a game against Richmond that the Tiger cheer squad's floggers caught alight, resulting in a duffle-coated ground invasion whilst the blaze was dealt with. But the more the crepe paper floggers were waved and shaken, the more the flames seemed to lick and spread. Schadenfreude set in and we "Bomber" supporters safely ensconced on the far side of the ground, laughed like drains.

Nothing announced the Essendon Cheer Squad with more precision than black duffle coats. These emboldened pearly kings and queens were glorious, with their garments emblazoned and sewn, adorned with players numbers, pinned and known ... Barry Davis, Ken Fletcher, Merv Neagle, John Williams, John Birt, Bill Duckworth and the Danihers all.

Down in the Croquet Club pocket stood the scoreboard, a giant blackboard filled with letters and numbers. At the top was the word ESSENDON and beside this stood a "G", for goals, followed by "B" for behinds, beneath this was often the abbreviation "Vis", which was short for visitors. I delighted in the dismissive nature of this act; to not even give the opposition a name was indeed the height of arrogance.

Further down this wooden edifice we watched encoded scores coming in from other grounds. A versus B, C versus D would provide added interest if a close game or an upset was unfolding elsewhere and the footy record supplied the cryptic answer as to which team was doing what to whom.

There was also a numerical code to unravel the mystery of which umpire was available to absorb our abuse that afternoon and it was always Jeff Crouch who was given the most generous "white maggoty" earful, lest he ever forget his wilful neglect of full-forward Geoff Blethyn's human rights during the 1968 Grand Final.

There were only two other sets of numbers on the board; first the winning digits of a thing called "Special Effort", this being the oddly named weekly prize of a portable telly or a donated electrical appliance of dubious provenance and usefulness. This was fund raising "Part A", while "Part B" saw the Cheer Squad carry an old army surplus blanket right around the boundary line, stretching it out like a fireman's safety net to catch the shrapnel hard coins hurled by the "Bomber" faithful, while opposition supporters lobbed the occasional empty beer can in the blanket's general direction.

The final scoreboard digits which I recall were the win and place numbers for horses running at Flemington, Caulfield, Moonee Valley or Sandown and I swear that one day during the late 80s I saw John Barnes take a "butcher's" at the winner of Race No:5 just before pulling down a screamer in the goal square.

This was the very goal square of the ground which we the mob, ritually invaded after the final siren of each and every game. This moment marked the beginning of the kick to kick of a thousand footy dreamers.

The THWACK, THWACK, THUD of uncountable treasured, weathered footies being booted all at once as improbable moments of the game and marks taken by heroes were replayed by the crowd who now trod the same sacred turf. Daisy-cutting stab-passes, wobbly drop-punts and spiralling torpedoes flew through the air while a small group of figures, solemn and reverent silhouettes, stood with their feet supported by the sticky centre square mud as they admired the pointillist embossings made by the innumerable boot studs which perforated our very own caucasian chalk circle.

As if witnessing the birth of a child or the creation of the universe they stared in wonderment at the universality and the nothingness of this big white ring. Here is the place where every game and each new hope within each game is given fresh life. The centre circle, now partly obliterated by the depressions of boots and impressions of the battered knees of tireless ruckmen, still signifies the next best chance, the hope of regeneration and therefore the continuation of life itself. A renewal which every "Same Old, Blood and Tar, Bomber" does so passionately embrace as they urge their "Dons" to rise once more, like those irrepressible memories recalling a place where at least for me, time sometimes did stand still, under a battered old wind sock on that windy, Windy Hill.

Bill Hay

In 1974 Bill Hay signed what was called a "Form 4" to play with Sandringham Under 19s in the wildly tempestuous VFA, but after a couple of practice matches and some tedious training sessions at the Beach Oval, he went to Art School where he discovered the mysteries of paint, pubs and wild bohemian parties.

Later during the late 1980s he was one of the instigators of the annual Artists versus Gallery Directors football matches and as playing coach of the Artist's Team was justifiably proud of their unbeaten record.

Throughout the many winters of his childhood Bill would kick the footy with his mates until well after the street lights came on and he likes to think that this rather than gout is the reason for the continuing pain in his preferred left foot.

Dr Susan Alberti AC, Vice-President of the Western Bulldogs Football Club.
Photo courtesy of Susan Alberti Foundation, used with permission

15

Love of the Dogs

Susan Alberti

My love affair with the Western Bulldogs began a half a century ago when my father was the local policeman based in the very working class suburb of Footscray and my brother Richard and I would spend endless hours at the Western Oval cheering on the red, white and blue.

We would make the trek from Melbourne's east every Saturday and spend our afternoon exploring the nooks and crannies of this magnificent ground, which would be full to the brim with the working class, new migrants, died in the wool doggies supporters and of course the occasional game supporter from one of the other 10 Melbourne based clubs or cats' fans who had caught the train up from Geelong.

In the early days Dad would drop us at the ground and come back to pick us up – as we grew older we would catch the train in from Holmesglen in the east, change at Flinders Street station and head out west.

My earliest memories are of this amazing ground and being part of the cheer squad, waving a flag and screaming my lungs out in support of Teddy Whitten and Charlie Sutton. They were big, powerful men who played a tough brand of football and yet I would have done anything to be able to get out onto the ground and kick the Sherrin football around with them.

We would play the occasional game amongst ourselves as members of the Footscray cheer squad – it was a great thrill. It ignited in me a passion to not just watch and appreciate the game, but to play it as well.

I also have vivid memories of my listening around the radio in 1954 when Footscray won its first and only premiership. I was very young, but the Grand Final victory still made a huge impression on me and obviously seared the club in my heart forever.

And so began my life-long love affair with the Footscray Football Club, which became the Western Bulldogs Football Club in 1997, truly cementing our role as not just a football club, but the community champion of Melbourne's west.

We have always been a working class club, which has made us resilient, never taking anything for granted. But it also has meant that at times we have not been far away from being 'foreclosed'.

The year following the death of the late, great Ted Whitten, the club was (again) on its knees. Poor on-field performances had crippled the club's finances and I joined with a group of committed supporters to rebuild the club and make sure it was financially viable, not just for the next five years, but forever. That was nearly 20 years ago and from that point in time I devoted much more of my life to the club to ensure there was future success both on and off the field. Our initial enthusiasm and passion to restore the finances of the Club coincided with an on-field resurgence and a Preliminary Final the very next year against the Adelaide Crows.

In fact, we should have beaten the Crows, with a controversial kick for goal from pint sized club legend Tony Liberatore deemed a point by the goal umpire – it would have put us 37 points in front late in the third quarter and well on the way to playing in our first grand final since 1961.

After the game I was unable to talk for over an hour. I was numb with what might have been. I regularly revisit this game in my mind as it was really was the 'one that got away'.

As part of the new regime at the Bulldogs we knew that we needed to do more than just have a training and administration base at Whitten Oval. Melbourne's west has its fair share of disadvantage and quite frankly a lack of investment in the basics – childcare, health care and community facilities – which most neighbourhoods take for granted, were simply not available to the residents of the western suburbs.

I was proud to be part of a major fundraising drive to establish a community 'hub' at the Whitten Oval. We raised money and sought contributions from State, Federal Governments, local Council and AFL. Many said we just wouldn't receive a single dollar from a Federal Liberal Government, given we were not located in a marginal seat, but in the lead up to the 2004 Federal Election, former Prime Minister John Howard pledged $8 million to help fund the facility which now includes a 120 place childcare centre, a conference and convention centre and a state-of-the-art sports, medical, and health care centre for the football team to use as a training base. We were also delighted to welcome back the Footscray Football Club VFL team in 2015, who played five home games at the Oval.

As I said at the start of my story, playing in the red, white and blue has been a dream of mine since I was a little girl cheering on the bulldogs in the 1950s and 60s. I have long been a supporter of women's football and the two grand finalists in the premier women's football competition in Melbourne each year play for the Susan Alberti Cup.

The game is the fastest growing sport in Australia. I am pleased to say that the Western Bulldogs continues to lead the way with four female directors. We have nine members on our Western Bulldogs Board. So women are now pushing through football's glass ceiling and taking prominent positions at the elite AFL level, within AFL Clubs, on the Board of the AFL and within its executive.

At the grassroots there are now more almost 200,000 female football participants. Nearly 20 percent of all footballers playing Aussie Rules are women and a staggering 163 new female teams were launched this year alone.

Australian Rules Football is now one of the top four most popular female sports in this country.

We are also seeing breakthroughs in the development of female coaching staff and umpires. I am personally supporting female umpires through the AFL Female Umpiring Academy that is also based at the Whitten Oval. It is designed to help talented female field umpires navigate a successful career in our game by developing their skills and providing a pathway to future senior appointments.

Just three years ago we finally had a breakthrough with the first annual exhibition match played between two sides; one representing the Western Bulldogs Football Club and the other representing the Melbourne Football Club. Women were chosen, according to their talents, from right around Australia via a special 'draft'. The level of competition to be chosen to participate in one of these games each year is fierce.

This initiative has been such an outstanding success that in 2015 there was not one, but two clashes between the teams, with the second game televised around Australia on Channel 7. I am delighted that an idea that was not taken seriously for many years is now not just a reality, but a runaway success. In addition to the 10,000 or so fans on hand to watch the match, more than 170,000 viewed it live around Australia, comfortably outperforming a competing AFL match being screened on Foxtel!

The next step is a national women's league similar to the AFL in structure. It can't come quick enough if we want to capitalise on the growth in our game, attracting not just participants, but spectators and supporters from every corner of our great country. Not to mention keeping a lid on the growth of other winter sports attracting record participation numbers, like soccer.

So you can see that my Aussie Rules 'heartfelt' moments are threefold; supporting the mighty Western Bulldogs and Footscray VFL through thick and thin, developing a culture of excellence for women in the AFL and driving the formation of a national women's Aussie Rules competition.

I won't rest until all three are achieved. Woof, woof, woof!

Dr Susan Alberti AC, MAICD

Dr Susan Alberti AC was born in 1947 in Bairnsdale, Victoria. Susan has supplemented her successful business career with a major contribution and commitment to fundraising and promotion of Type 1 diabetes research. She has been involved in raising money for research into diabetes since her daughter was diagnosed with the chronic disease in the 1980s.

In 2015, Susan was appointed President of the Footscray VFL Club, number one ticket holder at the St Kilda Sharks Women's Football Club, and number one ticket holder for the Coburg Cricket Club Women's Team. In August 2015, Susan was appointed Director of the National Australia Day Council. In April 2015, Susan was appointed President of the Footscray VFL Club. In May 2015, Susan was appointed number one ticket holder at the St Kilda Sharks Women's Football Club. In April 2015, Susan was also appointed number one ticket holder for the Coburg Cricket Club Women's Team. In August 2015, Susan was appointed Director of the National Australia Day Council.

16

When the Giants Shook Down the Thunder From the Sky

The Giants Greatest Win

Chris Bowen

Unlike the Adelaide and Perth teams, the Sydney Swans and the GWS Giants don't hate each other. Maybe it's because Sydney is not a natural AFL town and us AFL tragics have a grudging respect for each other and have to stick together. Maybe its because many Giants members are former Swans fans. Whatever the reason, the tribal hatred that leads Crows to hope that Power loses and leads Dockers to urge on anyone who is playing the Eagles simply doesn't exist in Sydney. The Godfather of the Giants Kevin Sheedy, took to twitter on Grand Final day in 2012 to declare "I'm a Swan today" and many of us turned up to cheer on our Sydney cousins.

All of this counts for naught, however when we are playing each other. All bets are off. Our respect and mutual regard being suspended for two hours of combat. And so it was on the 15th March 2014, the opening match of the season. The two teams slugging out the Battle of the Bridge.

This was no ordinary match. It was the first game for Buddy Franklin with the Swans. For months, we loyal Giants had speculated, had hoped and had planned that Buddy would join us. Everyone knew he wanted out of Hawthorn. We knew that boot that could kick a goal from 70 metres would be a huge boost for us. But it wasn't to be. Franklin was coming to Sydney alright, but to be a Swan and not a Giant. They had out-bid us. Secretly. Betrayal. "Bugger him! We don't need him!" was our unanimous response. But we knew that in this match he'd be kicking against us, not for, and we were likely to pay a big price.

Instead, using the millions saved by not signing Franklin, the Giants secured the former Swan Shane Mumford and Magpie Heath Shaw (brother to Swan Reece Shaw). It was Mumford versus Franklin, willing recruit versus the player who snubbed us. It was a contest that would end as few had predicted.

My daughter Grace and I are Giants tragics. Foundation members, our name on the wall. Attending every home game. We've been there for all the smashing 100-point plus losses. Every time we'd put in a respectable performance for three quarters only to see the young bodies of the Giants peter out for the final quarter and our team get smashed. After every defeat, little Gracie would turn to me "Don't worry Dad. When we win the flag, Kevin Sheedy will remember those of us who were here on the bad days." (She is also responsible for the "Bowen Plan" that she insisted I put to AFL CEO Andrew Demetriou "If they want to grow the game Dad, they've got to stop holding the Grand Final in Melbourne every year. It should be held at the home ground of the minor premiers. Got to show the rest of Australia it's not just a Melbourne game anymore". I didn't get very far with Demetriou.

But a Swans Giants game is a bigger event. The whole family. My wife Bec and son Max. My parents-in-law Brian and Jackie. Brian and Jackie are Swans since the South Melbourne days, so the game splits our family. Brian takes a $2 a bet with Grace and Max, confident in a Swans win.

We held them within striking distance in the first quarter, just a 13 point lead at the first break. But at quarter time the thunder is literally shaken down from the sky. Lightning strikes the field and the stadium. We're under cover but the rain falls in such gusty sheets that no-one is dry, regardless of how far under the stadium cover you are. The lightning crashes against the stadium, the noise and vibrations are like a being in a tinny during an air raid.

Quarter time gets delayed for 20 minutes to let the storm pass. I've never seen that before and doubt I will again for a long time. The field is flooded but good drainage sees the water dissipate in time for play to eventually restart.

When play resumes we hold our own. Mumford the Magnificent is worth the effort to lure him. Thank god we got him and it was great we missed out on Buddy we tell ourselves. "Mummy" we shout expectantly every time he touches the ball. He dominates the ruck. Franklin scores just one goal and one behind for the whole game.

Our star forwards Jeremy (Jezza) Cameron and Jonathon (General) Patton shine. Jezza finishes with four goals, the General with three.

At each break we are in touch. Seven points behind at half time ("A goal and a behind in it Dad" Grace says confidently), just three behind at the final break ("One goal and we can take 'em Dad").

But I dread the final quarter. Game after game we have faltered in the final term. The pit in my stomach tells me that the Swans will come good in the final quarter. I tip the Giants out of blind loyalty every game, but I retain enough rationality to know the odds are against us.

The odds maybe against us but the Gods are for us. We play a blinder final quarter. Goal after unanswered goal. Six of them, to be exact. The Swans miss consistently. With every miss, I lament to Brian "Too Bad", "Tragic" in the way only a son-in-law can to a father-in-law.

Brian knows the gig is up ten minutes before the end. He quietly slips the kids their two dollars each.

Being a supporter of an old, established club means you have plenty of history (and heartache). But being a founding member of a new club means we make the history. And the first time we beat our Sydney cousins, the reigning premiers, is the most heartfelt moment in our history so far.

Chris Bowen

Chris is the Federal Member for the seat of McMahon and the Shadow Treasurer of Australia. He is the father of Grace and Max and the husband of Bec. All four are foundation members of the GWS Giants. Chris joined Federal Parliament in 2004 and has held a range of ministerial portfolios including Treasurer. In 2013 he was Acting Leader of the Labor Party during the party's leadership contest. On weekends he has occasionally been spotted as a goal umpire at games of the mighty under 10's Parramatta-Holroyd Goannas.

Cardinal George Pell, on the left shoulder of Br William O'Malley, coach of the St Patrick's College, Ballarat first eighteen premiership team.
Photo courtesy of Tess Livingstone

17

Aussie Rules

George Pell

Nearly half Australia's population was not born when Richmond won their last premiership in 1980, but I remember the match well.

During my thirty years as a priest in Victoria from 1971-2001 I always managed to obtain a ticket for the grand final. On one occasion the best I could do was a seat near the Collingwood cheer squad. They weren't short of a word, the women as well as the men!

In 1980 I went with a good friend, my regular tennis opponent and a potato farmer near Ballarat. He too was a Richmond supporter and had been an excellent country footballer. A nephew of his, Danny Frawley, was a champion full back at St Kilda and a Richmond coach who did manage to take us into the finals.

Richmond had a crushing victory over Collingwood, which gave particular pleasure, after a spectacular finals series. Immediately after the game Maurie and I drove home to the farm, where the whole family, who knew football well, celebrated late into the night. We re-ran the match two or three times and Richmond played better with every replay.

By any standards the 1980 Richmond team was among the finest. Kevin "Hungry" Bartlett kicked seven goals in each of their three finals matches, including the grand final. I remember being somewhat frustrated as Michael Roach, our champion full forward, wasn't holding his marks. However time and again they spilled into Bartlett's hands as he sped by; but David Cloke also kicked six magnificent goals.

I tend to run together the teams and champions of that golden era. The star, to my mind, was Royce Hart. I am not sure I can justify this, but he remains my greatest centre half forward. He was poetry in motion, a different poetry from Maurice Rioli's, but poetry nonetheless. A spectacular mark, often coming in from the side, with a long, raking, left foot drop punt.

Years later I discovered that Tom Hafey, the coach, had a sophisticated match plan. The other forwards were to get out of the way and everyone was to kick to Hart. It used to work.

I still remember the names of many of the players. Kevin Sheedy and Mick Malthouse, who weren't great players but became great coaches; versatile champions such as Jimmy Jess, Barry Richardson, Mervyn Keane and the relentless Francis Bourke, a champion on and off the field. Geoff Raines played with great style and dash in the centre, while Mark Lee and Emmett Dunne were two fine ruckmen, although not quite the equal of Neil Balme and Michael Green.

Richmond has had my support for over fifty-five years, but I was anti-Collingwood before then. After signing to play with Richmond in 1959 during my last school year at St Patrick's (St. Pat's) in Ballarat, I was promised a place on their training list and financial help to attend Melbourne University, to supplement a Commonwealth scholarship.

While it was a hard decision for me to begin studying for the priesthood, and I loved my V.F.L., I never had exaggerated notions of my football abilities. While I would have worked hard to make the grade, and was big, strong and fast, I never had the skills of other St. Pat's champions like Mick McGuane or Matt Rosa. Professional careers, and not only my football, were the alternatives to studying for the priesthood.

In those days (as today, if for different reasons) it was impossible to combine A grade football and seminary life.

Corpus Christi seminary was in Werribee and our community of 120 philosophy students (the first half of the eight year course) lived isolated from the world for nine months of the year. We had no access to television, radio and newspapers. Speaking was forbidden from 9 p.m. until after breakfast, which like nearly all other meals was taken in silence, and the textbooks were in Latin. While the buildings had no heating, much less air conditioning, the food was good, the showers were hot, while the daily routine of prayer, study, recreation and exercise followed patterns decreed in the sixteenth century by the Council of Trent, a gathering of bishops to counter the Protestant Reformation. In those days most of us were happy most of the time and the atmosphere was generally good, but the daily-life routine was like that of a very strict boarding school. After the Second Vatican Council in Rome (1962-1965) the more repressive elements of this Tridentine model were abandoned.

Students had to be outside in the open air for a couple of hours each afternoon and during the winter everyone, without exception, had to play football once or twice a week. The standard of play for the annual representative game between philosophy and theology (the last four years of the course) was more than respectable, as such teams held their own against, for example, the Newman College XVIII from Melbourne University. When everyone had to play it was a different story.

Naturally some were not interested and some had no athletic prowess at all. These would be parked together generally on the wing, perhaps in a forward pocket, where they could relax and hope the ball never came in their direction.

The cleverest fellow in our year was also the least suited to playing football. During one of these compulsory games another seminarian friend was running the boundary. At half time he came to me full of excitement: "Do you know what Gerry was talking about out there on the field?" he asked. Without a pause he added "Bloody Spinoza!". Spinoza was a Jewish philosopher from the seventeenth century. Enough said.

But to get back to Collingwood. In the early nineteen hundreds many Irish Australians lived in Collingwood and Richmond and the antagonism probably originated there, provoked by too many Collingwood successes.

My mother was Irish-Australian and her youngest sister, one of twelve, married a very serious Collingwood supporter and the family came to share this passion. It was a serious business, as the television would be turned off if Collingwood had lost badly. The family were close friends as well as relations and we grew up trading good-natured football insults.

I suspect that then, even more than today, many loved to "hate"

Collingwood, but it was a strange love-hate relationship, even though I grew up hoping that Collingwood would be last or runners-up.

When Richmond was struggling to survive financially, Collingwood fans took up special collections to help us and I have never forgotten this. I was even a bit pleased when they broke their 32 year-old premiership drought in 1990; although I didn't confess that to many.

The hostility to Collingwood is a bit like the Australia-England rivalry in the Ashes. The results of this Ashes series in England were so completely remarkable that if the teams had been racehorses they would have been swabbed. And it was a day of national shame when the Australian team was bowled out for 60.

We find it deeply galling when the Balmy Army has too many first rate anti-Australian songs, humorous and insulting, while our own responses vocally are so pathetic.

But all this is only one side of the coin. We share a great deal. We have many English migrants happily settled in Australia, even if they make the occasional complaint, while London is one of Australia's largest cities with an Australian population of 300,000 as well as transient Aussie tourists. There is more in all this than meets the eye at first glance as I cannot imagine the A.F.L. without Collingwood and cricket would mean much less without the Poms as enemies.

During my nine years as assistant bishop in Melbourne, I used to spend an hour with each of the fifty or so grade six groups who would receive confirmation from me. In an attempt to maintain their attention I would use an adapted form of Dame Edna's approach, relying especially on their responses to questions. At that age both girls and boys are happy to answer. To balance our proceedings I always allowed them ten to fifteen minutes to ask me any question they chose.

Nearly always someone would ask which football team I barracked for. Eventually I adopted a standard routine for my reply, telling them I supported two teams and asking them for quiet. There was always a hush as I paused (hamming it up a bit) then explained that I barracked for Richmond… and any team which was playing Collingwood.

The results were predictable. Most of the children were delighted and the Magpie followers, usually a good number, were outraged. In one large primary school, where the Principal was a noisy Collingwood supporter, the applause, approval and delight of the students at my claim nearly did bring down the roof of the school hall where we were meeting.

St. Pats in Ballarat will always have a central place in the history of Aussie Rules. While Assumption College, Kilmore, had its nose in front for a while in producing more league footballers, St. Pats has won the Herald-Sun shield for the best football team in Victoria for the last six years. For forty-nine years in a row it was football champion in the small Ballarat Public Schools competition, before a team from Ballarat College wrested that title from them in 1954. As a young schoolboy I was a spectator on that black day when John Birt, later a long-term successful rover at Essendon, was unstoppable. The survivors of the College team had a celebratory dinner on the fiftieth anniversary in 2004, which was attended also by a table of representatives from S.P.C.

After being ordained as a bishop in 1987 I was welcomed back to the College, where the principal greeted me and explained to the boys that the College was famous for its two Brownlow Medal winners and (then) two bishops who were old boys (this was his order of priority).

Both Brownlow Medal winners played in the 1952 team: Brian Gleeson whose career as a ruckman at St Kilda was cut short by a knee problem and John James from Carlton where he played on a halfback flank. I don't know of any other school team who can boast of a similar distinction.

Both were champions, but James was also outstanding in many other sports, the best schoolboy athlete I have seen. He was an excellent cricketer, interschool champion as a sprinter, shot putter, hurdler and was in contention to represent Australia in the broad jump. He still holds the record for kicking thirty-five goals in one match against Ballarat High.

The 1952 coach, and my coach when I played in the team from 1956-9, was Br William Theodore O'Malley whom we knew as "Old Bill". For five or six student generations he embodied the football tradition and much else that was, and is, good in the College.

In those days Catholic schools received no funding from governments and the schools survived only through the unpaid labours of nuns and brothers.

Brother Bill was an effective teacher of "Inter A", the year ten class that studied Latin. He was no scholar, but very efficient in preparing students to pass the annual external exams. We had monthly tests in all subjects and we were graded on the results, with the dux sitting on the left of the front row, known as the Prime Minister, while everyone else had a place in descending order. Nobody seemed to complain about being in the back row, perhaps because the Latin-studying members of Inter A all felt (although this was discouraged) a bit superior to the Inter Bs!

Brother Bill was a simple prayerful man, much loved, who (we believed) could name every ex-student who turned up to greet him. He had a deep faith and taught me more about prayer than any other teacher; and he was a champion football coach.

He coached the first XVIII from the 1930s until 1959 and his principles were simple and effective. We were to play on at all costs (not the received way of doing things then) especially after a mark; we were forbidden to bounce the ball, so that those down the field would know when to lead and there was no kicking across goal in defence. Defenders were to stick close and everyone was to play in front.

He was an inspirational speaker despite a slight lisp or stutter, which disappeared as he became more animated, often comparing us to the champions of the past and urging us to emulate their achievements. The other schools were catching up when I was playing (I was in the first team to be beaten by Ballarat High). It might have been that we were slipping, although we still did well against traditional Melbourne rivals like Parade and St. Kevin's. In retrospect we probably won a few matches, which we didn't deserve to win, because we felt we couldn't be beaten and played above ourselves, inspired by the coach and drawing on our traditions.

In Melbourne a visiting South American priest, working as a chaplain in one of our secondary schools, surprised me by claiming that sport was the religion of young Australian Catholics. I don't know whether this was true of his school, but the idea that sport and Catholicism were alternatives never occurred to us; they came in the same package. In the eighties a young SPC boarder from the Western District told me that he was a typical Irish-Australian Catholic, with a football under one arm and a race book in his other hand. I am not sure how many of this breed still flourish!

I have watched quite a lot of European soccer and rugby union over the years. Union has lost some of its sparkle as most teams are now too defensive and disciplined to run the ball a lot and top class soccer remains a marvellous demonstration of skills. But neither sport can rival Aussie Rules for spectacle, when the best AFL teams are locked in competition with such a variety of hand and foot skills and the ball is moved around so quickly. Our Australian seminarians who live in Rome at the North American College have won quite a few converts to our game among their fellow American students.

Totti and Beckam and Balotelli are big names in Europe, but Gary Ablett (snr.), Dermot Brereton, Plugger Lockett and, of course, Royce Hart still top my list.

Cardinal George Pell

Cardinal George Pell AC was born in Ballarat on 8 June 1941. The Cardinal has a doctorate in Patristics from Oxford and a Masters of Education from Australia. Made a Bishop in 1987 he became subsequently Archbishop of Melbourne and from 2001 until 2014 served as Archbishop of Sydney. He was created a cardinal of the Roman Catholic Church in 2003 and has served on many Vatican Congregations and Committees.
In 2014 he was asked by Pope Francis to become the first Prefect of the newly created Secretariat for the Economy which oversees the finances in the Holy See and the Vatican City State.

Particularly interested in education, Cardinal Pell is a long-time Richmond supporter who signed to play football with Richmond during the last year of school at St. Pat's Ballarat in 1959. He made the difficult choice to forgo this to study for the Catholic priesthood for his Diocese of Ballarat.

Fitzroy's last game, September 1st, 1996
Photo courtesy of Fremantle Dockers Football Club, used with permission

18

Fitzroy's last game 1996

Les Everett

A lot of nonsense gets spoken at footy club marketing meetings. Often they come up with noisy notions to annoy the fans and disturb the peace at half time. But when the ideas people at the Fremantle Dockers got together late in the 1996 season a brilliant idea was hatched: "Let's do something for Fitzroy."

Footy clubs come and go. Country teams facing population shifts can be saved or gobbled up by mergers or simply disappear. But at the higher levels it's unusual for a competition to lose a team.

The last teams lost to the WAFL were North Fremantle in 1916 and Midland Junction in 1918. University was in the VFL from 1908 to 1914 while struggling VFL club South Melbourne was shipped off to Sydney in 1982 but it lives on in spirit and with SMFC stitched onto the back of the Sydney Swans jumpers. Woodville and West Torrens merged in the SANFL in 1991 but the last teams to leave that competition were Willunga (1885) and Gawler (1890).

The AFL has mainly been about adding teams – only one has been lost.

On 4 July 1996 the AFL, through administrator Michael Brennan and CEO Ross Oakley, announced Fitzroy – formed in 1883 and part of the VFL/AFL from 1897 – was to merge with Brisbane. Prior to the AFL intervention there were hopes Fitzroy could join North Melbourne and therefore remain in Melbourne.

Few Fitzroy fans saw the merger as anything but a takeover and when Brisbane Bears president Noel Gordon made some smug remarks about the footy and financial affairs of the Lions on Channel Nine's The Footy Show many hearts were hardened.

The Lions played their last game in Melbourne on 25 August 1996 against Richmond at the MCG and, cruelly it seemed, would play their final game far away at Subiaco Oval against Fremantle on Sunday 1 September.

Links between Fitzroy and WA were always strong. The club's first superstar Percy Trotter completed his career at East Fremantle, triple Brownlow winner Haydn Bunton later won three Sandover Medals with Subiaco, nine times Fitzroy best and fairest winner Kevin Murray was captain-coach of East Perth in 1965 and 1966 – he came back home and won the Brownlow Medal as a Lion in 1969. Ron Alexander, a premiership player with East Perth in 1972 and captain-coach of East Fremantle's premiership team in 1985, was the captain of Fitzroy in 1979 and 1980 and best and fairest winner in 1981.

Fremantle was in just its second AFL season but already there were ties that would bind the two clubs. Fremantle's first win was over Fitzroy in round three 1995 and Fitzroy's last win was against Fremantle in round eight 1996.

In the week before the game I spoke to Marj Dunstan who as a schoolgirl would head to Chandler's hardware store in Brunswick Street, Fitzroy just to catch a glimpse of Haydn Bunton who worked there. She was at the Junction Oval for the VFL grand final in 1944 when Fitzroy won its last premiership. "They were hard times and the team meant a lot to us," Marj said. She recalled buying raffle tickets for a penny to support the club and the ever-present enemy on the other side of Smith Street –Collingwood supporters. "There was bitterness and joy and a wonderful spirit about it all. I realise it was inevitable but I still fell bitter that now Fitzroy has been made to disappear."

I also spoke to Ron Alexander, then the chairman of selectors at the Dockers. "It will be like a wake," he said, "It's been a long hard fight by the Roys and a real war of attrition. It's just been so sad to see the blood sucked out of a terrific group of people."

Fremantle wasn't bad on the field in its first couple of seasons and was gaining a reputation for its pre-game ceremonies and celebrations that included a crew dressed as wharfies dragging a huge anchor out onto the ground.

In marking the occasion of Fitzroy's last game the Dockers assisted in bringing some past players and supporters across from Victoria. On the Friday before the game at a breakfast in Fremantle the speakers were Ron Alexander, Kevin Murray and another past Lion great Bernie Quinlan. Haydn Bunton jnr was there representing his father while young Fitzroy fans Tonya Stevens and Sian Bowen spoke of their love for the club and provided a reminder that Fitzroy wasn't all about history it was still firm in the hearts of many people.

Alexander tossed the coin to start proceedings and for a while it was just like any other game with the home team very much on top. At three quarter time Fremantle led by 88 points after playing some attractive football. After the break the mood changed. The crowd was subdued, the Lions lifted and kicked five goals in their last quarter – around me I saw Fitzroy fans crying.

The final siren sounded, the winning team's song came over the PA and then Fitzroy's mighty song to the tune of La Marseillaise as the Fremantle players and anchor crew formed a guard of honour for the Lions. A fan evaded the not very insistent security and ran onto the ground with a Farewell Fitzroy flag and then the crowning moment.

Sara Macliver from the WA Opera Company appeared alone on the roof of the southern stand and sang Auld Lang Syne. There were more tears. Then silence. And Fitzroy was gone.

Supporters of both teams were singing the same song as they departed Subiaco Oval on that day in September…

> We will always fight for victory
> We will always see it through
> Win or lose we do or die
> And in defeat we'll always try

The AFL's newest club had done something because it was decent not to appease sponsors or honour contracts. The AFL, meanwhile, contributed nothing to mark Fitzroy's last game.

> Ross Kelly (Fremantle chairman)
> "We want to tell Fitzroy people that our club respects and admires them and their club and that we share their loyalty to the tradition and achievements of one of the original VFL clubs."

> Rod Walsh (Fitzroy supporter, quoted in Maroon & Blue)
> "The Fremantle people were very sympathetic and handled the occasion with a lot of class. They put on a very good send-off."

> Ron Alexander (Maroon & Blue)
> "I can recall being on the ground before the game and I was talking to Kevin Elms (long time Fitzroy trainer) and Kevin Murray… Kevin Elms broke down and was crying and I put my arm around him and gave him a bit of a hug. Some photographer snapped a photo, I didn't even realise it at the time. I've got it up in my study at home, me with Kevin Elms and Kevin Murray just in the immediate background – that's something I see every day and reflect on."

> Steven Smith ((Fitzroy supporter, quoted in Maroon & Blue)
> "It was a very draining, hugely emotional, very hard week leading up to the game. The one thing that made it a little bit easier was the fact that Fremantle people went to such an effort to make us feel welcome. I was wearing my jumper and their supporters were very sympathetic, making comments like, 'We feel for you.' 'We understand how hard it must be.' They weren't gloating or anything like that."

> David Zampatti (Fremantle events manager, quoted in Fremantle Dockers: An Illustrated History)
> "It was powerful and such the right thing to do. A lot of work went into that and it was terrifically emotional."

Fremantle first grand final 2013

Tears flowed at Subiaco Oval on 21 September 2013. Fremantle was playing Sydney in an AFL preliminary final and it was clear from pretty early on that the Dockers were on their way to their first grand final.

Fremantle's play was so ferocious that Sydney found it difficult to make any progress. In fact when the Swans kicked a behind about a minute before half time it was their first kick inside the forward 50 for the quarter. Experienced football observers noticed. Speaking on ABC Radio four-time premiership coach David Parkin said: "I just think it's a manic pressure that we've never seen applied with or without the ball in the history of the game." Hawthorn premiership captain Don Scott speaking at a grand final lunch organized by the Footy Almanac said: "I've never seen a team play like that. They are mad."

While it was manic and mad on the field the crowd took the opportunity to move into celebration mode with chants and songs and movement for the last ten minutes of the game.

A few rows ahead of me at Subiaco Oval I saw a young man in the purple colours of Fremantle slumped in his seat and weeping. The seat beside him was empty.

Les Everett

Les grew up in Boulder and now lives in Fremantle. He is the author of *Gravel Rash: 100 Years of Goldfields Football* (1996) and Fremantle Dockers: An Illustrated History (2014).

In his spare time he takes photos of footy scoreboards for the website he founded with Vin Maskell – scoreboardpressure.com – one day they'll produce a book about scoreboards and the stories behind them.

Les is the author of *Fremantle Dockers: An Illustrated History*, published by Slattery Media Group in 2014.

19

The 1970 Grand Final

Paul Santamaria

The day began badly at 1207 Burke Road. Reasonable requests for errands and favours were met with unreasonable responses. There were no volunteers for simple domestic chores. Everything was just too much trouble. While none of us was prepared to acknowledge it, the tension in the air had nothing to do with the frustration of requests unmet. It had everything to do with the fact that Peter McKenna had kicked nine on us in the second semi final. The dreadful reality was that there was every chance he might do it again. The atmosphere had been sullen from the moment the sun had risen.

The Blues were to play Collingwood in the Grand Final. This would be the fourth time they had played in the 1970 season. Each of the previous three contests had ended in emphatic victories for Collingwood. When we had played them at Victoria Park, the Blues had managed to kick only 2 goals, 12 points. The Pies supporters on the outer wing had been merciless. Had it not been Carlton, they would have felt sorry for us. Because it was Carlton, they were vicious and relentless. Their laughter accompanying every missed Carlton goal resonated in nightmares leading up to the finals. Collingwood had persuaded itself, reasonably and on the basis of all the available evidence, that *"this was their year"*. And the unfortunate sacrifice on the altar of their ambitions was to be Carlton.

Aged 13 years, I had completed the Carlton banner, which I had been making out of crepe paper for most of the week. I then affixed it as an ensign to the upstairs balcony in a small act of defiance born of the love of the navy blue and white. A few cars tooted as I juggled the masking tape and scissors while attempting to attach the banner to the balcony. The Carlton thing was in the genes. My grandparents had owned a fruit shop in Sydney Road, Brunswick in the 1920s, a short walk from Princes Park. My Eolian nonna took my father to the outer where emigrant Italians were initiated into local tribal customs. My father, Bob Santamaria, became addicted and followed the Blues each week for the next 70 odd years. His eight children followed suit, although some were later to "marry out".

Dad retrieved the envelope from his sock drawer. He had placed in the envelope the tickets he had accumulated over the previous 5 or 6 days since Carlton had beaten a flu-stricken St Kilda team in the preliminary final. The gracious Laurie Kerr (himself a former Carlton champion) had stumped up 4 seats. There were another 2 seats from Adrian Wright (the St Kilda physiotherapist and a supporter of BAS). A couple more from elder siblings, who would each spend time away from their classes at Melbourne University that week queuing up around Princes Park for tickets. An MCC ladies' ticket from the Wood family in Nth Balwyn. We were covered; nine of us were going. My mother was the exception. She had grown up in Lisson Grove, Hawthorn and barracked for the Hawks. In those days, they were nothing. We called them *"The Sparrows"* to provoke her. Funny how things change. Dad solemnly removed the tickets from the envelope and placed them on the breakfast room table. They were counted several times over and shifted around the table as if a military manoeuvre was in preparation. The receipt of each ticket in hand filled one with a terrible sense of foreboding.

The planning then moved to transport and parking. We would travel in a 3 car convoy and park in the vicinity of St Ignatius Church, Richmond, an acceptable walk to the MCG. After the game, we would reassemble there. No one was to leave for home until we were all accounted for. We would gather ourselves, console each other, and nod in collective reassurance that we would be better next season.

Saturday, 26 September 1970 was bright and sunny. On arrival, the crowd was massive, the standing room areas were completely full – supporters were packed like sardines from about 12.30pm. The MCG fence was then of white pickets; there was not an advertising hoarding to be seen. The players ran out; Collingwood was wearing the black shorts of the *"home"* team reflecting their reward of a week's rest the previous week while Carlton had been occupied fighting off the Saints. There was only one field umpire: Don Jolley. Two boundaries and two goal umpires, the latter wearing full length white coats and hats as if they had come straight from a CSIRO laboratory. Ron Barassi's first major coaching decision was to play Kevin Hall on McKenna. Hall had never previously played at full back, but had the height and pace to put McKenna off his game.

Graeme *"Jerka"* Jenkin won the first kick of the game – a free kick against his nemesis, the Carlton captain, Big John Nicholls. Collingwood dominated the play from the outset kicking to the scoreboard end. The Richardson brothers, Wayne and Max, appeared to have bought their own football. Des Tuddenham kicked the first goal of the game, managing to avoid a Vin Waite *"special"* on the way. Vinnie had lots of accidents with his elbows. The Pies attack on goal began to look ominous.

In the whole of the first quarter, Carlton managed to get the ball into its half of the ground on only 5 or 6 occasions, prompting the TV caller, Mike Williamson, to say at the 15 minute mark *"Collingwood is playing as if they know the Premiership is theirs. They feel it"*. Too true. Carlton's forward line was non-existent. Carlton's first score (a point) only occurred at the 22 minute mark. By the end of the first quarter, the Blues had failed to score a goal. Collingwood had kicked 4 goals 8 points.

Things only got worse in the second quarter. McKenna started to take his marks. His third goal came in the third minute; his fourth in the tenth and his fifth by the fifteenth minute mark. Collingwood was in complete control of the game. Barry Price, the Collingwood centreman, a class player if ever there was one, was running amok. But two significant things happened during the quarter – Tuddenham collided heavily with McKenna, his team mate. It looked as if McKenna had been knocked out; the knock to his head had certainly dazed and unsettled him. Then at the twenty minute mark, Carlton's David McKay was paid a free kick on the half-back line. He kicked a long torpedo punt in the direction of the Carlton half-forward line. Jerka Jenkin positioned himself to mark the ball. But like a cat, Alex Jesaulenko leapt into the air, his knees on

Jenkin's shoulders, and took one of the greatest marks in the history of Australian Rules football. Williamson's exclamation, *"Jesaulenko. You beauty!"* was to echo through the years since. Jesaulenko's mark seemed to disturb the lethargy which had characterised Carlton's play until then. A goal to Silvagni quickly followed. Nevertheless, Collingwood regained its poise and went into the main break with a 44 point lead. The question for many Carlton supporters was not so much whether Carlton could win (it couldn't), but whether there was any point staying around for the second half.

Carlton looked bedraggled as they left the ground at halftime. Some players must have thought the game was over and that all that remained was to keep the inevitable loss to respectable proportions. Some must have been in trepidation of what was about to greet them in the changing rooms. As they traipsed up the race to be confronted by their coach, none could have foreseen the part they were about to play in the creation of a legend in Australian Rules football.

Ronald Dale Barassi was at the heart of a minor revolution in the game when, at the end of the 1965 season, he transferred from the establishment Club, Melbourne to Carlton, whose provenance was everything other than establishment. Barassi had played in six of Melbourne's premierships up to 1964 and was recognised as its best player. He had captained-coached Carlton's premiership in 1968 - its first since 1947. By 1970, his playing career was over. Apart from being a clever strategist, Barassi had one special quality as a coach: he was a ferocious orator, who had done everything on the field and feared no one off it. He understood how sportsmen thought and could strike the right key in choosing how to inspire dispirited players and orchestrate a revival. In contrast with other great speeches, there was no one present during Barassi's 10 minute half-time address who could record it for posterity. We know what Lincoln said in his 8 minutes at Gettysburg, because the scribes wrote it all down. But for this address, which has assumed its own Gettysburg status among the Carlton faithful, we must rely on the retrospective accounts given by players in some cases, several years after the event.

Despite the absence of a record, one could divine what Barassi said from what happened in the third quarter. First, he pulled Bert Thornley from the ground and replaced him with Ted Hopkins. It was a gamble. In those days there was no interchange.-only two reserves. Once a player was *"taken off"* he could play no further part in the game. In Thornley's case, he played no further part at Carlton. But Hopkins had shown previously his precocious ability to set fire to a game. Barassi then re-organised the team. *"Ragsy"* Goold, with his aristocratic demeanour and trade-mark baggy shorts, went to the wing. Waite to centre half-back. Swan McKay to a back pocket. Next, he told the players to handball as if their lives depended on it and to play on even when good sense said not to. The players were not to stop moving the ball forward, bombing the forward line in a blitzkrieg of motion. Finally, they were to tackle and hustle as if it were the last game they would play. If this Grand Final were to be lost, it would not be lost without a fight.

And so the breathless third quarter began. At the first bounce, the ball spilt to Carlton's Vinnie Waite. As if to signal his assent to the handball strategy now in play, Waite picked up the loose ball and handballed it backwards over his head 20 metres or so in the direction of Carlton's goals. Players who had seemingly never handballed before, or whose handballing was incompetent, started handballing over a mark instead of going back to take their kick. Silvagni, Crosswell, Hall and others dissolved the orthodox lines of fullback and centre halfback with the riskiest of handballs and by playing on.

Enter blond Ted Hopkins looking more surfer than footballer. He crumbed the ball repeatedly when it landed in the goal square pack. Within 10 minutes, Hopkins had kicked 3 goals. This willow incendiary had lit Collingwood's funeral pyre, a fire which burnt for years hence. Robert Walls began to dominate the forward line; Syd Jackson scoffed at the laws of metaphysics with his goal from the forward pocket. Walls' mark, baulk and goal at the 12 minute mark was sublime. The attack was relentless. More goals came from Crosswell and Jesaulenko. Carlton came within 3 points, only to see Collingwood regain its poise with goals to Twiggy Dunne and McKenna. Collingwood would not lie down. It scrambled a 17 point lead at three quarter time.

So how would Barassi play it in his address to the players at three quarter time? The carrot or the stick? According to Kevin Hall, Barassi chose a different approach saying something along the lines of *"Win or lose ,you blokes are magnificent"*. Beware the flatterer. No more was said – there was no need – to the players had decided there was unfinished business.

The last quarter belonged to Kevin Hall, Swan McKay and Vin Waite. Their defensive marking and attacking forays enabled the Carlton forwards to kick 5 goals for the quarter. Carlton's first goal came from a free kick to Big Nick in the goal square at the 8 minute mark; his second goal followed soon after from an authoritative mark over Peter Eakins only minutes later. That brought the Blues within 8 points. The battle of the back lines then began, with the ball moving from one end to the other at electric speed. At one point, Eakins went to clear the ball from Carlton's forward line, but it was smothered off his boot by Syd Jackson who followed the ball, handballed it to the waiting Ted Hopkins, who turned on his heels and kicked his fourth goal. Carlton were within a point at the 20 minute mark. The exhortations from the crowd were deafening. Minutes passed without a goal being scored. Then Des Tuddenham, who had had an ordinary day, snared Crosswell around the neck about 30 metres out from the Carlton goal. Crosswell's goal put Carlton ahead at the 25 minute mark – for the first time that day. Collingwood was out on its feet; heads were dropping; they had had enough.

The Police then entered the playing arena and paraded inside the fence, ostensibly to keep the crowd at bay at the end of the game, but in truth to perform their function as the official cortege once the loser's funeral rights had concluded. The *coup de grace* was then delivered by Jesaulenko. McKenna had been denied a controversial mark and the ball spilled to Silvagni. He picked it up and booted it aimlessly out of danger. The ball bounced awkwardly between two Collingwood players. Seeing his opportunity, Jesaulenko swooped past Jeff Clifton and with a slingshot left foot kick, sent the ball hurtling towards the vacant Carlton goal. The ball, now under the control of the teasing gods, bounced once, twice and a third time as it entered the goal. The game was over.

The party began in the car park behind St Ignatius, Richmond. Never before, and not since, had I seen my father in such unrestrained euphoria. He was embracing people wearing Carlton guernseys and scarves, whom he had never met, as if they had been lifelong friends. The convoy along Bridge Road was so noisy, the theme song being sung repeatedly in chorus with Carlton supporters on trams we passed, car horns blazing in jubilant euphoria. The joy of it all. The day that had begun badly finished well.

There was one unfortunate postscript. Days later a photo appeared of the Collingwood coach, Bob Rose, on the MCG after the game with his hands over an exhausted Twiggy Dunne, consoling and reassuring him. Rose was one of the finest men of his generation and endured much adversity in his life with grace and humility. Through the decades since that match, that moving photograph has continued to haunt me. In the swings and roundabouts of league footy, there will come the day when Collinwood will beat Carlton in a grand final and the wrong done to Bob Rose in 1970 will be avenged. I don't want to be at the MCG that day.

Paul Santamaria

Paul Santamaria is a Melbourne barrister who was present at the 1970 Grand Final and watched Jezza soar.

Atlantic 1958 Picture Pageant VFL
Football Card (#59 John Birt, Essendon)
Private Collection, used with permission

20

An extraordinary era of Grand finals and Premierships

John Birt

For me it began in June 1954 when I was captain of the Ballarat college first xviii on a cold wintery Wednesday afternoon and we defeated the famous St Patricks College in the Grand final of the Ballarat public schools competition.

The significance of this match was twofold. Firstly it was the first time in 49 years that Ballarat College had defeated St. Pats and therefore had won the premiership. Secondly after the game I was introduced to a man who was to influence my life in no uncertain way for the rest of my life, certainly my football life. This was Essendon's greatest, Dick Reynolds.

For the next two and a half years, Dick and Essendon battled the Ballarat football league authorities to get me clearance. However it was not until the beginning of 1957 that I was eligible to be selected for the 'Dons'.

I played in a premiership with Ballarat in 1955 and was a teammate of, three time Melbourne premiership player, Geoff Tunbridge. However in 1956, before I even got to Essendon, I sustained a serious shoulder injury which at the time, in the mid 1950's, was inoperable. It left me with the terrible thought of 'that's it'. Fortunately in 1956 an orthopaedic surgeon, Mr John Jens, had perfected an operation of pinning the shoulder together and I was ready to go to Essendon in 1957.

Fortunately I was able to play in four Grand Finals with Essendon, 1957, 59, 62 and 65, winning in 1962 and 1965.

Each had a special significance for me and for Essendon, with the losses in 1957 and 1959 contributing to the successes in 62 and 65.

I will begin this grand final story with the 1957 season and how in my mind this was a start to the extraordinary run of success at Essendon during the next decade.

1957- The first match of the season was against Collingwood at Victoria Park. I was thrilled to be chosen with three other rookies, Col Hebbard, Ken Timms and Frank Driscoll. This was a most significant game for Essendon and the VFL that season. Essendon won at Victoria Park for the first time in fifteen years and it was the first match of Australian Rules football televised after TV was introduced into Victoria in 1956. Therefore confidence was high and the club was desperate for a premiership as the then dominant VFL team from 1942-1950, hadn't played in a grand final since being defeated by Geelong in 1951. During the season we were very competitive and at the end of the 'home and away' we were second on the ladder to the all conquering 'demons' who were premiers in 1955 and 1956.

In the second semi final we triumphed over hot favourites, Melbourne, kicking 12 goals, 11 behinds (83) to 8 goals, 19 behinds (67). This match will always be memorable for me as I recall that the most outstanding player on the field, half back Mal Pascoe won the very prestigious award of a mattress. 'How exciting.'

Then in a memorable grand final two weeks later, Essendon made 5 changes, naturally all thought to be advantageous, the second semi final result was reversed. But how exciting it was for me to be playing in a grand final in my first year of VFL football.

Since leaving school in 1954 I was to play in two grand finals in my two full years of football, Ballarat in 1955 and Essendon in 1957. From this match I had great elation but then eventually the disappointment of losing. But there were three other memories I would like to share.

1. I was privileged to play in the last match in which my personal football hero, Bill Hutchison (Hutchie), played.
2. Over confidence in any game in dangerous. To win the second semi and having a better team on paper meant nothing; it's what happens on the day which counts. For those of us who played in this game we were to face a parallel situation in

1962 and a lesson had been learned.
3. I swapped my jumper with Peter Brenchley, kicked a goal and was amongst the best according to the scribes. I was proud to have played every game that season and to have won Essendons best first year player award. Great memories even though we lost.

1959 - On reflection the grand final in 1959, was miraculous and could be summed up as Dick Reynolds greatest coaching feat. Yet one year later he was unceremoniously sacked after taking a young Essendon team to fourth place in 1960. The 1959 team in that grand final was vastly different from the 1957 grand final team. Bob Suter, jack Knowles, Mal Pascoe, Geoff Gamble, Rob Fox, Stan Booth, Fred Gallagher, John Gill, Bill Hutchison, Jim Heenan and Leo Molony were replaced by Brian Sampson, Alec Epis, Ian Shelton, Barry Capuano, Alby Murdoch, Ken Peucker, Ken Fraser, Ron Evans, David Shaw, Barry Mackie and Graeme Leyden. That is eleven different players, all youngsters, with the exception of Ken Peucker, all with less than 40 games experience. Some even less than 10. On examination Melbourne from '57' only had five newcomers who were mainly experienced players anyway, with the exception of 'Hassa' Mann a second year player. It was a young enthusiastic team which met Melbourne in that grand final.

This group with another three years experience was the backbone of our first premiership team in 1962, the first for twelve years. Club officials, supporters and players should look back and feel very proud of the 1959 grand final effort. Coming from fourth place and being only one goal down at three quarter time was a truly remarkable effort and served well for the future. To reach that special day in September we had to defeat Collingwood in the first semi final 14:16 (100) to 8:14(62). We then stopped Carlton in the prelim final 8:9(57) to 7:8(50). On a personal note I enjoyed a satisfactory finals series being judged in the best players in each game, with a best performance being runner up to Bob Shearman in most awards as Essendon best in the Grand Final.

1962 - At last after twelve years a premiership was celebrated again by the Mighty 'Dons'. History quite rightly gives much credit to the genius of John Coleman for our success in 1962. His skill at developing the players at his disposal but apart from the brilliant Barry Davis and teenager Charlie Payne the backbone of the team was developing under Dick Reynolds from 1957 except for the three most experienced players Jack Clarke, Hugh Mitchell and Geoff Leek. But gone were some fabulous players in Bob Shearman, Reg Burgess and Col Hebbard. Colemans coaching style was different from Reynolds in that he encouraged a more rugged approach, with players such as 'Bluey' Shelton, Don McKenzie, Ken Timms given special roles to show the opposition that we had come a long way from the so called timid 'gliders' of the 50's, and we then became the feared 'Bombers' and so it happened.

We went into the game as favourites but the press made a big thing that Essendon's danger men were Carlton's ruck duo Graham Donaldson and John Nicholls, who incidentally were former Ballarat football league players. The press added that maybe this could be countered by Essendon's small men who had enjoyed stellar games in the previous finals, against Geelong with rover John Birt kicking three goals and judged in the top three for Essendon that day. Essendon was the dominant VFL team in 1962, being defeated only three times in the home and away season. However after a superlative performance in defeating Geelong in the second semi final, 14:21(105) to 7:17(59), Geelong played a draw with Carlton in the preliminary final.

This left John Coleman in a quandary, he was thrilled with two weeks rest, but three weeks? But the resourcefulness of Coleman came to the fore. As John and Norm Smith were close friends and Melbourne at the time were still in training for an exhibition game up north, the two coaches agreed to a practice match on the Tuesday afternoon prior to the grand final. A shortened game was played which incidentally Melbourne won and caused dramatics as star half forward Terry Rodgers was injured and ruled out of the grand final. Another mishap occurred on the Thursday night at training when the retiring vice captain, Geoff Leek, stood on a ball and severely injured his ankle. The match committee decided to wait until Grand Final day before making a ruling on Geoff's fitness. After a vigorous workout prior to the game he was passed fit to play. Geoff's take on the fitness test was as follows.

> I was asked to kick a medicine ball to ascertain whether I could

withstand the shock of kicking a ball in the match. I passed with flying colours. Little did the match committee know I kicked with my good foot.

The match committee's decision proved to be a triumph for Essendon. As it turned out Essendon's all around strength, Geoff Leeks valiant efforts to nullify Carlton's superior ruck strength and Essendon's small men, with John Birt kicking four goals with two in the first quarter and Jack Clarke being a candidate for the modern 'Norm Smith' medal was enough to foil the blues. Take a bow John Coleman, second year of coaching, a premiership.

Apart from the dramatic lead up to the grand final and the game itself, there are three other memories which I would like to share.

What does a player do on the morning of a grand final?

No doubt every player has a different routine. In my case, because I'm a bit of a music freak, I spent the morning with a close friend and Essendon player George Spero. George and his family lived across the railway line from me in Brewster St, Essendon. All morning we played on his gramophone Ray Charles, Country hits. I still feel nostalgic when I hear, "I can't stop loving you", "born free" or "take these chains from my heart" and so on.

What does a player do on the night of celebrations?

I was so excited. I was in love with a young commerce student from Melbourne University, I had plucked up the courage to ask her to the post match celebrations and she had accepted. Although it was my only date with her it was still a pleasant memory of that grand final day.

What does a player do the day after a Grand Final?

Being a Christian and with most Sundays having the opportunity to speak at Sunday Schools, Preaching or speaking to Men's groups I had a Sunday school anniversary, I was to speak at on the Sunday morning. After this it was a rush to the old Essendon airport to board a plane for our end of season trip to Surfers. I felt very special to be a part of Essendon's first premiership in twelve years. As we were walking up the steps to the aircraft I was presented with a premiership cake on behalf of grateful supporters, for the players.

1965 - 1963 and 1964 were less than spectacular years for Essendon despite making the finals in 1964. Therefore a premiership was a must in 1965 with the talented team we had in that era. Personally 1965 was the most memorable year in any of my eleven years at Essendon. In March I was married, one of the happiest days of my life, to a beautiful young Christian lady Karen Robottom. At the end of 1964 the famous and wise Fergie Speakman, a committee man and the doyen of foot running trainers suggested that I should train with his elite group, five nights a week during the summer of 64 and early 65.

The hard work certainly paid off and it proved to me how unfit I had been in earlier years. I now saw the reason why Bill Hutchison and Jack Clarke, both athletic devotees, had been so successful. For me it was the start of a new era. In my final 6 years of football 1965-1970 (three played at west Torrens) I was four times best and fairest and was third twice. My other personal triumph was of course being a member of the 1965 premiership team. The game itself was a triumph for all those involved; the coaches, the players, the supporters, officials and staff. However most of the other football people, excluding Essendon, were no doubt hoping for a St Kilda victory.

What a fairytale that would have been, their first premiership ever. They had finished minor premiers but alas had to wait until 1966 for their first ultimate victory. We held sway in the ruck where Brian Sampson and Don McKenzie were dominant with great support from Hugh Mitchell and Charlie Payne also with match winner Ted Fordham kicking seven goals. St Kilda had no answers. John Coleman's record of two premierships in five years was phenomenal and adding this to his stellar playing career there is no doubt that the great culture and success of Essendon was due in no small way to the three greats, Dick, Hutchie and Coley. The final scores were Essendon 14:21 (105) to St Kilda 9:16 (70).

In looking back on the game John Coleman, in 1962, showed great courage with his selections. He gambled on the fitness of his enforcer Bluey Shelton, who at the time had a suspected shoulder injury but was selected at centre half back. This forced Geoff Pryor, who had been a satisfactory replacement for Bluey and had previously had a good record on St Kilda champion Darrell Baldock, to half back flank. This meant regular half back Alec Epis to the wing for the first time. Alec was superb with his pace and dash and one wonders if it could have been his natural position. In this position he was the fore runner to "Dipper", a Hawthorn Brownlow medallist. At a recent celebration of the premiership (50 years) Ken Fraser thanked half forward flankers Graeme Johnston and Geoff Gosper for keeping out of his way. Coleman's instructions to play out of the way of brilliant marking Ken Fraser who was our forward thrust target as much as Tommy Haley's famous line, "kick it to Royce."

Essendon was a well-disciplined team under Coleman, you knew what he wanted of you and he took a no nonsense approach. He wasn't averse to dragging you if you showed weakness or failure to carry out team rules. Yours truly found this out early in 1961. As history shows us the great man sadly passed away early in the 1970's at a relatively young age, all that knew him knew he had a certain health problem even in his glory coaching days. Well done Coley.

My premiership involvement was with four different clubs, two at Essendon in 1962 and 1965, hawthorn in 1978, Carlton in 1981 and Collingwood in 1990. A truly fortunate career as a player, coach and administrator.

John Birt

John has conducted a long and distinguished career in Australian Rules football, amounting to 42 years of continuous service at the top-level as a player, coach and administrator.

He played with Essendon in 194 games over an 11-year period from 1957 to 1967, and was best and fairest for the club three times. He played for Victoria on 11 occasions.

He went on to play for West Torrens in the SANFL as captain-coach and then held down a series of senior non-playing positions with Footscray, Hawthorn, Carlton, Collingwood and Brisbane Lions Football Clubs.

21

9 games

Peggy O'Neal

I became president of the Richmond Football Club in October 2103. We had reached the finals that year (after finishing 5th in the regular season) for the first time since 2001 and things were looking up for a Club that had been regarded as underachievers for longer than bearable for any self-respecting supporter. We lost the Elimination Final in 2013 but we had met a goal that had long-eluded the Club as we hadn't played in a final since 2001.

The general tenor of the chatter outside the Club and among supporters was that we were on the cusp of fulfilling our promise.

By Round 14 of the 2014 regular season, Richmond was 3-10 and the chatter had changed to "typical Richmond" and everyone wanted to proffer a view as to the magic pill that would cure our ills. Much of it ill-informed; not much of it constructive.

Was the promise of 2013 a mirage? Was the foundation for the future built not on rock but sand? We didn't believe that to be the case but the mounting losses made it difficult to banish all doubt about our approach and our plan. After all, we had lost to Melbourne, Gold Coast, and, in one of our worst performances in many years, to Essendon in the Dreamtime game. We lost to teams that we were expected to defeat, teams that were (at the relevant time) below us on the ladder and, most worryingly, we showed none of the dash and drive that had identified us for most of 2013.

A successful season was slipping away quickly and, with only 9 games left, we knew that our opportunity to play in finals in two successive seasons was fast evaporating - if it wasn't already vapour.

After our Round 14 loss to Sydney, we were 16th. No club in the history of the game had come from so far down on the ladder to make the 8 and while we believed that our team was improving, it was too much to count on much less to expect.

Our focus became winning as many games as we could, playing attacking footy and regaining some respect.

1.   Round 15 Saturday, June 28 ST KILDA

At the start of this game, both teams had 3 wins on the ledger and were equal 16th. Saturday night at Etihad, we were the visiting team and the pundits had opined that this would be the battle of the wooden spooners. However, we came away with our fourth win of the season and our captain led our first steady, four-quarter performance of the season.

> *St Kilda 11.7 (73)*
> *Richmond 18.9 (117)*

2.   Round 16 Saturday, July 5 BRISBANE

A grey afternoon at the MCG that featured our annual game in support of our charity partner, the Alannah and Madeline Foundation. As the week before, the two teams went into the game with the same record but the Tigers prevailed and, for the first time in the season, we had two wins in a row. Perhaps we were starting to show the improvement that we knew was inside us somewhere.

At the end of the game, we were 12th, ahead of Carlton and the Bulldogs on percentage.

> *Richmond 12.7 (79)*
> *Brisbane Lions 7.12 (54)*

3.   Round 17 Sunday, July 13 PORT ADELAIDE

It was a gloomy winter Sunday at Etihad and I was scheduled to stop by one of the function rooms and to say a few words to some of our loyal supporters in one of the coterie groups. Despite the 2 recent wins, the mood of the room was low and despite my exhortations to stick with the Club as I was sure that we were improving, I could tell that the long-suffering, faithful members were, at best, dubious. They had heard it all before.

We won our third in a row. Port Adelaide had been on top of the ladder for most of the first half of the season and was still in the top Four.

At the end of this game, we were 12th, ahead of the Bulldogs on percentage.

Richmond 19.12 (126)
Port Adelaide 16.10 (106)

4.　　Round 18 Friday, July 25   WEST COAST EAGLES

A trip to the west and this would be a true test - travel and playing the Eagles at Domain Stadium. The Eagles were 11th and we were 12th. However, the Eagles had started the season in fine form and had played finals the year before. Even though they had slid down the rankings in the 4 preceding weeks, the Eagles were expected to win handily and to start to progress up the ladder. It was pelting rain and the Richmond contingent was small.

We won. We looked tough and our skills in the wet were impressive.

West Coast Eagles 6.6 (42)
Richmond 8.11 (59)

5.　　Round 19 Saturday, August 2   GREATER WESTERN SYDNEY GIANTS

It was our first game at the MCG since 5 July and it was a 4:40pm match in the fading winter twilight and, as if to emphasise the gloom, midway through the second quarter, two of the MCG light towers failed but were restored at the half so that the game wasn't played in semi-darkness. The Giants were in their second season and this was one of those games that we were expected to win so, of course, the media assumed that we would return to our earlier-in-the-season form and lose.

At this point in 2013 we were 7th in the competition and after this game, we were 12th.

After 5 wins in a row we were still languishing in the pack forming outside the eight but some television commentators started to speculate that, mathematically, it was still possible for Richmond to make the finals. Most people believed that such prognostications were to build some drama and interest in the run to the end of the season and no one took it seriously considering the teams that we still had to face. Rohan Connolly of the Age had us staying 12th and winning only one more game for the rest of the season.

Richmond 13.11 (89)
GWS Giants 8.14 (62)

6.   Round 20 Friday, August 8 ESSENDON

A great Friday night game at which we celebrated the centenary of our great sash jumper and which brought our sixth win in a row. We hadn't won six in a row in 20 years. Fittingly, the win was against Essendon, not only one of our fiercest rivals but also the team that had humiliated us in round 11 with a 50 point win at the Dreamtime game.

Essendon had been ahead of us on the ladder all season (as had most teams at one point or the other) so to defeat them instilled belief that if we played our best and if we could do that for long enough, we could win games and, perhaps, we could win against anyone in the league. The team had produced a desperate, want-it-more performance that denied Essendon a season where they beat us twice.

We were within a game of the 8.

Richmond 14.11 (95)
Essendon 11.11 (77)

7.   Round 21 Saturday, August 16 ADELAIDE

Rainy and cold at the Adelaide Oval and it was our first game there since the Oval had been redeveloped. It definitely had the feel of a 'home ground' as the Crows supporters out-numbered the Tigers by multiples and they seemed comfortable, if not relaxed, in the expected result of the contest to be played there that night.

The Crows had been in the top 8 for most of the season and they needed this game to stay there and we needed this game to get there.

The team believed and played accordingly. We didn't lead for the whole game but we led when it mattered: at the end.

As I walked back to the hotel across the footbridge from the ground, I remember remarking to our CEO "you know, if they continue to play like this, we could just do it".

We had 10 wins and 10 losses and were out of the 8 on percentage, with Adelaide still clinging to that spot we badly wanted. All we could do was continue to play the best football we could.

Adelaide Crows 9.15 (69)
Richmond 10.19 (79)

8. Round 22 Sunday, August 24 ST KILDA

Last home game for the season and a danger game in that we risked again losing one of those 'unlosable' games that had stymied us so often.

We won. The last time we had won 8 in a row was 1980, which was also the last time we won a premiership.

A glimmer of hope and a return of spirit to supporters who had felt the flame extinguished many rounds previously.

Richmond 15.8 (98)
St Kilda 10.12 (72)

9. Round 23 Saturday, August 30 SYDNEY

If we won this game, and if a few other results fell our way, we would be in the finals. We were 8th on percentage only - just ahead of Collingwood. West Coast, Gold Coast and Adelaide were lurking just below on 10 wins each.

However, the reality was that Sydney was ladder leader, where they had hovered for much of the year.

It was a dreary grey afternoon spitting rain as many of us made our way in a mini-bus down Parramatta Road to ANZ Stadium. The traffic was terrible (as it always is on that Road) which gave us plenty of time to think and to try to contain our anxiety while mentally chasing the demons over and over again. None of us dare give way to those dark thoughts by articulating them.

When we last played Sydney at the MCG in round 14 and lost, we sunk to our lowest ebb of the season and winning this game had the power to bring us home on a high tide that we dare not think about all those weeks ago.

In Richmond Victoria, the streets were empty as the pubs were full of the faithful banding together to share elation if we won or to offer succour if we didn't. There were those good souls who weren't Tiger members but who wished us well because, honestly, they felt sorry for us. Everyone can rally around the underdog from time to time.

In a game for the ages, we won. How the team repelled wave after wave of Sydney advances in the last 4 minutes of the game when bodies were breaking down can only be attributed to mental fortitude that, somehow, engendered a super human effort that withstood the pressure.

The ability to handle challenges and to find a way to win had been developing through all the consecutive wins and did not desert us when we needed it most.

Against all expectations, we would be in consecutive year finals for the first time since 1975 - and we made history by doing so in a manner and from a starting point that no team had ever managed before.

Sydney Swans 9.11 (65)
Richmond 10.8 (68)

Peggy O'Neal

Peggy is the president of the Richmond Football Club where she has been on the board since 2005. Peggy is a lawyer who is presently a consultant to Lander & Rogers as well as a director of several financial services companies and not-for-profit organisations.

22

Robbie Flower

Robert Pascoe

On wintry mornings I haul my unathletic 62-year-old body around The Tan, a 3.7 km circuit of Melbourne's Botanic Gardens. Running and jogging past me are dozens of young fit people, one or two of whom call out, rather cheekily, 'Go Dees!', when they make out in the half-light the navy and red colours of my tracksuit top.

The top is marked XL in size and it boasts the names of the club's sponsors from several winters back. More importantly, the top once covered the rangy frame of Robbie Flower, perhaps Melbourne's greatest player, with his name now etched in the Members stand at the MCG following the 1990s reconstruction of the Northern Stand. Flower died at the age of 59 in the week after the 2014 Grand Final. Like the proverbial man who would give you the shirt off his back, Flower gave this top as a gesture of thanks to one of my son's friends who had taken him on a wilderness trek. The trek leader confessed that he himself belonged to the tribe called The Saints, but that he knew just the man who would want to wear it, and so he accepted it on my behalf.

Every time I pull on that top, my mind races back to an afternoon in Footscray and a famous match in the last round of 1987. This match has swelled in the memory of many Melbourne supporters. At a recent funeral the brother of the deceased recalled that moment in his sibling's eulogy; Flower's great game that day, taking marks on the goal line, kicking 3 goals, and getting Melbourne into the finals for the first time for 23 years. That visitor's stand on the eastern side of Western Oval, with its rickety platform for the opposing coach, is now a patch of verdant grass.

These brothers, my son, and some other friends stood with me that afternoon. We had stopped for lunch at the Plough Hotel *en route* to the Western Oval. The morning newspaper joked that Porsches from South Yarra would nose their way cautiously into Melbourne's western suburbs that day. I had been teaching in Footscray for four years and knew my way there only too well. And the magnitude of the challenge awaiting Melbourne, whose promising but up-and-down year saw us a game shy of the Final Five.

That season the crowd at Western oval was usually about 15,000. On this day, 29 August 1987, 31,249 of us squeezed into the ground. When the Melbourne coach 'Swooper' Northey and his senior players came out to feel the conditions at half-time during the Reserves match, they were surprised by the buzz we were creating. 'Several of them [the players] remarked to Northey that they had never experienced such a feeling before or during a match, and that the noise as they ran on to the ground had almost lifted them into the air.' Not only did we have to defeat Footscray at their kennel, down the Geelong Road Hawthorn had to defeat Geelong at the cattery. A few minutes before the Footscray game ended, we broke into applause when news of the Hawthorn win at Geelong, by just three points, came through on our trannies. Again Northey and his brains trust were confused, as the news came through during a lull in proceedings at the Western Oval. It was the fans who once gain played an active part in this match.

Stories of the day became apocryphal. Melbourne's Jamie Duursma was supposed to have bet Hawthorn's Jason Dunstall a case of beer that he could not get his team over the line at Kardinia Park, but Duursma's career at Melbourne did not officially start until the following season. But the best stories of that day belonged to Flower.

What was Flower's talent? He grew up a Melbourne supporter in Murrumbeena, in Melbourne's south-eastern suburbs, and he had no other loyalty than to this one club. Barely 68 kg in weight, his frame was light and rubbery (rather like that of Gavin Wanganeen), and he bent his supple body in the act of marking, of baulking, of dodging, and of running. Watch him on YouTube. A prodigious kick from full-back Danny Hughes spots up his tiny chest in mid-field at the MCG. He handballs to Sean Wight and runs on to receive the Irishman's handpass.

At the Western Oval (on the famous afternoon in question) the ball is held up by the onshore wind from Port Philip Bay at the southern end and twice Flower floats up above the goal-square to snare it. His light physique earned him the nickname, 'Tulip'. He controlled the ball with a deftness that defied easy description, and he could kick powerfully on either foot. His marking was prodigious, plucking the ball from above a pack with consummate ease; his running was electric, as he zig-zagged down the wing; and his kicking at goal, close in or further out, was deadly in its accuracy. My son-in-law owns a footy skills book from his playing days, authored and signed by Ron Barassi, featuring photos of players showing young boys (and the occasional girl) how to kick, to handball, to tackle to shepherd, and more besides. In the centre of these photos, with his silky skills on display, is Flower, by then six years out of the game.

In Flower's last season we had moved to a new house in an eastern suburb, Glen Iris. It was a lovely Californian Bungalow, apparently undistinguished. At a conference held in Warrnambool the month after Flower retired, the 1987 season a dashed hope for Melbourne, I learned that the Hay brothers, Phil and Sted, had grown up in that very house. The Hay boys were heroes in Hawthorn's first premiership side, that of 1961. I began to imagine their shoulders bruising the central corridor of that house. My son was aghast. 'Why couldn't we have bought the house where Wobbie grew up?', he asked with all the wide-eyed innocence and incredulity of an eight year old.

Over successive seasons we would catch glimpses of Flower in the Melbourne crowd. He was there among us, usually attired in a leather jacket. He never aged. He was just as we remembered him on the playing field. He was a constant reminder that the years might hurry past, but memories of his exploits were burnished in our brains. Sponsors might come and go. The club's colours changed a little with the advent of colour television, and then reverted to the traditional dark navy. Presidents came and went, as the club's factions wrestled for control of the numbers. The 1996 proposal to amalgamate Melbourne and Hawthorn came and went, supported by the corporates at Melbourne, but not by the diehard ordinary members. (Flower never gave his consent to that merger.) Melbourne rose to giddying and humiliating defeats in both the 1988 and 2000 grand finals. Flower lived on through all these tribulations.

And then he suddenly died, after a series of illnesses that eventually took his battle-scarred body.

Where does 'Tulip's' death in 2014 leave us, as mere supporters? In recent years we also lost other celebrated players, such as Todd Broadridge, Jim Stynes, and Sean Wight, and an ex-coach in Dean Bailey. Why? These are weighty questions. A clue came in an article about Jesse Hogan, Melbourne's promising goal kicker of 2015: he was, according to one journalist, Melbourne's new 'Tulip'. Flower was not forgotten. He and Hogan could not be more different in body shape and field position. And yet they are joined by their dedication to the Melbourne club.

One of my great fortunes in life is that my son's daughter, now aged 8, comes with me to Melbourne games and has imbibed the passion her father felt in the 1980s. Recently she asked me what the true purpose of football was. 'Why do we have football, Babar?', was the exact phrasing of her question. I was lost for words. 'Every week we go with the same people, make the same jokes, tell the same stories, and share in the game', was the best answer I could offer. 'You know, Babar, I think the reason we have football is to work out what is right from what is wrong.' Her logic was compelling. She never saw Flower play, but he embodied that sense of steadfast loyalty to an aspiration he had also felt when he too was an eight year old, running around in suburban Murrumbeena.

We want our lives to be guided by a sense of what is right and what is wrong, and Flower embodied that ideal. He played with a purpose and a sense of the elegance we need in our own lives. When he passed over that tracksuit top to me, it was as prophetic as Joseph's coat of many colours. Whatever our colours, we need to wear them in the morning's early light. The seasons will come and go, the heroes will be emblazoned on the verdant green of the playing field, but who we are, and what we aspire to be, will outlive those moments. Vale, Robbie Flower. Thank you for all you were, and all that you taught us.

Robert Pascoe

Robert Pascoe is Dean Laureate and a Professor of History at Victoria University, Melbourne, author of *The Winter Game* (1995). He would like to add a thanks to the gang who accompany him each week: Scott Baker, Rosemary Clerehan, Nina Pascoe, Ross Williams.

23

Heartfelt Hawthorn moments

Richard Allsop

Football success is measured in terms of Premierships but heartfelt football moments are not always to be found at the end of September.

For instance, I still get a warm inner glow from remembering a seemingly meaningless late season Hawthorn win at Windy Hill in 1979. Injuries and poor form meant Hawthorn had no chance of making the Finals, whereas Essendon was gearing up for its first Finals' campaign for six years. It was a typical 1970s football day, standing in the outer in the rain, copping lots of abuse from opposition supporters. On the field, the game also seemed to be going to form. Essendon led at every change and was still almost four goals ahead half-way through the final quarter. Then, suddenly we began a run of goals which culminated in a booming kick from Michael Tuck which actually put us in front. Essendon attacked from the restart, but now Tuck was deep in defence taking a soaring mark to preserve the lead he had given us. It was a truly heartfelt win for the small band of brown and gold true believers who were there that day.

A few years earlier, my Hawthorn-following career had moved from the social norm of going to some games to what some might consider the eccentric practice of going every week, no matter what compelling reasons there might be to do something else. This commitment had many consequences over subsequent decades but, in the short term, its main impact was journeys to all the grounds in Melbourne, including a first trip to Victoria Park. As I was only 12, my father had to take me and during that inaugural visit the Collingwood supporter behind us 'accidently' punched Dad in the back whenever the mood took him. We kicked a measly 3.9.27 that day, but I was glad I was there rather than anywhere else.

By the mid-1990s, most of the suburban grounds had disappeared from the fixture, leaving the trip down to Geelong as an annual highlight. In this period Hawthorn was struggling and Geelong going well, but several of these games met the criteria for heartfelt moments being played in a hostile environment, having close finishes and, most crucially, delivering upset wins. Hostility was not just confined to the ground, as we discovered after a particularly heroic victory in 1995. Returning to our car, parked in one of the surrounding streets, we discovered that some local had tried to steal it, doing quite a bit of damage in the process.

Of course, a normal reaction would be to regard this as putting a dampener on the day. Our reaction was to see it as adding even greater moral vindication to the win the team had just achieved. Even the couple of hundred dollar repair bill could not shake this feeling. In a famous speech at half-time in the 1989 Grand Final Allan Jeans implored the players to "pay the price". As a supporter, whether it was car repairs after a trip to Geelong in 1995, or inflated airfares to get to Perth for Finals in 2015, you are likely to feel increased vindication from success, the greater the personal price you have paid.

Despite the loss at Victoria Park late in the 1975 home and away season, Hawthorn made that year's Grand Final. Losing is often said to be character-building. It possibly is; it is certainly character-forming. Getting beaten by the underdogs North Melbourne in my first Grand Final was bad enough, but what made this loss particularly galling was that all the neutrals wanted North to win. One commentator even said that Hawthorn supporters, when they woke up the next morning, would not begrudge North their success. No true partisan would ever make such an inane comment. The pain of Grand Final losses doesn't just dissipate overnight. I spoke to an elderly Hawthorn supporter on the evening of our 2008 Grand Final victory against Geelong. He remained completely unreconciled to our loss to them in 1963!

The public popularity of North in 1975 is not the only time a sense of injustice has been engendered by our opponent being an unjust sentimental favourite. The 1987 Preliminary Final was a classic of the genre. No problem with the ten thousand or so genuine Melbourne supporters at Waverley that day, the ones readily identifiable as loyalists as they were wearing the royal blue that Melbourne had worn for a decade after the introduction of colour television. But, as Melbourne had just reverted to the darker blue, it was easy to spot new merchandise. So where had these other forty thousand people barracking for Melbourne come from? I felt it would be the height of inequity if this fair-weather crew triumphed over our long record of commitment and success, particularly given that it was only our Round 22 victory over Geelong which had allowed Melbourne into the Finals at all.

For a long time the fates seem intent on allowing injustice to reign, even to the extent that the wind changed direction at quarter time meaning Melbourne had it for three of the four quarters. When we finally got a turn with the wind in the third term, we could not make any inroads on the scoreboard, the margin still being 22 points at the final change. Even as we edged closer in the last quarter, victory still seemed unlikely, but finally the fates began to change their attitude. Melbourne began to miss very gettable shots at goal; we began to score more regularly; and finally Jim Stynes ran through the mark giving away a 15 metre penalty, allowing Gary Buckenara to goal after the siren. Justice prevailed.

Preliminary Finals seem to have a habit of delivering heartfelt moments. I never thought any would quite match the 1987 one, but then 2013 came along. Much had changed in the world and in my life between 1987 and 2013. Much in football has altered too, sometimes for better, sometimes for worse. In that time, Hawthorn had even had a near death experience, narrowly surviving the 1996 proposal to merge with Melbourne. Nothing that has ever happened on the field quite matches the weeks of stress and anxiety when it seemed likely that our football club would be destroyed; nor the sheer sense of relief when the members voted the proposal down.

Yet, despite all the changes, at its very core the football experience has tremendous continuity – the same sense of anticipation in the lead-up to the game and the same range of emotions during it. The ball is in dispute and every thought has gone out of your head, apart from the desire for your team to win the next contest.

What defined the 2013 Preliminary Final was the need to overcome the 'Kennett Curse'. After our upset win against Geelong in the 2008 decider, our President Jeff Kennett had made comments about how

Hawthorn had the mental edge against Geelong. As if Geelong did not have enough incentive for revenge. They began building up an impressive list of narrow wins against Hawthorn, and the gravity of the 'Kennett curse' grew greater and greater. However, one little saving grace remained. Only one of Geelong's 11 consecutive wins had been in a Final, and it was a Qualifying Final, not a knock-out game. So we could hang onto the dream that we might end the curse when it really mattered.

For much of 2013 it looked like Hawthorn and Geelong were destined to meet in the Grand Final, but then Geelong lost a home Qualifying Final meaning any meeting would be a week earlier. From the moment Geelong won its Semi Final ensuring a Hawthorn versus Geelong Prelim, the nerves kicked in. A loss in this game would be the most humiliating in forty years of following Hawthorn.

Until the 20 minute mark of the third quarter the game failed to deliver a decisive break. Then suddenly, as in 1987, the fates appeared to turn against us, this time courtesy of a howler of an out-on-the-full decision. The resulting goal was one of three we conceded in the final minutes of the quarter. Tears began flowing around me, not just from the eyes of my own young children, but even from our teenage family friend, overwhelmed by the prospect of another loss to Geelong, an imminent defeat of colossal magnitude.

A goal apiece kept the margin constant for a good chunk of the final quarter, but general play started to create a slither of hope that that we might be capable of another surge. Within minutes we were in front. Yet, in a weird way, this only increased the tension. Throughout the 'Kennett Curse' we had generally got a lead and then thrown it away. Now, we were in front at the 23 minute mark, with at least another five minutes for this wretched recent history to repeat itself.

We continued to dominate the play, but only added three more behinds to take the margin from two to five. In our febrile state this seemed surely to be building up to a conclusion where we would lose by one point, on the basis that losing by four would not be quite cruel enough. At the 28 minute mark, a further behind made the margin six points. Watching the replay of the game, I was struck by the commentators saying that getting the point was bad for us, as it gave Geelong the ball. It certainly did not feel bad at that moment. At least a draw would buy some time, and extra time would lengthen the period when we could still hope. Indeed, what happened next would have unbearable if the margin had only been five points. Geelong did manage to break out and surge forward. The ball got to an unmarked Travis Varcoe who seemed to have an age to steady and shoot.

Varcoe missed. This was not much of a relief. Once again losing by a point seemed a highly likely outcome. The clock had still not reached 29 minutes. It was easy to imagine an intercepted kick out and Geelong goal. Fortunately, Shaun Burgoyne, the man who had kicked the goal to put us in front, now had the ball in the defensive goal square. There might have been a handful of better Hawthorn players over the past forty years, but never has there been a person I would rather have with the ball in a crisis. If ever a wordsmith were looking to coin a term for the opposite of panic that word could well be 'burgoyne'.

Burgoyne calmly passed the ball to Luke Hodge. Hope began to rise. Hodge went long to a pack near the boundary, right in front of us. It was at the moment that the ball came off the back of that pack that I knew. It might have been a few more seconds before the siren actually sounded, but I knew. I knew that feeling which makes all the years of thinking about it, talking about it, writing about it and going to it worthwhile. Lots of other people clearly felt it too, because I have never seen anything quite like the lengthy impromptu party which took place in the back of the Southern Stand that night.

The fact that the Preliminary Final had been such an emotionally draining experience made the lead-up to the Grand Final an oasis of calm. We beat Fremantle, and have won the next two Flags too. Sometimes heartfelt moments can be in meaningful games too.

Richard Allsop

Richard Allsop is the co-author of two books on aspects of Hawthorn FC history and for the past 12 years has contributed the 'Footy Flashbacks' column to the Hawthorn website. He is a Senior Fellow at the Institute of Public Affairs and an Adjunct Research Fellow in History at Monash University, and has written on Australian politics and society for a range of publications. He previously worked as an adviser to state and federal politicians.

Amanda Vanstone wearing her Port Adelaide colours.

(Photo courtesy of Amanda Vanstone, used with permission).

24

The Port and the Passion

Amanda Vanstone

The Port Adelaide Football Club is based at Alberton in the Federal seat of Port Adelaide. It's one of only two seats Labor could hold in South Australia against the incoming landslide of the Howard government in 1996. It's a very solid Labor seat. Someone from interstate might be surprised that a former Howard government Minister is a committed Port supporter and presently on the board. Local people know better.

Yes, Port Adelaide has its roots in the port. We have the fighting spirit that comes from having a home base full of battlers. We are the postcode but we are much bigger than that. We have the biggest membership in South Australia and the eastern suburbs are very, very well represented.

I started supporting Port Adelaide when they first went into the AFL. Prior to that we had been a one team town. We were a bunch of unthinking, one eyed supporters largely because we only had that one team. In life, if you find yourself in a pack it's best to get out of it. A pack mentality is just so unattractive. I decided that when it came I would support SA's second team. I thought it would be based around the SANFL Norwood area where I had spent most of my childhood but got that badly wrong. Port Adelaide became mine in the sense that politicians are always asked at Showdown time who they support.

Greg Bolton, the President invited me to a few games. I had hardly been to the football before that. My father died when I was quite young. Not long after my mother remarried and then he died. So there were five of us, my mother, brother, two sisters and myself. My brother wasn't into football, he was a car fanatic. We just weren't a football family.

Nonetheless when the invitation came I went and absolutely loved it. After a while I joined up, only letting my membership lapse when I was in Italy for three years.

On my return and to my great surprise David Koch invited me to join the board. Port had had a shocking run and were really in the doldrums but people were keen for change. I was delighted to join. Having spent twelve years in opposition I was very familiar with the idea of coming from behind and working hard to win.

My first AFL Grand final was back when Port won in 2004. A Melbourne mate who is also a Port man asked if we could catch up over the AFL weekend. I told him Tony wasn't a mad football fan and not a Power supporter so we didn't try and get tickets. He was in government relations and had thought the club, having a cabinet Minister on side would have invited me. It had never entered my head. Anyway, I don't know who said what to whom but an invitation arrived and we went.

How can anyone forget their first Grand Final and when their team is playing? And wins. The buzz around the stadium was electric. Up until that time the biggest and best team event I had been to was in the eighties. It was a baseball game in San Diego with a pre match concert by the Beach Boys. Plastic beach balls bobbed around the stadium and between levels and crowd waves just kept on coming. The crowd was happy to be there, munching hot dogs and living the American dream. But the Beach Boys final song sent the crowd into overdrive. You guessed it, "I wish they all could be California girls" had just about everyone on their feet, joining in. It crossed my mind that the stadium could collapse! Switch to my first grand final in 2004 and "Up there Cazaly" had a similar, uniting impact.

I remember after the lunch we filed in to our seats in the stadium. Tony and I ended up immediately in front of the Prime Minister and the Governor General. My fox whistle which is discreet in size but not sound and I felt a little inhibited. They were far more polite and clapped when either side did anything great. I thought perhaps it was a Sydney thing but then with them holding those jobs I suppose a bit of decorum was to be expected.

If there's one thing about that game that will stick with me forever it is Gavin Wanganeen. One guy, out in front of the pack, he's got the ball and there's no one there. He just keeps running and bouncing, running and bouncing and then kicks it onward and upward like a fly ball in San Diego. It's coming down and he's belting down the ground and marks his own ball. It was breathtaking. There were other great plays and spectacular team work but Wanganeen's effort is indelibly implanted. Tony and I were sitting behind the then PAFC board members and one thing is for certain, grown men do cry.

I am not big on crying in public but when we get our second premiership there will be tears from me for sure, oceans of them. Or I may throw up. Since I can't remember when that last happened you'll understand how the commitment from our players and coaches just draws you in. They, no doubt like other clubs, are giving it all they've got. And then Ken Hinkley asks for more. Our admin people are as committed as you could find anywhere. We work both on the football because we exist to win premierships and to give the fans a better game day experience. We want to make our community proud. I get excited just thinking about how fantastic that second premiership day will be.

A Showdown isn't a grand final, but it's as close as you get in a local sense.

One of the last showdowns at West Lakes, before we moved to the new Adelaide Stadium was unforgettable. It was early in the final quarter and it looked as though we were set to lose. Kochie and I had to get to the airport. We hopped in the taxi, had the radio on and bang a few minutes from the ground and we'd kicked a goal. From the commentary you could tell our guys were putting everything into it. Every minute in the taxi was excruciating. We never ever give up, so 20 points down with six minutes to go and we were coming at them fast. Angus Monfries had a shot from outside 50 that must have been touched by the wing of an angel. It bounced at right angles to go through for a goal. With less than 30 seconds on the clock Chad Wingard kicked the final goal and handed us victory.

Kochie and I had missed being there at one of the best comebacks of all time. Oddly the tension of racing to the plane added to the tension of the last few minutes of the game. It epitomised how we play, we never, ever, give up. It is one of our most admirable qualities.

This year however has seen Port Adelaide finish a disappointing ninth. How did that happen when we beat the reigning premiers twice? We just lost too many games and to teams that were way down the ladder from us. It's been a salutary reminder that in football, as in life, it is not good enough to have capacity to do something unless you can draw on that capacity when you choose. Capacity on demand is what's needed. Occasional capacity, capacity that you are unable to call on as needed is just not enough. For our players I can only imagine the heart ache. You beat the premiers, twice ... so you know you can do it. You would look where you finished up on the ladder and there would be some deep thinking going on. Souls would be searched.

Having said that, the first quarter of round four against Hawthorn at Adelaide Oval this year was some of the most exhilarating football I have ever seen.

The first goal was like a cannon shot, and six more followed before Hawthorn could really respond. It is like being in a dream when your team plays as a team, smoothly perhaps perfectly against last years premiers. Hawthorn, being the team they are soon found themselves and we had a battle on our hands. The tension was terrible, just terrible. They just wouldn't give up and I admire that.

We won but it was tough. All through the match there was fabulous football, from both sides. It was the sort of football that the crowd just loves to watch. The entire game was spectacular, on the edge of your seat stuff.

But nothing, nothing, will beat that cannon shot, followed by six more, before Hawthorn woke up. Well, there is something that would top it ... being Premiers next year. I live in hope.

Amanda Vanstone

Amanda Vanstone is a former federal politician.

A Liberal Senator for South Australia from 1984 to 2007, following the 1996 election Ms Vanstone was the only female member of John Howard's coalition cabinet. She held several ministerial portfolios including minister for employment, education, training and youth affairs, minister for justice and customs, minister for family and community services, minister assisting the prime minister for the status of women, minister for immigration and multicultural and Indigenous affairs, and minister assisting the prime minister for reconciliation.

After her resignation from the Senate in 2007, Amanda served as the Australian ambassador to Italy until July 2010.

Ms Vanstone is a regular newspaper columnist and the presenter of the program "Counterpoint" on ABC Radio National.

One city, two teams - Adelaide Crows and Port Adelaide share one banner in honour of the late Phil Walsh. Adelaide Oval. July 19, 2015.
Courtesy News Ltd

25

Born to be Rivals

Chris Kenny

He is as tough a man as ever played the modern game; but skillful too. He has hurt opponents on and off the field. He played 312 AFL games, all with the Crows, and won a Brownlow medal. He is an eight-time All-Australian (twice named captain) and he captained Adelaide. One year he cried from the sidelines as his teammates won a grand final and the next he returned to hold the premiership cup. When the AFL allows cloning the Adelaide Football Club's first draft pick will be Mark Ricciuto's DNA sequence.

He is known simply as Roo – a name that can part crowds and open doors – but it is his full name that graces the AFL Hall of Fame and a grandstand at Adelaide Oval. He is the sort of bloke who is miserly with his words but people hang on them; Roo can make a player's reputation from the commentary box just by saying "he's all right."

Yet as we discuss one particular game, Ricciuto's voice trembles with emotion and his words convey compassion and tenderness, as well as footy pride. I suggest this match might have been Adelaide's greatest victory outside the finals. "Maybe it was bigger than the premierships," he ponders, and goes on to recount bittersweet memories.

Yet he didn't even pull on his boots for this one. Rather, he looked on as a TV commentator. "Everything about the day was perfect," he explains, listing the weather, record attendance and crowd generosity. "It was as hard a game as you get," he stresses, "but played in brilliant spirit." This was a Showdown – Adelaide versus Port Adelaide – and

Roo notes that even with no Victorian club involved, commentators far and wide agreed it was the best game of the season.

The intensity of Crows antipathy towards Port – and vice versa - is beyond words. It is more easily conveyed in a Tony Modra mark, a Mark Bickley tackle or the imprint of Port captain Josh Carr that was once left on the bonnet of a Mercedes Benz. Roo infamously invited Carr into the car park of the Ramsgate Hotel the day after a 2002 Showdown loss. "Carr used to tag me pretty closely," remembers Ricciuto, "in a game there's not much you can do about that but I just wanted to let him know that it's a bit different off the field."

For all the bruising encounters, what often escapes Crows and Port supporters is that theirs is a classic love/hate relationship; born of a shared love for the game and hatred of the other's success. The history is vital. Rather than developing over time, this animosity is the very foundation of the Crows. It was the 1990 revelation that Port Adelaide was secretly trying to dud the other nine South Australian clubs by entering the AFL that saw the Crows conceived and cobbled together by the SANFL. We Crows didn't learn to hate our cross-town rival; the desire to beat Port was our inception.

In sport such tensions can be wellsprings of motivation. It is surely no accident that the Crows' first premiership came in the first year Port joined the competition. Losing the inaugural Showdown helped spur the Crows to the top. Showdowns come around twice a year; must-win matches with finals-like intensity.

Over the summer of 1990/91 a football state conditioned to rivalry against the AFL had one pre-season to put a team together and join it. On Friday March 22, 1991, travelling to the first game, we saw Hawthorn supporters waving scarves and spoke enviously about how Victorians might be the greatest beneficiaries of the new team – they'd have a weekend in Adelaide and four easy points. The Hawks were a powerhouse and in a controversial pre-season deal had snatched one of Adelaide's most promising talents, Darren Jarman, before the Crows could sign him. So Darren lined up with the 1988 and 1989 premiers against his older brother, Magarey Medallist and former North Adelaide teammate Andrew, one of the leading foundation players for the Crows.

That first night turned out to be joyous, as the red, gold and blue hoops ran amok at West Lakes making the Hawks look slow. Surging a wave of crowd enthusiasm, the Crows' quick hands and fast legs delivered a staggering 15 goal win. At one stage Darren Jarman ran towards an open goal for the Hawks and hit the post. "We got the real Jarman," we screamed, deliriously joking about how, having conquered the AFL, we'd need to find a better competition.

The divergent fortunes of the Jarman brothers tell a remarkable story of heartbreak and joy that would have been inconceivable as elder brother Andrew took best field honours that night. Adelaide won nine more games in that first season and didn't play finals, Darren went on to play in Hawthorn's grand final team and snare a premiership medal, something that cruelly eluded Andrew. In fact, it was the prodigal son, Darren, who years later would return to Adelaide, deliver glory and make history. In a handful of the finest finals performances in the modern era, he would star in two more premierships – with Adelaide.

Adelaide first made the finals in 1993 and experienced the agony of losing a preliminary final against Essendon after leading by 42 points at half time. They returned to the penultimate final at the MCG four years later against the fancied Western Bulldogs. Adelaide's superstar full-forward and newly-crowned Coleman Medalist Tony Modra was lost to a serious knee injury early in the game, the Bulldogs were all over the Crows and 31 points up at half time. Starting the last quarter 22 points down, Adelaide were all but written off. Crows fans at the ground were pessimistic and resigned: winning in Melbourne was always tough, "Godra" was gone, Darren Jarman (in his second season back at the club) was quiet and little was expected of others (Andrew McLeod, Simon Goodwin, Tyson Edwards and Kane Johnson) who at that time had 50 games or fewer under their belts.

Halfway through the last quarter Bulldogs Brownlow Medalist Tony Liberatore snapped what might have been the clincher and was hoisted by teammates in a triumphant, fist-pumping celebration. The ball sailed over the post – a behind. This was the moment of Libber's premature exaltation; tempting the footy gods. The Crows were 23 points down with 11 minutes to go and they sensed the Bulldogs' hubris. In an astonishing comeback, including two crucial goals by Jarman, they grabbed a grand final spot by just two points. Outside the MCG, Bulldogs fans were broken and Crows fans hugged strangers in the right colours.

Planes, trains and automobiles got Crows fans to the MCG in numbers on Saturday September 27, 1997 to take on the minor premiers, St Kilda. Having won only one premiership, 31 years earlier, the Saints were Victoria's sentimental favourite and the form side. They'd cruised through two finals with star on-baller Robert Harvey picking up the Brownlow Medal along the way.

The Crows were the disrupters. New coach Malcolm Blight upended the club in the previous off-season. The Magarey and Brownlow medalist, who'd coached Geelong to three grand final losses, arrived and quickly said goodbye to three All Australians seen as the heart and soul of the club - inaugural captain Chris McDermott, successor Tony McGuiness and foundation playmaker Andrew Jarman. Blight wanted a new culture and paid no heed to reputation.

With Adelaide trailing by 13 points at half time the grand final seemed on a predictable path. St Kilda looked too strong for a Crows team without All Australians Modra and Ricciuto. Yet there were signs of Blight's innovation; ruckman David Pittman was fashioned as a defender and was keeping Stewart Lowe quiet, leaving other backmen such as Peter Caven, Brett James and Ben Hart to generate offensive run. In the third quarter Adelaide lifted and played their way into a 10 point lead.

Still, for Crows fans there was a deep abdominal feeling of dread. Adelaide might be out-muscled in the last quarter, as was so often the case across the border. Certainly, the Saints believed they could bring it home. Perhaps nothing epitomized the new against the old better than a trim Darren Jarman dancing around St Kilda's monolith of a fullback, Jamie Shanahan. Minutes into the final quarter, the Crows' run was evident. Chad Rintoul played on, bounced and drove the ball deep where Jarman propped and judged the flight of the ball while Shanahan lost him, took his eyes off the ball and grabbed at Jarman's jumper. Jarman kicked only his second for the day and Crows fans dared to hope.

Soon the Saints got it back to nine points but then it came again, that fearless run out of defence; this time Caven to Kim Koster and a pass to Jarman. Shanahan saw Jarman run back toward goal over his right shoulder, then looked over his left shoulder but he was gone. The full-forward had changed direction, led to Koster and left Shanahan 10 metres and another football era behind. Jarman goaled again and everyone expected St Kilda's coach Stan Alves to put a more mobile player on him. He didn't. The Crows were more nimble on the field and in the coach's box.

Adelaide supporters were about to experience MCG ecstasy. A ball-up on the forward flank, a scramble, a punch forward by Matthew Robran, and there he was – Jarman, one grab, wheeling on his left and splitting the middle. It was artistry. With 11 minutes to go, Adelaide's lead was similar to the one they'd snatched from the Bulldogs the week before. There was no time for premature celebrations.

Shane Ellen, almost unheard of till that day, was a Blight masterstroke. He'd snuck forward and kicked goals, then he drifted back and provided run. And now, midway through the last he got on the end of some Shaun Rehn courage, accepted a sweeping handball, skipped to the centre circle, and kicked long to the danger zone where Nigel Smart contested for the Crows with three Saints jumping against him. One of them was Shanahan. In the blinking of an eye, 98000 spectators saw this and wondered the same thing – so who's on Jarman? As the St Kilda defender landed and turned, he had the same thought. Too late. One nanosecond; the ball was over the back. Two nanoseconds; it was in Jarman's hands. Three nanoseconds; he powered to goal. Four ... forget it, it's over. Delirium; for the Crows this was history.

Crows fans would never disrespect his older brother but now, surely, Darren was the real Jarman. He instantly transformed his reputation from frontrunner to big game match winner. It was party time. McLeod ran amok, Ellen bobbed up for another, and Jarman's sixth; a right foot snap that was spiraling over his shoulder and through the goals before anyone knew he had it.

Adelaide's unlucky injured list watched from the sidelines – Modra, Matthew Liptak, Peter Vardy, Jason McCartney (who would write his own extraordinary chapter on AFL courage six years later), and Ricciuto.

"One minute we were cheering," says Roo, "the next minute we were crying." Their mates and club were triumphant but victory would not be theirs. "We were excited by the victory but crushed that we were going to miss out on living our dream." The pain is still evident as Roo speaks. "We were really cut up; as an outlet I spent ten hours in a Hindley Street tattoo parlour, with a mixture of aggression, frustration and anger, getting my first tattoo – it was probably a mistake."

The frustration burning away in Ricciuto's mind – and etched into his back – was one of the driving forces behind the club's ability to go back to back. There was no chance of a premiership hangover when Roo and Modra, in so many ways the vital organs of the team, had not drunken from the cup. "Because we had missed out," says Ricciuto, "we were so hungry." In 1998 he tasted grand final triumph. Godra – like that other footy "God" and high-flying Blight charge, Gary Ablett – never did.

Seven years after he retired, while successful in business and media work, Ricciuto took up a place on the AFC board. The club's most decorated player wanted to make more history. He was after a coach. "I went digging across Australia, ringing and catching up with lots of people and I kept hearing the best bloke they'd worked with was Phil Walsh (who was assistant coach at Port)," says Ricciuto. "But they told me we'd never get him, so I tried three or four times and eventually he said he'd catch up."

Walsh had played at Collingwood, Richmond and Brisbane, and coached at Geelong and West Coast. But in two stints at Port Adelaide, including a premiership, the Power had become his home. Roo lured him to the senior coaching role with Port's arch-enemy at the late age of 54. And early in the 2015 season the Crows promising squad started to deliver – attack, run and intense pressure were the attributes. The spectacular new Adelaide Oval brought fresh excitement to routinely packed home games. The optimism was palpable.

Then the unthinkable; people in Adelaide woke to news of an overnight stabbing murder in a suburban home. Soon came the shocking revelation - the victim was Walsh. And, horror upon horror, the suspect was his 26-year-old son. The Crows coach was gone, suddenly, tragically and in the most gut-wrenching of circumstances.

People were numb with shock, character took hold. From club and

AFL management to players and supporters, everyone just did what they thought would help. The club got around the Walsh family; the AFL looked out for the players; the community got around the club; the players supported each other and the football world mourned. The next game against Geelong, just two days away, was cancelled and the clubs split the points.

The first post-Walsh game for the Crows was eight days after his death in Perth against one of Walsh's former clubs, the West Coast Eagles. As with matches across the country for the previous 10 days, there were tributes at match's end with all players embracing around the centre circle. Soundly beaten, the Crows players looked lonely and worn as they walked from the centre-circle to the players' race with the Eagles crowd applauding their bravery. Players were openly weeping and consoling each other - on-field warriors looking, at once, courageous and vulnerable.

Looming the following week was Adelaide Oval and Showdown XXXIX (39). "These were young men who had spent 40 to 50 hours a week with Walsh, staring into this bloke's eyes, listening to him," recounts Ricciuto, "and suddenly he's not there – there was no playbook on how to deal with it, for the CEO, the coaching staff or the players, no one had been through this." There was uncertainty leading up to the Showdown. "We knew Port were ready to play (they'd just won a tight game against Collingwood) but we really didn't know about the Crows."

One state, one city, one oval and one game – but two teams. The Showdown rivalry is fierce and visceral. Yet on Sunday July 19, 2015, Crows and Port players ran onto the ground before a crowd of 54,468 through a shared banner. The inscription was stark: Vale Phil Walsh, 1960-2015. The teams came together in grief and respect.

At the end of this epic match there would be only three points between the teams; the tightest Showdown margin ever. "Both coaches went for an attacking, fast and high-scoring game," Roo recounts. "Port made a typical late charge, Travis Boak stood up and tried to lift his team, Scott Thompson stood out for us; it was enormous."

After the game, the record crowd stood, opposing teams applauded on the field, the rival club presidents embraced and alongside them a young woman wept and forced a pained smile of appreciation. Her name was Quinn Walsh and she had lost her father just 16 days earlier. After an intense battle between her father's final club and another where he'd been loved and respected, Quinn summoned courage her father surely would have admired to present the specially-minted Phil Walsh Medal for the best player. Thomson wrapped Quinn in his bulging arms, bowed to accept the medal then stepped to the microphone to praise his team, the opponents and the crowd. He said the game was played in the "right spirit" had been a celebration of the "life of a fantastic man" and was "overwhelming" for everyone. "How Phil's daughter did it," Ricciuto recalls, "how she managed to hand over the medal, for her to do that in honour of her dad, blew everyone away, including Scott."

"I think the Phil Walsh story is incomplete," says a steely Roo, "we found a diamond, he would have been a premiership coach with a bit of luck; he was a brilliant leader of men." Ricciuto took great comfort from words spoken at Walsh's funeral by Port Adelaide's Rob Snowden. "He said Phil had told him, not long before he was killed, that he had never been happier, that he was going to be a long term Adelaide coach and that he was pleased he had finally become a head coach; I was very pleased to hear that." Ricciuto believes that although Walsh's time at Adelaide was tragically shortened to just eight months, his influence will endure. "We'll continue to implement his plan."

In the wake of the Walsh tragedy, perhaps more than any time in Crows history, that line in our club song about being "respected by our foes" rang true. As Walsh used to exhort the players; they got the job done. Showdown XXXIX will remain an exemplar of how the game should be played and how sporting rivalry engenders deep respect. And, best of all, the right team won.

Chris Kenny

Chris is a footy tragic, journalist and former wingman and political staffer who has spent more than 30 years in politics, media and the nation's grandstands following his beloved Adelaide Crows since their inception. Associate Editor of *The Australian* and host of *Viewpoint* on Sky News, Kenny has published two books; *State of Denial* about the downfall of SA's Bannon Labor government and *Women's Business* about the Hindmarsh Island bridge controversy. Kenny claims that after raising four sons his greatest achievement has been his appointment as an official Crows Ambassador.

Kevin Sheedy is recognised for playing and coaching a total of 1000 games, August 4, 2012.

Courtesy of the GWS Giants

26

A Thousand Giant Reasons

Gabrielle Trainor

The GWS Giants have at least one major advantage over most clubs. The memories we have so far created are still as crisp and clean as newly minted dollar bills.

For most other clubs, the full catalogue of decades of milestones, triumphs and tragedies, impossible goals, premierships and other accolades can't be brought to mind with ease. Once glorious, exhilarating moments now sit as faded dog-eared photographs in an old chocolate box. Unidentified groups in unrecognisable guernseys gaze up through time, from a game no-one now can quite recall, from an oval which no longer sees the heroic combat of our game. Names of champions that once thrilled are now mispronounced, unfamiliar to all but the most ancient or obsessive fans.

But Giants supporters don't have to strain to recall our best moments. We can summon up the taste of that very first win in May 2012 as though it was breakfast today. We can still count all the games we've won on our hands – a nice round twenty. Most of us can cite the margins. We've had four B&F winners, two All Australians, a third in the Coleman medal. We beat the Swans. We beat the Hawks the year they went on to the threepeat.

While all our fledgling victories have been sweet, for mine, it is the Giants' second win, in Round 19 of our debut season, 2012, that was the most deeply heartfelt for the club. In fact, it was all about ticker - the will to win when we barely knew how to, and to win for the man who in many ways gave the AFL's newest team, our heart.

Sheedy. At that point, forty-five years in the caper – first as a ruffian player – at his best, ruck roving, unbeatable – and then as maestro coach. Unconventional, passionate, tireless enthusiast, with a brilliant but quirky natural intelligence, decent, media darling, man of the people, household name – even in parts of Greater Western Sydney. Having Kevin Sheedy as the inaugural coach of the Giants was a masterstroke.

Plenty of experienced people from the top shelf of football were involved in the genesis of the Giants but it was Sheedy, appointed in November 2009, who breathed life – and a good measure of necessary courage - into the wide-eyed group of talented, but mostly green as grass teenagers who had thrown their lot into football's newest adventure.

Not even mid-way through the inaugural 2012 season, the Giants still without a win, the commentators were regardless hailing Sheedy's role - part senior coach, part evangelist - as a triumph. At the time, former Port Adelaide premiership coach Mark Williams who signed up as Sheedy's senior assistant coach summed him up: "He deals with Premiers, he deals with heads of government, he deals with heads of companies, he deals with the common man and he has a great connection with them all. He continually surprises me and everyone. His energy is one thing, his diversity is another, his willingness to invent he has never lost and it's still one of his highest priorities whether it's a way to get a crowd, a way to stimulate the media or a way to beat the opposition."

The Giants' first win, against its slightly older sibling club, the Gold Coats Suns, took place at Manuka Oval, Canberra, on May 12, 2012 in round 7. Of course, it was a history-making day. The jubilation of the young team, for the first time singing the words of the Giants' anthem off prompt sheets, made for great images. Beating the Suns that day was both a watershed and a relief but to some extent unsurprising as they, too, were suffering growing pains. They had not won a game in 2012 at that point and went on to post 14 straight losses. Still, we were thrilled to have opened our account in the AFL history books.

Twelve grim rounds later, the Giants' premiership points still totalled that measly four and we had suffered some brutal drubbings including from the Lions (92 points) Hawthorn (162), Adelaide (119), Fremantle (95) and Collingwood (120). As was said on a fan site at the time, "very often that walk to home games felt like a death march." Commentators began to murmur about psychological damage to players under such punishment. But Sheedy and the player group kept positive, believing a breakthrough would come.

It's no secret that Giants CEO, David Matthews, loves Kevin Sheedy. It is a fine bromance. He had been the first to suggest back in 2008 when Matthews was Director of Development for the AFL, that Sheedy return to coaching at the Giants. Matthews himself is no slouch at marketing the game and recognised that Sheedy was not only what the club needed on the field, but was that rare manner of man who could inculcate the players with a love for the game, a culture of strength and community and embed in them the importance of winning - not only games, but also the hearts and minds of Western Sydney and Canberra. Unprecedented for an AFL coach, Sheedy would leave the coaches' box at half time and call in at the Chairman's function, grab a microphone, and explain to the footy neophytes how he was seeing the game, what moves he might consider and his assessment of the key contests. Then he would make his way to the rooms. Such was his realisation of the breadth of his role and the scale of the club's challenge.

Early in 2012, Matthews recognised Sheedy would pass a significant AFL milestone on August 4, in the fixture against Port Adelaide to be played at home at the Giants' newly-opened boutique home ground at Sydney's Olympic Park, Homebush. Including premiership, pre-season/night and international games, Sheedy would be the first person in VFL/AFL history to have been involved in 1000 games as player and coach. This extraordinary achievement by a legend of the game, Matthews figured, deserved recognition by not only the Giants, but by the whole football community. The club promoted it, urging Kevin fans everywhere to regard the game as a tribute to him.

Port, the proud, long-established South Australian club which played its first game in 1870, winner of 36 Premierships including six on end, was having an absolutely awful year under coach Matthew Primus. But given the Giants' had only won one ever game against the novice Suns, and the Giants' most recent outing, against Collingwood, ended in a 20 goal deficit, hopes for a Giants' victory were not high.

While Sheedy did not much mention the milestone game, the

leadership group of the players talked about it at length during the lead-up week. Sheedy burst through the banner as the teams came on to the field and both formed a guard of honour for him. The crowd rose. Game on.

Two early goals by Tom Bugg saw the Giants grab the opportunity. At quarter time we led 34 points to 8 and extended our lead to 44 points at half time. It was our first ever lead at half time and our tails were up. Former Port ruckman, Jonathan Giles, played a blinder. He had something to prove, having been on the Port list for four years without senior selection, and he punished his old teammates in the centre, where it hurt. A member of South Australian football royalty, now Giant, Chad Cornes, also played well against his former side, including slotting a wonderful goal.

Port's pride at stake, they regained ground in the third quarter, getting at one stage to within five points. Hearts began to sink in the stands as we foresaw the familiar pattern of game-hardened experience making the difference in the final term. Then Jeremy Cameron goaled to steady, from a cracking pass from Callan Ward, but our lead had been whittled to two straight goals as we went into the huddle at the last change.

While Sheedy was not drawing attention to his record game, the Giants knew they wanted to make this a memorable day for him, for Western Sydney and for themselves. They pledged to finish the job. The last quarter was magnificent. Booting six, the Giants topped 100 points for the first time in their history. Their strong and confident attack left Port, looking leaden and demoralised. A roar on the siren. The winning margin was 34 points.

"There's a big, big sound from the west of the town..." blared across the ground as it had never done before, its rhythm conjuring up mental images of beaming Cossacks, decked out in orange, dancing wildly. Fans hugged and kissed. Players flung their arms around each other in elation and looked, marvelling, at the scoreboard, by then the target of thousands of phone cameras. Port players slumped to the ground, humiliated, knowing there would be consequences.

"I never think of the (milestone) games that much, but it was monumental for the Giants of western Sydney to win in western

Sydney," Sheedy said after the game. "It's just great for the GWS fans ... (and) it's great for the team and we'll gain an enormous amount of confidence out of it."

The media went into raptures over a win they labeled "incredible." "In a debut season of many firsts this was the biggest and best of them, the Giants' first win at Skoda Stadium in just their fifth match at their new home ground," the News Limited papers recorded. "Giants earn famous win over Port Adelaide in Kevin Sheedy's milestone match." "Sheedy received the ultimate respect from his young charges by overrunning Port."

Giles, who vied with Callan Ward for best-on-ground, routed his old club with 26 hitouts, 23 disposals and two goals. Asked about the part Sheedy's milestone game played in the result, he said: "It's been talked about all week and before the game we mentioned it ... so it was great to get a win for him."

It was put to him at the post game presser that it was a fairytale win. Sheeds remarked cryptically: "I live in fairytales and actually it's very lonely because no one bothers me when I'm dreaming." Nobody cared whether that made sense or not. The moment was magic, anyway.

Gabrielle Trainor

Gabrielle is an inaugural director of the GWS Giants. Both her father and grandfather were Presidents of North Melbourne Football Club (Frank 1938-1951 and Tony 1965-71) and AFL Life Members. She was a member of the AFL Commission NSW/ACT for about ten years from 2000 during which time the concept of a second AFL team in the west of Sydney took root. She sat on the advisory committee that led to the creation of the GWS Giants. She is a lawyer (recovered), former journalist and consultant, and nowadays a professional non-executive director.

27

Freo Dockers
Purple, Pain and Possibilities

Sally Murphy

My life's passions include poetry, children's books and footy. An odd mix, I was told recently. Maybe, but that's how I roll – I love lots of things, and the things I love I am really passionate about. And boy do I love the Dockers.

But back to the other things – kids' books and poetry. As part of my work I spend a lot of time talking to both kids and adults about my books, and I've realised that using a footy story or two to illustrate my point can be a wonderful tool. Many of my books are about topics which seem a bit serious to kids: a grandmother with dementia, a mother in a wheelchair following a car accident, a boy fighting cancer. "Why do you write stories about sad stuff?" a kid will ask me almost every time I do a school visit. And every time I'm asked, I reply: 'Because I'm a Dockers supporter.'

There have been lots of sad stories in the Dockers relatively short history. The obvious one to start with is premierships. We haven't won one, have no big trophy in the cabinet, as our West Coast frenemies like to constantly remind us. Yes the 2015 minor premiership and Brownlow have cheered us up somewhat, but we still yearn for the big one. And we'd love to have it while Pav – who has bled Purple the longest of all Dockers players – is part of the team. We've come close, with a heart-breaking Grand Final appearance in 2013, and six other finals series. But there's no prize for second, and a minor premierships is only a small thing compared to holding that cup aloft some September.

Then there were our early years. I have to digress here to say why I became a Dockers supporter. Although my love for Fremantle played its part in my decision, my love for the underdog was a stronger factor. And Fremantle was very definitely the underdog. When a decision was made to grant a second franchise to Western Australia, it seemed to many supporters of the fledgling club (myself included) that the powers that be, including the West Australian Football Commission, were determined that this be a second rate team. The resources that were poured into establishing West Coast were nowhere near matched by what was spent on establishing the second club. No training ground, no change rooms, almost no staff. When West Coast was established, the AFL's decision to grant them the pick of all West Australian born players ensured a top quality team from the outset, with finals campaigns and their first two premierships in their early years the result. As well as top players, the money poured into West Coast's establishment was nowhere near matched when the little brother team was established. As I've said, the team was set up to be the underdog, and the underdog it was – to the delight of West Coast fans.

Back to the sad stories. Freo entered the AFL in 1995, and fans like me were excited. Our new young team, the pride of Fremantle, was going to do us proud. Sadly, though, our excitement wasn't matched by on field success, and Freo were well out of contention until 2003, when they finally made their first finals appearance, having finished fifth in the home and away season. They've since played in seven finals campaigns, but only a Freo player knows how painful it has been to come so close so many times – including a Grand Final appearance in 2013 and the minor premiership in 2015 – without having a premiership to show for it. Heartbreaking doesn't come close to describing it.

A proud West Aussie, I cheered for West Coast in each of their three Grand Final wins, glad to see a team from my state take on the eastern staters. But, since then, my tune has changed a bit. I've yet to hear a West Coast supporter barrack for the Dockers when they are doing well, and the pain of having to listen to West Coast fans remind us of their three premierships wins every time footy is mentioned means that it's darned hard not to prefer a Victorian team win the grand final rather than the Eagles. I tried for many years to maintain my support of the Eagles when they were playing anybody but us, but failed miserably in 2015 when I heard not only West Coast supporters but also the majority of the West Australian media so broadly panning the team which had managed to win its first minor premiership, well before we'd dropped out of the finals campaign with a heartbreaking loss to the Hawks in the preliminary final. Deep down I'd still rather see West Coast win than an east-coast team, but never have I cared less about a Grand Final outcome than in 2015 when the pain of missing out again was just too much.

Then of course there are the derbies. Nothing brings out cross town rivalry more than an AFL Western Derby. West Coast and Fremantle play each other twice every season, and the interest in those games rivals that of the Grand Final. The first nine times – yes NINE times – the two teams met, West Coast were victorious. But as a Freo fan I didn't give up. I kept believing, as did so very many other Dockers fans. And the sweetness of that first win in 1999 was (almost) worth the wait. Of course, since then there have been highs and lows – most recently, the pain of West Coast winning our home derby in 2015 – but, ever on the lookout for the positive stat, I must note that since that horrible nine loss streak, Freo have had the upper hand, winning 20 derbies to West Coat's 14. Even with the dismal first nine counted, West Coast's lead in head to heads is only two. That could be rectified in just a single season. Or, of course, blow out to four just as quickly.

Rivalries aside, being a Freo supporter is a tumultuous thing. The pain of seeing Michael Barlow dash his Brownlow hopes with a leg fracture so terrible it is still talked about even by people with no interest in footy – and the joy of seeing him make his return to the game. The pain of seeing Nat Fyfe, arguably our best ever player, miss out on the Brownlow after being suspended controversially for an accidental head clash, the agony of waiting to see if his late season injury the following season would once again see him miss out, and the absolute ecstasy of seeing him become the first Dockers player to take home the Brownlow, and making the best ever victory speech to boot. The lows of losses such as that in 2009 where our lowest ever score of 1.7 (13) was embarrassingly only a tenth of Adelaide's 19.16 (130,) and the euphoria of big wins including the Anytime, Anywhere win over

Geelong in the first week of the 2013 finals campaign. That win was particularly sweet given that the AFL's decision to play the game in Geelong was controversial, reversing a decision that no final would be played in Geelong, where no final had been played since 1897.

There have been many other controversies, painful to watch. In 2006, in what came to be known as Sirengate, Fremantle were seemingly robbed of victory when the umpires failed to hear the final siren, and allowed St Kilda to score a game-tying point ten seconds later. Freo players, staff and fans were joined by commentators and the media in questioning how this could happen – and two days later the AFL reversed the result of the game, for only the second time in history, awarding Fremantle the win. More painful for all concerned was the sudden sacking of the popular coach Mark Harvey and his replacement with Ross Lyon. The way this was done seemed harsh, and left Harvey shattered, and this fan's heart a little bruised, though Lyon's success since has shown it was probably a good move for the club.

Back to where I started: what being a children's book author and being a Fremantle Dockers supporter have in common. After the kids have stopped laughing at my explanation that I write sad stories because I'm a Dockers supporter, I explain myself. See, for more than 20 years I have lived with great disappointment. At the start of each new season I've believed that my team, the mighty Dockers, can win the holy grail: the AFL Grand Final. And, year after year, we've missed out. It's a sad sad story – just like the stories I write which deal with the tough stuff kids have to deal with: death, disability and family struggles. But I've had two choices: to give up, and go barrack for another team or turn my back on AFL altogether – or to keep the faith, keeping believing that one day my boys in purple will come through for me, for the rest of the Purple Army and for themselves. Just like the characters in my books, I choose to live in hope. There will be a happy ending.

Sally Murphy

Sally Murphy is a proud West Aussie, children's book author and mother of six. Her books include picture book Fly-In, Fly-Out Dad, and verse novels Pearl Verses the World, Toppling and Roses are Blue, as well as historical fiction including Australia's Great War: 1915. Her books have won awards including the children's book category of the West Australian and Queensland Premiers' Book Awards. Sally's website is www.sallymurphy.com.au and she also runs a book review site called Aussiereviews.com

Gary Ablett makes sure Robert DiPierdomenico pays the price in the 1989 Grand Final. The other Hawk is Andy Collins.
Picture Sebastian Costanzo,
Courtesy of The Age.

28

Heartfelt Moments

Michael Gordon

I can't remember the year I became hooked on Hawthorn, but I can recall the moment. I was in grade two of primary school when we moved from Box Hill to Hawthorn and, one Saturday, I wandered down to Glenferrie Oval and caught a turnstile-framed glimpse of Ian Law: hunched over the ball, blonde-headed and moving fast. From that sunny afternoon, I was utterly, unequivocally committed.

Pre-teen reading of newspapers was confined to the training notes and focused almost exclusively on Hawthorn. Twice I played on that sardine can of a ground at half-time, representing Auburn Central in the pre-Little League days. Posters of John Peck and Graham Arthur, purchased from the tiny yellow souvenir stand on the wing, adorned my bedroom walls. The day my old man, Harry, presented me with a brand new Sherrin (or was it Ross Faulkner?) signed by the team, I slept with it.

Even now, it is hard to say which odour was the more alluring: the smell of the leather of the brand new footy, or the liniment-laden aroma in the old Hawthorn change rooms when we, the boys from Auburn Central, took on Glenferrie State.

What I can say is that more than half a century of devotion to the Hawks has delivered a huge emotional dividend, mostly happy but often sad. That is the nature of sport. The invitation from Ross Fitzgerald was to select my most heartfelt memories and "perhaps start with Peter Crimmins, and then move on from there". I can think of no better place to begin.

1. 1965

The record books tell us Peter Crimmins played 176 games between 1966 and 1975, kicked 231 goals, captained the club and, with Leigh Matthews, was one of the most formidable roving combinations of his time. But the contribution can't be measured in statistics.

The simple truth of it is that no Hawthorn player better personified the qualities that were formally adopted as the trademarks of the team that won three consecutive flags between 2013 and 2015: he played "commando football", was open and honest, was selfless to a fault and left his ego on the hook when he entered the club.

My Crimmins moment came well before he was among Hawthorn's best in the 1971 grand final and the tragedy of his battle with cancer a few years later that led to the toughest decision of John Kennedy's coaching career: to leave him out of the grand final team that lost badly in 1975.

I was still in primary school and ran out on to the ground seeking autographs on my Graham Arthur poster after a game, before following the players into the rooms. Crimmins had just emerged from the shower when I approached him and, towel wrapped around his waist, ushered me to a quiet corner where he could sit, signed the poster and apologised for the drips.

2. 1971

Conventional wisdom would have it that the 1989 epic against Geelong was the most physical of Hawthorn's 13 premiership wins, but 1971, my first, was every bit as brutal. As the captain and future premiership coach, David Parkin, expressed it, both teams included seven or eight of the toughest players in the toughest period of AFL football. "The first half of the 1971 grand final was played without the ball," he quipped.

If there is a more self-effacing or good-natured champion in the history of the competition than Peter Hudson, I would be very surprised. In this game, he was denied both the all-time AFL goal kicking record and the memory of being part of the premiership victory by the brutality of Kevin "Cowboy" Neale, who remarked in a candid interview in the remarkable documentary *The Final Story: 1971* that "you can't kick goals if you're unconscious".

Much to Neale's surprise, Hudson bore no ill-will to the man who hit him so hard in the first quarter that his ear was split in two and, for the rest of the game, "when I tried to focus on the goals, I was seeing too many posts". Nor did Hudson harbour any regret about being unable to surpass the 150 goals of Bob Pratt.

"Really, it wouldn't have been a true record anyway," he told my father in *The Hard Way*, the club history we updated together as *One for All*. "Pratt kicked his 150 in fewer matches than I did. I'm happy enough to have my name bracketed with his."

Looking at the replay all these years later, the most logical explanation for Hudson kicking into Lawrence, the man on the mark, from point blank range in the final term, and for splaying another shot shortly after, is the concussion. My most enduring memory of the day is of Hudson embracing Lawrence after the game.

3. 1978

I watched the 1978 grand final from the couch, having torn every right knee ligament off the bone in a club footy grand final the previous week. After North Melbourne outscored the Hawks, by five goals to two, to take the lead in the second quarter, beads of perspiration trickled down my ankle-to-thigh, plaster-covered leg and into the stitches. They itched like crazy.

Early in the final term, Knights was so heavily concussed that it looked like he would be unable to play any further part in proceedings. With the grit that Dermot Brereton displayed 11 years later, he stayed on and moved to the forward line, where he took one of the marks of the year and kicked a running goal that combined athleticism, skill and kamikaze courage in equal measure.

Knights would play in another premiership, his third, in 1983, but to my mind, those few minutes of brilliance amid adversity summed up the way he played in an injury-plagued career spanning 267 games.

4. 1985

"The end for a slightly soured Leigh." That was the headline on a piece I wrote about Leigh Matthews that appeared on grand final day in 1985. I was the sports editor of *The Age* and Matthews agreed to an interview before what would be his last game. It had been a tough year for the man who would be judged footballer of the century, and Matthews was typically candid as he reflected on the low of his career: being charged with assault after breaking Neville Bruns' jaw midseason at Princes Park.

I was at that game and wrote at the time that the shameful end to the game, including Matthews' nose being broken in retaliation, could have been avoided if field umpires had the power to order players from the field. In my view, it was Mark Jackson, throwing haymakers at Gary Ayres and Chris Langford who bore responsibility for what followed.

Matthews had seriously considered not playing again after the controversy but came back, he told me, because he wanted to "show them Leigh Matthews the footballer, so that that (the Bruns incident) was not the last memory".

The very last memory was a tearful Leigh, being carried off on the shoulders of Russell Greene and supported by grim-faced team mates after the Hawks were thrashed in the 1985 grand final. The photograph provided the cover shot for *The Hard Way*.

5. 1989

"You'll always get knocked down in life," Allan Jeans said many years after the 1989 grand final. "It's how you get up and what you do after (that counts)." He was talking about Dermott Brereton, who suffered a serious kidney injury and bruised ribs in the opening seconds of that epic encounter. But he could have been talking about Robert "Dipper" DiPierdomenico in what Malcolm Blight called "the last seriously brutal game of football".

Mark Yeates payback hit on Brereton (for an action every bit as violent earlier in the season) set the tone for a truly gladiatorial grand final, perhaps the last in the history of the game. But, perhaps because I was sitting nearby, the most enduring memory for me was Dipper running backwards to mark and being hit with such force by Gary Ablett that he sustained broken ribs and a potentially life threatening punctured lung. The difference was that Dipper knew Ablett was coming.

Over the years, I have heard Dipper tell the story many times at functions, mostly fundraisers for charity. It just gets better and it's true.

6. 1998

Jason Dunstall was reluctant to have a farewell game at the end of the 1998 season. In his 14th year at the club, Dunstall had played 268 games, become the third highest goal kicker in VFL/AFL history and been the spearhead in four premierships. But his last two seasons were marred by injury and he was reluctant to take to the field for a final 269th game. After suffering a broken collar bone in round 14, he did not consider himself to be fit enough.

The game was at Waverley, where on countless occasions I had sat with my kids in the forward pocket, changing ends each quarter so we could have a good view of the Hawthorn full forward.

Coach Ken Judge had other ideas, persuaded Dunstall to play and invited Allan Jeans to speak to the players about Jason's contribution before the game. Jeans gave such a moving address that, when the lights came on after a video package of career highlights, Judge recalled: "There were 22 players and six or eight officials in the room and you would have been struggling to find one or two who were not crying or visibly moved by it all. And I remember thinking: 'I've put these blokes over the top'."

Although Dunstall kicked an early goal, he was so spent at three-quarter time he approached Judge and asked to be taken from the ground. "I'm no value to you," he said. Judge had none of it and made the gesture the centre-piece of an unforgettable address. "He's been the consummate team man to the end," he said of Dunstall. "It's his day and he wants to come off because he wants us to win. We owe him! WE OWE HIM AND HE'S NOT COMING OFF! AND WE'RE GOING TO WIN!" The response could hardly have been more emphatic. The Hawks kicked 11 final-quarter goals against Fremantle to provide the perfect send-off.

The moment: a humble Dunstall applauding the crowd as he was carried from the ground on the shoulders of Jonathan Hay and Trent Croad.

7. 2004

It was Allan Jeans who called football "a game of heartaches" and no one appreciates this better than Peter Schwab, who played in three premiership teams, but was denied his place in the 1989 grand final by a cruel decision of the tribunal, despite having had an unblemished record through 10 years of senior football. It was Schwab who suggested I update *The Hard Way* and, after he was appointed coach in 2000, who gave me the access to team meetings that continued under Alastair Clarkson.

As a coach he experienced some blissful highs and gut-wrenching lows. The Hawks played in the finals in his first two years and could very easily have won a spot in the 2001 grand final. The highlight, and Schwab's greatest performance as a coach, was in the semi-final against Port Adelaide that year, just after the world changed on September 11.

The heroes of that away-from-home, come-from-behind victory were Daniel Chick, who lost the man who was going to be his brother-in-law when the World Trade Centre came down, and John Barker, who suffered a migraine early yet managed to kick a miracle goal from the pocket where goals were strangers at Football Park.

Years later, I asked Chick how he managed to shut out the grief and play with such an intensity. He wasn't sure, but paid tribute to Schwab, describing him as "an amazing coach in the way he is able to alleviate pressure and put things in perspective and tell stories of life".

My most emotional memory of Schwabby's period as coach came in the rooms after the final loss in the horror year of 2004, after the Hawthorn board had terminated his contract. The mood was one of shared grief that it had come to this, and sorrow that a list of players that was in urgent need of renewal had been unable to match the commitment and character of the coach.

My friend (and Schwabby's) Martin Flanagan covered Schwab's final press conference and wrote in *The Age*: "He gave me a wink on the way in and I knew he was all right. We both like boxing and, in the language of that tough game, I knew he had taken a big hit but he was still on his feet."

8. 2008

It is easy to forget, given Hawthorn's success in recent decades, that the club had to wait 17 years to win its 10th premiership in 2008. Shane Crawford arrived in 1993, just as the club's most golden era was coming to an end. He played under five different coaches and waited 305 games, a record for the competition, to realise his premiership dream. For most of that period, his irrepressible spirit shone like a beacon of hope.

For many supporters, the most memorable Crawford moment was when the four-time club champion and Brownlow medallist received his premiership medallion and declared: "That's what I'm talking about!"

The more heartfelt for me came a few weeks earlier, when Crawford became the sixth Hawthorn player to notch up 300 games. The achievement was all the more extraordinary because, only a few weeks earlier, it seemed his career was over. It was Rick Ladson who conjured a way to deliver the ball to Crawford in the final minutes to give him a chance to goal in that milestone game, and it was every single member of the team, including Trent Croad running from full-back, who rushed to him afterwards to celebrate the moment.

9. 2013

Max Bailey was my favourite story of the 2013 premiership: the big boy from the west who fought back after three knee reconstructions to realise the dream. Like Shane Crawford in 2008, he knew from just after halfway through the season that there was a serious prospect that he would not be able to see out the season. And, like Crawford, his presence in the team and ability to play his role was the result of a collaboration with the Hawks' fitness guru, Andrew "Jack" Russell.

Max's capacity to endure hardship and focus on doing whatever was required to reach his goals was matched by his ability to accept the hand he was dealt and roll with the punches. In this regard, he was very like Brendan Whitecross, who suffered knee injuries in the 2012 qualifying final and the 2013 preliminary final.

On both occasions Whitecross put the team first and congratulated team mates, masking the seriousness of his injury so as not to diminish the moment. The grin on his face when players walked from the field after that epic prelim win over Geelong prompted Cyril Rioli to run to his mate, give him a bear hug and declare: "It's your time now, cuzzy. You've been waiting a long time."

"I'll be waiting a little longer," Whitecross whispered.

It was only when the players entered the briefing room to hear from the coach that Whitecross succumbed to the emotion and shed a silent tear, prompting Alastair Clarkson to break the news. "There's plenty of emotion in this game. We cry with you, Whitey," he said softly, ruffling his hair. "He's hurt his knee. It's a fuckin' roller coaster, isn't it?"

10. 2015

I watched the grand final with Ray Wilson, a member of the 1971 premiership team, and his son Tony. For the third year in a row, there were good judges of football who predicted a Hawthorn defeat. This year, so the argument went, the emerging West Coast side that had soundly beaten the Hawks in the qualifying final had too potent a forward line, too much pace and would cope better with the expected heat.

What they had not factored in (again) was the value of experience, the pride of captain Luke Hodge and the entire playing group and the ability of Alastair Clarkson and his assistants to prepare for the contest. There were many moments to savour and, for me, two stand-out performances: the mesmerising brilliance of Cyril Rioli, the deserving Norm Smith medallist, and the four-quarter contribution (delete: performance) of Ryan Schoenmakers, who suffered a season-ending knee injury in 2013, was overlooked in 2014 after playing a majority of games in the home-and-away season and faced the prospect of losing his place in the grand final team to Jack Gunston.

Rioli has always been a favourite of supporters, and the joy was simply to witness him deliver his very best on the biggest day and the biggest stage, especially after the hamstring challenges he had faced in the previous two seasons. Schooey, in contrast, was not so blessed in the skill department and had not enjoyed the same unqualified regard of the Hawthorn faithful because he made the odd mistake. What he did on grand final day, emphatically, was win over the doubters and the undecided with a performance that reflected his own self-belief and work ethic and the faith of his coaches and team mates. Awesome, I reckon.

Michael Gordon

Michael is a Melbourne journalist. He is political editor of *The Age*, a Walkley Award winner and five-time winner at the United Nations Association of Australia Media Peace Awards.

In 2005 he won the Graham Perkin Award for Australian Journalist of the Year.

He is the author *of Playing To Win: The Inside Story of Hawthorn's Journey to an 11th Premiership* (2014); *One For All: The Story of the Hawthorn Football Club* (with father, Harry) (2009); *Bells: The Beach, The Contest, The Surfers* (2011), *Layne Beachley: Beneath The Waves* (2008), *A True Believer: Paul Keating* (1996), *Reconciliation: A Journey* (2001) and *Freeing Ali: The Human Face of the Pacific Solution* (2005).

The author tossing the coin before the West Coast Eagles v Gold Coast match, round 7, 2015.

Image: Courtesy of the West Coast Eagles

29

Home and Away

Julie Bishop

There is no shortage of commentators who will happily engage in the eternal debate around the predominant football code in Australia. The fact is there is only one code with roots that are purely Australian – Australian football. While it may be seen as a curiosity around the world, within our shores it is an essential part of our psyche. Simple in concept yet complex in execution, a free-flowing game of Australian Football is a truly entertaining spectacle and has inspired intense loyalty amongst its fans for generations.

My father Doug first introduced me to the great game of Australian football. Dad is a passionate supporter of North Adelaide in the South Australian Football League and he has barracked for the Adelaide Crows since the team entered the national competition in 1991.

One of my fondest memories was attending the Championship of Australia match with my father in 1972 between North Adelaide and Carlton at Adelaide Oval.

The Championship of Australia was contested between football clubs from state football leagues from 1968 until 1975. It was played in Adelaide almost every year but had been dominated by Victoria since inception. North Adelaide had made the final in 1971 but was beaten comprehensively by Hawthorn. The following year was North Adelaide's chance.

Fathers of teenage girls often acknowledge that it is not always easy to find common ground, but Dad and I have always been able to bond over our love of football. So in 1972 together we cheered North Adelaide home to a one-point victory over Carlton. I recall standing alongside

Dad cheering ourselves hoarse as our team triumphed, with the final score 10 goals 13 points to 10 goals 12 points!

Another time when I felt a similar rush of adrenalin and pride over a football game was in 2006 when I witnessed the West Coast Eagles win over the Sydney Swans by one point in the Grand Final, just a year after suffering a heartbreaking 4-point defeat against this determined rival.

My journey to becoming a die-hard West Coast Eagles supporter began in 1987. Family and work ties lured me from South Australia to Western Australia in 1983 and at the time there was no AFL team to follow in either state so I supported the Claremont Tigers in the West Australian Football League.

I was working with law firm Robinson Cox (now Clayton Utz) in 1986 when the VFL voted in favour of two new clubs in the competition, one from Western Australia and the other from Queensland.

The WA Football Commission was required to provide $4 million up front and was given just 160 days to assemble a team and its supporting infrastructure.

My law firm was approached to help with the establishment of the first West Australian Football Club, an historic step in the VFL becoming a national competition.

There was an initial public offering, heavily subscribed by Western Australians, eager to see a WA team compete against Victoria, and we provided the legal advice.

It was an exciting time, and our law firm signed on as early supporters of the Golden Eagles Club. I attended the first Golden Eagles function, and delighted in the birth of the West Coast Eagles - finally a team that would represent Western Australia in a national competition.

I followed the Eagles fortunes closely and without hesitation arranged to attend our first Grand Final appearance in 1991. It was unprecedented for a number of reasons. Reconstruction work at the Melbourne Cricket Ground meant the game was played at the smaller Waverley Park for the first and only time. Angry Anderson's performance of 'Bound for Glory' aboard a mock batmobile was memorable for all the wrong reasons. More importantly it was the first time a Grand Final had been contested by a non-Victorian side - the newly formed West Coast Eagles -and it was not a popular development with Victorian fans. The Hawks were a football force and were seeking a third premiership in four years.

I made what has now become a regular migration for West Australians across the Nullarbor for finals football. The reception by the Victorians to this influx of interstate invaders was not something for which I was prepared. The mood was extremely tense, the parochial Victorian media, anticipating the unthinkable (the flag going West) sought to undermine the credibility of the Eagles side, painting them as a 'state-side' in the lead up to the match.

When the big day finally arrived as I walked through the mud-soaked Waverley car park, Eagles scarf proudly flung around my neck, I felt a light shower on this cold September day. The weather was not responsible – the spray had originated from a disapproving Hawthorn supporter.

While the Eagles started the match strongly we were blown away in the last quarter to lose by 53-points. It was a very bedraggled group of Eagles supporters who made their way back home to the West. Of course in the following year the Eagles were Premiers, a feat repeated when we lost in 2005, only to win the Premiership in 2006.

The 2015 Grand Final provided a certain sense of déjà vu when my beloved Eagles, against the odds, made it to another Grand Final against Hawthorn, this time chasing its third straight premiership.

I hope that next year the Eagles can respond with the same maturity as the 1991 and 2005 versions, learning from the gut-wrenching disappointment that only a Grand Final defeat can provide. The 1991 defeat in particular ushered in a golden era for the Eagles – one which saw us win two Premierships and reach the finals each and every year.

In 2008 I was asked to join the board of the Eagles. The Club was in a rebuilding phase following a period of prolonged success, but while the team struggled with its two worst seasons in 2008 and 2010, the Club continued to thrive, achieving record profits.

Despite external pressure, the board stood by the only constant in all three of its Premierships in our 1992 and 1994 captain and 2006 coach – John Worsfold. The record turnaround in fortunes in 2011 proved the decision was the right one. In a rare feat, the Eagles rose from wooden spoon status in 2010 to the top four in just one year. Many were surprised by the change in fortunes but I was not. Of all the boards on which I have served, the West Coast Eagles was one of the most professional and experienced. It is a club that prepares for success and has a plan to rise to the top of the competition. This has been proven time and again through the Eagles relatively short but successful history.

One of my only regrets in becoming Foreign Minister was having to step down from the Eagles board due to extensive travel and parliamentary commitments. While I can no longer serve the club as a board member I remain a committed advocate of sport, football and the West Coast Eagles in my current role.

In 2011 President Barak Obama made a historic visit to Australia and gave an address to a joint sitting of the Australian Parliament in Canberra.

Then Opposition Leader Tony Abbott and I, his deputy and shadow minister for Foreign Affairs and Trade, were invited to meet the President prior to his address. The President's security detail provided strict instructions not to bring any gifts or other items into the meeting but I was determined to ensure there was one exception to the rule.

The situation required some creative thinking. I neatly folded my gift, a customised West Coast guernsey, into the shape of what appeared to be a little blue clutch purse. At the exact moment the photographer lifted his camera to capture the moment, I unfurled my purse to reveal a West Coast Eagles guernsey with Obama and a big number 1 emblazoned on the back.

Before the President had time to react, I explained the West Coast Eagles were a bit like his NFL team the Pittsburgh Steelers and he broke into a broad smile and proudly displayed the jumper for the photo. Needless to say the photo went viral, appearing in Australian and international media and shared widely across social media.

In 2014, as Foreign Minister, I made my first official visit to Fiji to enhance the relations between our two nations which had been frozen for about eight years, following the 2006 military coup in Fiji.

In considering how to approach my meeting with Prime Minister Bainimarama, the first by an Australian Minister since 2008, I decided that there could be no better way to commence our conversation than by presenting him with a Number 9 West Coast guernsey signed by Nic Naitanui, the Eagles ruckman and Australia's most famous Fijian-Australian sports star.

The headline in The West Australian newspaper read 'Nic Nat the diplomat' and the title stuck. Nic has become an unofficial ambassador between our two countries, having been part of our first steps in normalising relations with Fiji, a nation that is an important friend and partner of Australia.

Sport has the power to transcend politics, cultural differences, economic circumstances and religious outlooks. Sport can bridge the deepest divides. Sport can inspire, it can transform, it can capture the imagination of a nation, a region, the globe. Sport is increasingly playing an important role in what is known as "soft power" diplomacy – building stronger relations between countries around the world. It is becoming an essential component of the art of diplomacy. Australian Football is an exemplar.

Julie Bishop

Julie Bishop is Australia's Minister for Foreign Affairs and Deputy Leader of the Liberal Party.

She has held the seat of Curtin in the House of Representatives since 1998 and has previously served as Minister for Education, Science and Training, the Minister Assisting the Prime Minister for Women's Issues and Minister for Ageing.

Before entering Parliament, Minister Bishop was Managing Partner at Perth law firm Clayton Utz.

She holds a Bachelor of Laws from the University of Adelaide and completed the Advanced Management Program for Senior Managers at Harvard Business School.

She was a board member of the West Coast Eagles AFL Club from 2008 to 2013.

Simon Black the first player in AFL/VFL history to win a Brownlow Medal, a Norm Smith Medal, a Premiership Medal and play 300 games.

Photo News Limited, used with permission.

30

The Brisbane Three-Peat

Chris Griffith

May 19, 2001. Circle it. It's a turning point that propelled Brisbane to three consecutive premierships and a further grand final appearance.

Simon Black, the unassuming yet brilliant Brisbane Lions champion recalls the rise of the Lions, and that turn around from mediocrity to stardom. It began with a massive 74-point loss to Carlton on May 19, 2001.

After making the Preliminary Final in 1999 and the Semi Finals in 2000, the Lions in 2001 had lost four from eight matches and were sinking. And coach Leigh Matthews was bitter.

"I remember the talk by Leigh after the Carlton game", said Black "He went through a few individuals and laid down the law, and said it wasn't good enough. The players were a pretty proud group even then, but they were frustrated. Leigh said to everyone go look at yourself individually. I remember the presence he had on that occasion. It was really powerful."

The talk was like a bomb under Brisbane which played heroically the following week, coming within a whisker of beating Adelaide, although still losing, making it five losses from nine.

But, says Black, the positive energy at Brisbane had begun flowing. Preparations were afoot for round 10, an epic match against Essendon, the reigning premiers. "It was a highly publicised game." says Black. "They were a fantastic side. They were being spoken about being as one of the greatest Essendon teams. The year before they had only lost one game in the season."

Matthews resorted to Hollywood, getting his charges to watch the 1987 alien blockbuster Predator. He adapted Arnold Schwarzenegger's famous quote: 'If it bleeds we can kill it" to the Lions' cause. It was as if Essendon were being relegated to a bunch of hunted extraterrestrials.

"Having the greatest player of the century coaching you, having him in your corner, it gave the group a lot of confidence," says Black.

"On the night before the game he got the Essendon team up on the board, he got our team up on the board and he went through the amount of games each individual player had played. He said that we as a group had played more football than they had. If we could beat the best, we could beat anyone.

The rest is history. Brisbane belted Essendon by 26 points and was destined never to lose again that year, winning the next 13 home-and-away matches and three finals. It was the first of three magic Brisbane seasons, an incredible ascendancy as the Lions had been last three years beforehand.

Black was a linchpin in this historic team's three-peat success. He is one of the AFL's most decorated players, with 3 Lions premiership wins, a Brownlow Medal in 2002, a Norm Smith Medal, and a member of 3 All-Australian teams.

Simon Black was born at Mt Isa in 1979 while his parents were travelling around Australia. His home was Perth where he went to school and played various sports before settling on Australian football. "I was a big West Coast Eagles fan growing up, I loved it," he says.

In 1997 he was draft pick 31, playing for East Fremantle when he was chosen by Brisbane, debuting in the 1998 season. Black played well that year but it was a bittersweet experience with Brisbane languishing at the bottom of the ladder. Coach John Northey was sacked mid season and former Bears captain Roger Merrett acted as caretaker coach. Black says he was drafted with Luke Power and both played nine games, getting their chances through other players' injuries.

The following year, the modern Brisbane Lions era began in earnest when Matthews began as coach. Michael Voss and Alastair Lynch had become co-captains the year before. Black says Matthews had an immediate impact.

"One of his great hallmarks as a coach was that he brought clarity to his players as a playing group, Leigh came in with a clean slate, he wasn't big on a whole lot of rules but he was high on expectations," says Black.

"He was obviously a very revered man and I deeply respected him. Some players might well have been found out early on because of Leigh's player expectations.

"One of his great saying was 'you've got to know your role, you've got to accept your role and then perform your role'. That was a large part of Leigh's coaching."

Did Matthews bring with him the more modern science of coaching to the Lions? "Black says that in 1999, the game wasn't analysed like it is now. But he credits Matthews with appointing pivotal coaching staff such as former Essendon captain Gary O'Donnell and former Bears champion Michael McLean.

In those early years, Brisbane evolved a tough yet free-flowing brand of football, an attractive style that became hallmark Brisbane. The team occasionally kicked 10 goals in a quarter, with players streaming down the ground and kicking to goal accurately on the run.

"In '99 we had a fantastic year, we made the Preliminary Final and we beat Carlton the first week of the finals, and the Bulldogs the week after and we took it up to North (Melbourne) until late in the game," says Black..

"That era gave us confidence because we did find that we could score quickly. Our attacking ability really came to the fore."

Black talks about the trust and bonding that developed in that amazing era of three premierships. Brisbane's charismatic midfield of Black, Voss, Jason Akermanis and Nigel Lappin became commonly known as the Fab Four. Three of the four became Brownlow medalists.

"I certainly loved playing with each of those guys, they were great, wonderful players," he says. "I guess we were the four who played inside with rucks and rovers the most, I guess that's how that came about."

But Black quickly acknowledges other star midfielders such as 2001 Norm Smith medallist Shaun Hart and Luke Power who were brilliant in that role.

"If you talk about the four of us, we had a bit of chemistry, we had ball winners, Acker was more our outside runner who would get the ball. You'd get to a stoppage and we knew where each other was and we had an understanding of space with each other. We could figure things out quickly."

He said Brisbane developed the knack of moving the ball really quickly from stoppages. Premiership ruckman Clark Keating would thump the ball forward when opponents loaded up the defensive sides of contests.

"We kicked a lot of running goals in that era and I think a lot of that was the fact that from stoppages we'd get the ball forward and it became a running race into the forward 50 (metre) area."

In 2001, despite its 13 home-and-away consecutive wins, Brisbane was the underdog coming into the grand final. And in the second quarter, it looked like the Bombers were slipping ahead.

"They were competitive until half time. Alistair Lynch had kicked a goal to bring it back to 14 points. We started to drag the momentum back to us and we were really buoyant at half time.

"We came out in the third quarter, got on top, and got to three-quarter time. In the huddle we felt we could push them, and push them harder and take it to them, but we had to win it. And in that last quarter we ran away with it." The 2001 celebration was euphoric. Black remembers the Fitzroy Lions supporters coming out in droves. Given the previous Lions premiership was in 1944, most were not alive the last time they'd won. "It was unforgettable," he said.

Black remembers getting one hour's sleep in the ensuing revelries before greeting "thousands upon thousands" of fans the next day. "The first one was just sheer elation because it was the first time."

Year 2002 was a different scenario. "It's amazing how the psychology changes. We were the red hot favourites against Collingwood and it was a pressure game. I remember waking up on the Saturday morning and seeing the rain coming down, the drizzle and the fog out there and thinking it's going to be a tough slog today. And that's what it was all day," says Black.

"It was a close game. At no time was there a big lead. When Akermanis snapped (a goal) in that last quarter, that gave us a nine point lead.

"It was more relief. Don't get me wrong, it was still an enormous amount of exhilaration but there was an element of relief to it, given that we were favourites going into it."

In 2003, with fine conditions prevailing the Lions easily ran away from Collingwood to score a 50-point victory with Black voted best afield with an amazing 39 disposals. But it hadn't been all easy going for Brisbane that year. Three weeks before the Grand Final, the Magpies had defeated the Lions by 15 points in a qualifying final.

"We had a month of pretty average footy." Black says, recalling another significant discussion, this time with captain Michael Voss who questioned whether his players were still prepared to put their bodies on the line, a doubt that appealed to their pride. "It was just one of those significant discussions with the playing group that probably realigned us and helped us get back on track."

Another was Leigh Matthew's appeal at three quarter time in the Preliminary Final against the Sydney Swans. The game was in the balance with Brisbane leading by just three points: 58 to 55.

"At three quarter time Leigh said: 'Don't underestimate where we're going now. We're back-to-back premiers'. He said you guys can get the opportunity next week to win three in a row and write yourself in history. It really struck a chord with me. and I think it struck a chord with the playing group."

It certainly did because in that final quarter of the Preliminary Final, Brisbane blitzed Sydney scoring 6-6 to Sydney just one behind, turning a 3-point lead into a 44-point thumping. But there was a downside. Nigel Lappin had suffered broken ribs, a condition that Brisbane unsuccessfully tried to keep a secret during Grand Final week. However the injury didn't deter the super-tough Lappin who played with painkillers and his ribs strapped.

Black holds great respect for Voss as captain. "There was the way he played the game, his toughness as a player, his skills as a player, his on-field leadership, his expectations demanding of his teammates. But ultimately any great leader is judged by his actions and Michael's actions were as good as anyone I've seen play the game."

He said Alistair Lynch, who earlier co-captained the side with Voss, was respected for overcoming chronic fatigue syndrome that impacted his ability to play in previous years. "It was more admiration, the way he got through it, he had a really difficult two or three years."

Black cites the three premierships as the most memorable moments of his career, but finds it hard to pick between them. "Obviously the first one is special because it is the first one, but it's harder to do it the second time around and the third time, so I'd just have to say the premierships, the campaign and the journey together."

Brisbane would play a fourth Grand Final and have a chance to equal Collingwood's four-in-a-row victories from 1927 to 1930. But it wasn't to be and Brisbane lost to Port Adelaide, fading in the last quarter to lose by 40 points.

Should Brisbane Lions have won? Black is philosophical. "They were the better team on the day. But looking back in hindsight, we were a pretty beaten up team going into that week, we played a Preliminary Final in Melbourne we should have had the right to play in Brisbane, that's something that can't be underestimated.

And there were injuries. "Jonathan Brown could hardly run, Alistair Lynch had torn his quad. We had a lot of injuries going into the game and we just tried to hold on."

Black himself didn't get many kicks that day; he was well held by Port tagger Kane Cornes, whom Black says he enjoyed a rivalry with over the years. But it was a rivalry full of mutual respect with Black texting Cornes when the latter retired in 2015, saying he helped make him a better player. Cornes was quoted as saying "that's the way I feel about him".

All 2001-2003 Brisbane Lions premiership players have now retired, with Black being the second last to go, in October 2013. He remains with Brisbane as an assistant coach.

Chris Griffith

Chris Griffith is *The Australian* newspaper's Senior Technology Journalist. He began studying computers at school in Melbourne in the 1960s before working in the computer industry, teaching computer science and running his own software business. He has pursued a second career In journalism, writing extensively across rounds for *The Sunday Mail* and *The Courier-Mail* in Brisbane. He was also founding editor of the indigenous publication *Land Rights Queensland*. Chris Griffith has been a friend of Professor Ross Fitzgerald for 25 years. The two met campaigning together for equal voting rights in Queensland.

31

The End of the Affair? Reflections on a Grand Final

Geraldine Doogue

"History doesn't repeat itself but sometimes it rhymes." Mark Twain.

Etiquette matters in life, as in football. So when your team is defeated, you're supposed to say, in sanguine fashion: 'It's only a game' or 'there's always next year'. But I couldn't do that when defeat hit like a machete, during the 2014 grand final between my Swannies and Hawthorn.

This was more than a defeat, it was a drubbing, without dignity and I haven't put it behind me. Will I ever really, that is the question?

This loss was epic in scale, more akin – or so it seemed on the day – to a collective panic attack by much of my team. It defied easy recovery, soiling my enjoyment of the subsequent season. The club could have helped supporters recover better too: more later.

It wasn't the loss itself. In its own way, the chasm between the two scores – 21.11 (137pts) to 11.8 (74pts) – did say it all. But even I could bear that gap. It was the *manner* of the loss, so complete in nature, that was so acutely, so utterly, devastating.

And it all came flooding back during the *2015* Grand Final when the West Coast Eagles replaced the Swans as Hawthorn's play-things. Yes, it was déjà vu all over again, as the comics say.

I saw the same exuberant hope, the same complex travel plans to cross the country To Be There To See History Being Made, the ecstasy of reaching the last weekend in September (except this year by an odd quirk it ended up being the first October weekend) with the dream that the young, running team just might pull off the flag. Yet within a couple of hours, I sensed via the television, the Sandgropers' shock, that this had been Utopian: nothing like that outcome was possible, probably never was.

The great Australian writer Gerald Murnane produced a lovely memoir this year on his love of horse-racing; and he told me on my Saturday Extra programme just before the Melbourne Cup, about the particular joy of the mounting-yard. Here, he said, was that golden experience of "potentiality", where for a short time, as the horses paraded, everyone could dream that their horse might win. Anything was possible, that was the drug of it all.

So it is as one rolls up to the majestic MCG, having battled to secure one of the club's precious assigned tickets, then altering one's schedule to prioritise being there above all else, then just absorbing the wondrous atmosphere of one of Australia's incomparable rituals. Oh, the joy of it all: and yes, I had experienced that in 1996, 2005 (oh bliss it was to be alive that year!) 2006, 2012 (more bliss), book-ended by the 2014 nadir.

True, some special circumstances maybe accentuate all the feelings. The man who drove much of our devotion, the footy fanatic who regularly came near the top of the big footy tipping comps, my lovely husband Ian, died of pancreatic cancer in August 2011. This Collingwood-turned-Swans-tragic could analyse a game as well as the best from Fox Sport's 'On The Couch'.

We honoured his memory by continuing our commitment, because his love of the game was so contagious; I too, like him, had been introduced to it around the age of 12 in WA. Thankfully he experienced that wonderful 2005 final and even the one point reversal the following year. The 2012 triumph was almost too much for me to bear, because he felt so near and yet so far away.

I channelled him and his uncanny ability to 'pick' crucial shifts during the 2014 season, when about round 9 I decided: we're in this! I *know* we're going to be there in September. Our boys were playing beautifully. Everything was flowing. Our tackling was intense. Our passing up the field to Lance 'Buddy' Franklin and his pyrotechnics, was assured.... even though I wrote a piece for The Age warning 'we're more than

Buddy Franklin', which I came to regret. But at the time, my personal favourite, young Dan Hanneberry, simply never missed a beat, nor did Teddy Richards in defence, nor did Adam Goodes, who kept improving despite less outright speed.

So back in July, I booked my air ticket to Melbourne, feeling smug at my perspicacity and budget.

On the day, Sept 27, my little mob of friends struggled so hard to get there too. Clad in my vestments, a taxi sped us from my RN studios to Sydney Airport at the end of my show at 9am.

Red and white bunting, scarves, socks, hats, umbrellas – it was Melbourne after all – dotted the airport. Excited men, women and children all lined up to board the planes. Qantas and Virgin had scheduled extra flights, such was the demand.

Our queue moved nicely till suddenly, the ground staff stopped processing people. Over the public address system came the announcement: boarding on all flights has been temporarily suspended. We apologise for the inconvenience.

What? All questions to staff went unanswered. They seemed as bewildered as we were. Many minutes went by with no more information. Then came the next announcement: clear the airport! Ohmigod. It's finally happened, I thought to myself: the terrorists are hitting a big ritual Australian event.

I called the ABC News Desk and urged them to get out to Mascot fast. A Channel Nine News crew was already on the scene and started questioning us all as the atmosphere became more tense.

The problem, it turned out, was nothing like as dramatic as we'd imagined: merely a freak event in which a traveller had apparently walked *in* through the *out* doors (don't ask me how) without being security-checked. All hell broke loose as we were re-checked. All was well except for the one outstanding question: would we make the grand final?

It was now exceptionally tight for time. We were still on the ground in Sydney and it was by now about 11.30 with the magical 2.30pm MCG start. A special Qantas announcement was made, which I won't forget: be assured we *will* get you to the grand final!

I've always wondered whether Alan Joyce, the airline's doughty leader, personally intervened. They certainly did well that day and indeed, they did get us there ... some of us may have wished they hadn't.

I re-tell all this to lay out how much effort, dedication and money was expended on our date-with-destiny, on one of the biggest days in Australian life. The teenage boy beside me, sitting in the 'gods' of the MCG about nine rows from the back, had travelled throughout the night down from Indonesia, to be there.

And then ... the disaster unfolded before us. None of the Swans' game plan seemed to work, none of our running players could break out, we had our usual flubbing in front of goal. Hawthorn was super-humanly dominant. The energy visibly drained away from the Swans. Buddy Franklin, who'd so broken the hearts of the Hawks' fans by defecting to us, was one of the few capable of withstanding right through the game. Maybe he could see into the belly of the beast because he'd been formed there and was not afraid. I have sometimes wondered how much the shock of that day affected Buddy's whole morale, a more vulnerable thing than we may have imagined, we now know.

The Hawks simply crushed the Swans to death. That collective panic attack I described earlier, was heart-rendingly evident. I had a sliver of hope at half time that a small miracle of metamorphosis might occur, that 'Horse' Longmire might be able to tap some set of psychological possibilities thus far elusive, much like the famous Jackson/Jesaulenko fightback for Carlton back in 1970, when they won from seven goals down against Collingwood in the final quarter.

But no. I should have heeded my RN sporting commentator colleague Warwick Hadfield's on-air warning the day before about the seriousness with which Hawthorn coach Alistair Clarkson approached his every task, with big ambitions at every turn: for his club, the whole league and beyond.

By three-quarter time, I could take no more. I told my friends I'd meet them somewhere in Melbourne, that I'd liaise on the mobile phone as to where precisely. Then I stumbled out the gate and started that lovely walk back towards Federation Square. I wasn't alone. A few others had decided on something similar but I suppose most people simply felt it was a sacrilege to leave a grand final so early.

I would have once too. But age confers both some powers of prediction and maybe a readiness to act on them, no matter what convention says. The game was well-and-truly over, I could see that. Only humiliation lay ahead. I didn't have to expose myself to that. So I didn't.

Avoiding the big screens at Fed Square was a challenge, pumping out triumphant scenes to the copious brown-and-gold tribe. I escaped to a coffee shop somewhere in Exhibition Street I think, and awaited my friends' eventual arrival. The detail may escape me but the overall memory is painfully clear.

So when the latest iteration of this unfolded in 2015, when the Hawks thumped the Eagles (which could have been my team had I stayed in my native WA in the 1980s) it was re-lived awfulness ... without the numbing demoralisation. There but for the grace of god went I, oh yes.

At least by then I was better prepared. I'd rehearsed during a mid-year outing against the Hawks at the ANZ Stadium. Again, the Swans were travelling pretty well. We'd beaten Hawthorn earlier in the season. I thought we had a hope and there was always that residual desire for some relief from the dreadful memories.

But it happened all over again. It wasn't the collective panic attack but once more, the tell-tale Hawks' intensity erupted, our usual game plan looked like a bonsaied thing and with spectral certainty, I knew that my Swannies would not make the grand final.

One of my friends lamented afterwards that 'we were hopeless'. No, I said, they were just too bloody good. We're in the presence of a super-team, just as I'd felt in the 1990s when we played a preliminary final against Leigh Matthews' Brisbane Lions, another rare winner of a flag trifecta.

Whether or not my club ever scales those heights remains to be seen. Certainly I don't think it handled the aftermath of the 2014 disaster well, behaving more as if this had been merely a bad-day-at-the-office when, to my eyes, senior officials should have explicitly taken responsibility for fans' astonished shock, even an apology.

I'm not a sadist. I expected the president or similar rank, not the players, to turn up to what I imagined would be hastily arranged: namely, one or more functions at the club-houses of both Melbourne and Sydney by mid-October, where people could share their sorrow.

Call me a girl but this type of 'workshopping' of grief, some semblance of a wake, is what would happen in a decent family. So it should have at the club, a community of souls if ever there was one.

Instead, by way of foreshadowing Christmas functions, the then captains, Kieren Jack and Jarrad McVeigh, sent word on-line "of some disappointments at the end of a good season" and then seemed to resume normal life. The club withdrew in other words and the fans were left to themselves – not good enough.

I wonder whether the acute disappointment of Sept 2014 triggered some detachment in me. Or was it brewing before, as life becomes increasingly something to be fully lived every single day, especially having watched a loved someone's days cut short. After all, football competes in the realm of *distractions* from life and hooray to that.

Maybe the game should be shorter, except for finals. Maybe clubs have to morph a little, to imagine themselves offering new, cut-through affiliation events for disconnected and busy 21st century moderns.

Truly, it's not the consistent winning that I wish to experience. But the contest at the core has to seem worthy of my commitment. Because there are lots of draws on my time. And right now, between seasons, I just may not saddle up again next year. Incredibly, I am just not sure.

Geraldine Doogue

Geraldine Doogue is the presenter of ABC Radio National's 'Saturday Extra' program broadcast from 7.30-9am and of ABC TV1'S Sunday evening program 'Compass', which covers Religion, Spirituality, Beliefs and Values.

While originally planning a career as a schoolteacher, in 1972 Geraldine applied for a journalism cadetship with The West Australian. Within ten years Geraldine had carved out a reputation in print, television and radio, including two years in London working for the Murdoch group.

While covering a story for 'The Australian', she was interviewed on Four Corners. Head office was so impressed that they offered Geraldine the Perth compere's position for ABC Television's new program Nationwide. She then moved to Sydney. After playing a major role in ABC TV's coverage of the Gulf War in 1990, Geraldine was awarded two Penguin Awards and a United Nations Media Peace Prize. Since then she has been awarded a Churchill Fellowship, an Officer in the Order of Australia, and an Honorary Doctorate of Letters by Macquarie University and her alma mater, the University of Western Australia. In 2014 Text published her book *The Climb: Conversations with Australian Women in Power.*

John Coleman depicted on a Nabisco breakfast cereal swap card in 1951. It was one of a series of 64 cards placed in Kornies packets that year, one a pack. The more Kornies purchased, the more swap cards obtained.
From Paul Henderson's football card collection.

32

John Coleman and the Ghosts of Princes Park

Gerard Henderson

I've never got over the events of Saturday 1 September 1951 and Tuesday 4 September 1951 – even though I was just five years old at the time. And, I guess, I never will. It was the occasion when a young Catholic boy came to grips with the consequences of The Fall, original sin, human imperfectability and all that.

On the first day of Spring 1951, Essendon travelled to Princes Park to play Carlton. It was the final round of the home-and-away series which preceded the finals. Essendon had won the flag in 1949 and 1950 and had prevailed in enough games in 1951 to make the Final Four, while Carlton had no chance of finishing in the first half of the League Ladder. So, in a sense, it was a "dead" contest.

But, alas, not one without fire – with fights on and off the ground. Yet only one really mattered. Just before half time, on the outer side of the ground in the forward pocket near the northern goal posts, star Essendon full-forward John Coleman clashed with Carlton ruckman Harry Caspar. Both players were reported by a goal umpire and a boundary umpire for striking each other. Essendon was trailing Carlton at the time of the incident but went on to win the game 16.12 (108) to 9-10 (64). Coleman kicked seven goals in all, six in the second half.

On the following Tuesday, Coleman and Caspar appeared before the VFL Tribunal at Harrison House on Spring Street in the Melbourne CBD. A crowd of 200 gathered outside the VFL headquarters. According to *The Argus*, many Essendon supporting women turned up, including "a score or more of 16 and 17 year old bobby-soxers". As Dough Ackerly points out in *Coleman: The Untold Story of an AFL Legend*, at the time "John Coleman was football's Frank Sinatra".

Caspar's case was heard first – he received a four match suspension. Then it was Coleman's turn – and he received the same penalty. This meant that Essendon's star full-forward, a brilliant high mark and a great kick of the ball, who had topped the goal-scoring list in 1949 (his first season) and 1950, would be ineligible to play finals in 1951. I learnt of Coleman's suspension on the morning of Wednesday 5 September 1951 – my memory of the occasion has never faded.

I grew up in Melbourne's eastern suburb of Balwyn – not all that far from Glenferrie Oval, the home ground of Hawthorn. My mother Pauline Henderson (nee Dargavel) had no interest in sport. My sister, Veronica, brother Paul and myself supported the team of my father. Norman Henderson had grown up in Essendon and barracked for The Bombers. My uncle William Dargavel supported Carlton, the suburb in which he was born. In the first half of the 20th Century, football allegiances in Melbourne were very tribal.

In September 1951, without Coleman, Essendon defeated Footscray in the First Semi Final (by 8 points) and Collingwood in the Preliminary Final (by 2 points) but lost the Grand Final to Geelong (by 11 points) – less than two goals. At the end of 1951, Coleman had averaged five goals a match. I can recall listening to the 1951 Grand Final on the radio urging The Bombers on – while wondering why some of my Essendon heroes didn't do something desperate – like kicking their Geelong opponents in the head. I was as desperate as that.

But it was not to be. Essendon coach Dick Reynolds (unwisely) came out of retirement to become 20th man in the Grand Final team. Jack Clarke, who soon became one of my heroes, was 19th man. In the years before the interchange bench, both the 19th and 20th men happened to get on the ground in the last quarter. Reynolds assisted Greg Tate to score a goal but soon after spoiled his team mate Keith McDonald marking on his own in front of goal.

The ball returned to the Geelong forward line and Geelong full-forward George Goninon (whom Essendon had cleared to Geelong in

1950 because it did not need him as well as Coleman) kicked a behind, the final score of the match. Goninon had a great finals series, kicking 11 goals in the Second Semi Final and four goals in the Grand Final.

Goninon also played in Geelong's premiership team in 1952 but was dropped from the 1953 Grand Final team which was defeated narrowly by Collingwood. He later maintained that that Geelong dropped him when it found out that he was having an adulterous affair with a female nurse. Well, it was 1953 and, according to Goninon, there were many conservative Catholics in the Geelong Football Club administration.

It's likely that Goninon's career would have lasted somewhat longer had he remained at Essendon. There were few Catholics at Essendon in the 1940s and 1950s and rumour had it that the club had attachments to the Masonic Lodge. Protestants had a somewhat different view on sexual morality. As the writer Malcolm Muggeridge once joked – the Anglican Church regarded the Ten Commandments as akin to an exam paper, with only eight to be attempted.

In September 1951, I was primarily upset by the unfairness of life. My father told me about the evidence given at the VFL Tribunal. Caspar hit Coleman with several punches some 60 yards behind the play. Then Coleman retaliated. In short, Coleman was the innocent party who had been physically provoked.

Boundary umpire Herb Kent told the Tribunal that, following the first punch, "Caspar struck Coleman a second time, and then Coleman retaliated by striking Caspar with a closed fist, he threw a hook after he'd been hit twice – Coleman only punched Caspar because he had been provoked". Goal umpire Roy Allen told a similar story. He recalled that Caspar hit Coleman in the stomach following by a left and a right to his head. Allen added that Coleman responded with two punches in defence.

The Tribunal, chaired by Tom Hammond, sat for just over ten minutes before disqualifying Coleman for four matches. In other words, the aggressor and the retaliator received identical sentences. Some thought that Coleman would be suspended for only two games – in which case he would have been eligible to play in the 1951 Grand Final. But it was not to be. And, to someone who turned six on 10 September 1951, it seemed so unfair.

An emotional John Coleman was photographed departing Harrison House in the company of Essendon Football Club committeeman Ted Waterford. He was said to have broken down after the hearing. My mother occasionally remarked sarcastically that my hero Coleman had cried in public. In the early 1950s, real men didn't cry – or so it was said. Monica Coleman (nee Fernando) told *The Sporting Globe's* Kenneth Joachim in 1975 that, after the Tribunal verdict, Coleman "went quiet, he just clammed up; you could see the hurt and it wasn't just for himself – his grief was that he had let the team down and cost it a premiership".

In contemporary parlance, Coleman had a short fuse. On Saturday 18 August 1951, in a game against Geelong, Coleman was reported after having told one boundary umpire to "shut up" and another to "pull your head in". This followed directions by the boundary umpires to let Geelong full-back Bruce Morrison get off the ground after a marking contest. Coleman, who was reported for disputing an umpire's decision, was acquitted because he had not disputed the field umpire's decision and only field umpires made decisions about the play. The role of boundary umpires was to determine whether the ball went out of bounds. Many fans resented boundary umpires involving themselves in the game – the comment: "Get back on the boundary line, you mug" was sometimes heard at matches I attended in the 1950s.

Coleman's anger with umpires was understandable. As Essendon's star player, he was often subjected to violent assault by opponents in days when field umpires were reluctant to give free-kicks to forwards close to goal and there was no filming of matches to determine unfair play.

It's possible that Coleman's frustration fired up at Princes Park on 1 September 1951. I was at school with Murray McInerney. As I recall, he was the only person among a 98,385 strong crowd at the Melbourne Cricket Ground at the 1965 Preliminary Final who saw Collingwood's Duncan Wright knock out Essendon's John Somerville well behind the play. I was there that day – and was one of the remaining 98,384 spectators who saw nothing beyond the Essendon half-forward lying unconscious on the ground.

Murray McInerney's mother's first cousin was Herb Kent – the boundary umpire who reported Coleman for striking Caspar. McInerney told Ackerly about a family get-together in 2001: "Herb told me that he did not tell the VFL Tribunal the full circumstances of the clash. He told me that Harry Caspar had been involved in a car accident and Coleman had goaded him several times during the game, calling him "Killer".

It's possible. Harry Caspar (1926-1988) was driving on 9 May 1951 on Lygon Street, Carlton when he hit and killed 41 year old Alfred Edward Miller. The day was a public holiday – Jubilee Day – to celebrate the 50th anniversary of the Commonwealth of Australia. The VFL upheld the occasion by playing a knock-out Lightening Premiership at the MCG between the 12 clubs. Caspar played in the first game which saw Carlton eliminated by Footscray.

Caspar told Victoria Police that he had around ten to fourteen beers at the MCG after his game concluded, followed by "two or three beers" at the Nicholson Hotel in Carlton on the way home. He then drove to Lygon Street newsagent to buy *The Herald* (Melbourne's top selling evening newspaper) and collided with Miller. According to reports, the victim was also drunk and darted across Lygon Street where he was hit by Caspar's car travelling at low speed.

In the 1950s, sobriety was gauged by whether a person could walk in a straight line and touch his/her nose with eyes closed. Caspar passed both tests. Despite a blood alcohol reading of 0.212 (well above today's legal limit of .05), the doctor declared that the Carlton footballer was not incapable of controlling a vehicle. In time, Miller's death was regarded as due to misadventure. It was, after all, 1951.

It's possible that Coleman verbally provoked Caspar at Princes Park. Certainly this makes more sense than the conspiracy theories that spread at the time that Caspar was paid to have a go at Coleman by the teams that finished first and second on the League Ladder at the end of the 1951 home-and-away series. Namely, Geelong and Collingwood.

The real fault in Coleman's suspension lay with the VFL Tribunal. It disqualified the game's most famous player from taking part in the 1951 final series on account of a brief punch-up in which no injuries were sustained. Also, the Tribunal refrained from giving a reduced penalty to the player who retaliated, as it had on some previous occasions.

The VFL Tribunal which sat in 1951 comprised of L.P. Whitehead (chief of the Metropolitan Fire Brigade), Bill Somerville (secretary of the Discharged Serviceman's Employment Board) and chairman Tom Hammond (a stipendiary magistrate). Only the latter had played in the VFL. According to Ackerly, Hammond subsequently conceded to *Herald* football writer Alf Brown that he and his fellow members had erred in not giving Coleman a lesser penalty for retaliating. This was Coleman's position. Ackerly quotes Alf Brown as reporting a comment made to him by Coleman on the day after the disqualification:

> I am still greatly upset at the tribunal's decision. It was clearly established that I was not the aggressor and yet I received the same punishment as the player who first struck me. When Caspar received four weeks disqualification for striking me, I expected to receive two. I had broken the rules and was ready to take my punishment. But, four weeks – I was amazed. I still am.

So was I in September 1951. And I still am today – a mere six decades or so later. At a young age, I learnt all about disappointment and injustice and the foibles of humanity. After The Fall, that is.

John Coleman did not play in another Grand Final. His last VFL game took place on Saturday 5 June 1954. Playing against North Melbourne at Essendon's Windy Hill ground, Coleman seriously injured his knee. As a young boy, listening on the radio, I hoped and prayed he would recover – but, alas, in vain. Coleman never pulled on an Essendon guernsey again.

However, I did see Coleman play on a couple of occasions in 1953 – once at Hawthorn and once at the MCG. And I was present in September 1962 when Essendon won its first grand final since 1950. John Coleman, at age 33, was coach of the Essendon team which defeated Carlton. Under Coleman's coaching, Essendon won two premiership flags in seven years. He died, of a sudden heart attack, in April 1973 at age 44.

Early in 1962, after The Bombers had defeated Carlton at Princes Park, former Essendon player Jack Harrington, accompanied by his friend Caspar, approached Coleman. Harrington told the Essendon coach that Caspar wanted to apologise for what happened at the ground on 1 September 1951. But, as Harrington told Ackerly, Coleman looked angry then turned his back and walked away. Obviously Caspar was an unwelcome ghost from Coleman's past.

As someone yet to recover from the Caspar/Coleman encounter of 1951, I can understand John Coleman's approach. Time, after all, rarely heals all.

Gerard Henderson

Gerard Henderson is executive director of the Sydney Institute. He writes a column for *The Weekend Australian* and appears regularly on the ABC TV program *Insiders*. His *Media Watch Dog* blog comes out every Friday. Gerard Henderson's most recent book, *Santamaria: A Most Unusual Man*, is a biography of B. A. Santamaria (1915-98).

John Elliott sings the club song with Les Lofts and Dick Pratt after a Carlton win.
Photo: Private collection of John Elliott, used with permission

33

We Are the Navy Blues

John Elliott

When I started school in 1947, age five, there were only two sports, football in winter and cricket in summer. My two brothers, Ross and Richard and I were sports mad. I vividly remember my late father Frank in 1947 telling me that all our family barracked for Carlton.

As he had been going to Princes Park since the early 1920s to watch the Mighty Blues he became a passionate life-long Carlton supporter. As a young boy he was taken to Princes Park by Paddy O'Brien who played 167 games for Carlton between 1913 and 1924, including two premierships in 1914 and 1915.

My father's life long connection with Carlton not only influenced me becoming a passionate life-long Blues supporter but also influenced my father to tell me when I accepted Carlton's invitation in 1983 to become President "of all the things you do in life, being President of the Carlton Football is the most important". At that time I was CEO of the merged Elders & Henry Jones Group, Elders IXL which had acquired 100% ownership of CUB following a $1 billion takeover. At the time, I thought my fathers statement was very strange as on the face of it, all of these positions seemed far more important than being president of a football club.

However, the passing of time this has served only to confirm the truth of his words. What he knew then and what I have come to appreciate is that, if you are prominent in a successful football club in Melbourne you become part of the lives of a great number of people. I was Carlton President for 20 years where I learned that what you do is hugely important to the army of club supporters, from the major sponsors to the young kids.

In Melbourne, Aussie Rules permeates everything as people are identified by the club they support. You have to a Blue, or Magpie or Tiger to name a few. Football is a great leveller as it provides a bridge between social classes, suburbs, occupations and the sexes. It also is a common topic of discussion in boardrooms, bars and even bedrooms!

One of the key credentials as President is to accept the premise that the sole purpose of a football club is to win matches and premierships. Win enough of them and the financial performance follows. Lose for whatever reason and the supporters want to know why and don't turn up.

Being president of Carlton was a privilege, not a pastime. During my time as a passionate Carlton supporter there have been many highlights and lowlights. When I was President from 1983 to 2002, I treated the highlights and lowlights as "successes and failures" as you do in business.

During my lifetime, Carlton has won 10 Premierships but there were and have been several long periods between winning premierships. During my term as president, we played in 11 finals, 5 grand finals, (1986, 1987, 1993, 1995 and 1999) and won 2 premierships, 1987 against Hawthorn and 1995 against Geelong.

Unfortunately, since 1999 Carlton has not played in a grand final. Our performance, on and off the field has been very disappointing – a big lowlight. However, attending the recent 20-year 1995 players Premiership reunion was one of my few highlights since 1999.

My first VFL game as a Carlton supporter was in 1949 when my father took me to see Carlton play Richmond on the day Richmond's famous player Jack Dyer set a new record for most games played in the VFL. Richmond supporters turned up in great numbers at that unforgettable day at Punt Road oval. They also wanted to renew the battle with Carlton because Percy Bentley, Richmond's champion ruckman before Dyer, had come over to Carlton as coach and had won two flags in 1945 and 1947.

Although we arrived at Punt Road before the gates opened and raced into the Richmond stand, the record crowd of 46,000 – more than 10,000 turned away – forced the fence to collapse, resulting in fans standing there deep in the walkway in front of me. I saw nothing, but what I did know was that Carlton won by 15 points. I did however see two young boys fall out of a tree outside the ground!

This game was my first Carlton highlight. I have never seen so many people so excited or argumentative, and never felt such an electric atmosphere.

One of my heroes was Carlton's captain and ruckman, Ken Hands whose nickname was Solvol, the great grease and grime removing soap. I have never seen a tougher player. After boundary throw ins, opposing ruckman lay inert on the ground after play moved on despite nothing untoward appeared to happen. Ken Hands blows only went 4 inches, but were effective.

I also watched the then young John Nicholls develop into a strong ruckman and a terrific mark. I was at Princes Park when the Blues were playing South Melbourne (the Swans or Bloods) the day Ken Boyd, the Swans tough ruckman ran half way up the ground to knock out Nicholls. Boyd got a 12 week suspension.

Another unforgettable event at Carlton was when my father's work colleague and 'Sporting Globe' football writer, Alan Fitcher took us into the Carlton changing rooms at Princes Park. It was a great thrill to meet my heroes firsthand – especially Chooka Howell, Laurie Kerr, Ray Garby, Bill Milroy, Fred Davies, Arthur Hodgson and the great Ken Hands himself. As a result of this experience, during my time as president I always made sure the young Carlton fans got into the rooms to see their heroes.

Although my Father was reluctant to take us to the away games as we would argue with opposing supporters, in 1954 we went to Victoria Park to watch Collingwood play Carlton.

This was my most memorable day at an away ground – since I saw my first VFL game at Richmond in 1949 as an seven year old. After the Magpies champion Bob Rose ko'd Carlton's centre-half forward, Max Wenn, a melee broke out between the righteous Carlton supporters whose man had been wronged, and the tattooed brigade who barracked for Collingwood.

1960s

During the early 1960s I continued playing football for Old Carey while completing my Commerce Degree and MBA at Melbourne University which restricted my time to go and see Carlton.

However in 1965 there was a major highlight in Carlton. Ron Barassi was controversially appointed as Carlton's Captain-Coach. His appointment was a major catalyst in reviving Carlton's future by installing a winning culture and a new approach to training and tactics which he learnt from Melbourne's record winning premiership coach Norm Smith.

Barassi's appointment was vindicated in 1968 when Carlton defeated Essendon to win our first premiership since 1947. It was the first time I saw Carlton win a grand final and I never forget sitting on hard concrete at the City End stand in front of the MCG main scoreboard. When you win premierships, all spectator pain is forgotten.

This victory was the instigator of Carlton's turnaround. In 1969 we played Richmond in the grand final but lost to the tall, long kicking Richmond side.

1970s

Carlton's remarkable turnaround against Collingwood to win the 1970 grand final, was in my view, Carlton's greatest victory. The only lowlight was that I was living in Chicago and couldn't be at the MCG to see Carlton beat our arch rivals. I also missed seeing Jessa (Alex Jesaulenko) take that famous screamer over Jerker Jerkins. This colossal grab, with Jessa rising to an unbelievable height over the Collingwood big man, is still rated by many as one of the greatest marks of all time.

When I was in Chicago, my father-in-law used to send me audio tapes of each Carlton game where they would arrive in Chicago the following Saturday. That evening my wife and I went out for dinner and came home at 11.30pm when I started listening to the audio tape. However, I went to bed at half time in disgust as Carlton were trailing Collingwood by 43 points. Next morning I restarted the tape for the second half while feeding my two young children their Sunday breakfast of toast with vegemite and cornflakes. When Teddy Hopkins kicked three goals and Carlton adopted aggressive handball tactics to regain the lead I got so excited about their comeback that I left my kids on their own throwing their vegemite toast around the kitchen, much to my wife's displeasure.

The 1970 grand final was possibly eclipsed by the 1972 grand final between Carlton and Richmond. I vividly recall standing in the concrete MCG stand with my father behind the Carlton goal in the first quarter to see John Nicholls pull off one of the great tactical achievements of all times to defeat Richmond in the highest scoring grand final ever.

Nicholls decided to pull all of his star players, including himself, into the forward line leaving Percy Jones as the sole ruckman. It was attack at all costs. Carlton kicked 8 goals in the first quarter and by half time led by 43 points.

Throughout the mid to late 1970s, Carlton's performance was disappointing. However I had taken a Corporate Box and used to take friends there. I had lunch a couple of times with Carlton president George Harris, mainly about sponsorship.

But it was the great Jezza, Carlton's captain-coach that restored my love of and pride in Carlton after the fantastic 1979 victory against Collingwood which ultimately involved me more into the clubs affairs.

Another major highlight was in early 1975 where I influenced Australia's future prime minister, Malcolm Fraser to become a Carlton supporter and number 1 ticket holder. This followed the same status that Sir Robert Menzies enjoyed as a long term Carlton supporter when he was Prime Minister.

Malcom replaced Billy Snedden as Liberal Party leader in early 1975 when I was Vice President of the Victorian Liberal Party. He knew I was an ardent Carlton supporter and told me he had to support a football club. I said, it is simple Malcolm you should barrack for Carlton. As he was unsure about this, I invited him to my corporate box on the next Saturday at Waverley Park. We watched Carlton win the match. The press were there in force and when I arranged to take him down to Carltons rooms, I arranged for Malcolm to be photographed with Alex

Jesaulenko. This photo was in the following Monday's *Sun* front page. Malcom rang me a few days later to tell me he would barrack for Carlton. When we won consecutive flags in 1981 and 1982, Malcolm invited the premiership players and officials to a dinner at the Prime Minister's Canberra Lodge on both occasions.

1980s

A big lowlight to Carlton's start for the 1980 season was Alex Jesaulenko's, (the 1979 premiership playing coach) decision to resign as Carlton captain-coach. His allegiance to George Harris's ill-fated attempt to merge the Social and Football Clubs (which was soundly defeated by members in February 1980), resulted in Jezza going to St Kilda. This left Carlton without a Coach two months before the season started.

George Harris also resigned as President and was replaced by well-known Melbourne businessman, Ian Rice. I had been approached to become President, but declined due to my business commitments at Elders.

Percy Jones, Carltons long serving premiership ruckman, was appointed coach where Wes Lofts played a key support role with Percy during 1980. Carlton finished second on the ladder, 17 wins, 5 losses. Despite expectations of winning two flags in a row, we lost the first semi final.

Percy only lasted one year and was sacked when David Parkin was appointed coach achieving instant success by winning flags in 1981 and 1982. However Carlton could have won the 1980 flag (and equal Collingwood's long held record of four consecutive flags) if Jezza had not been the casualty of the Harris 'Blue'.

The three years from 1983 to 1985 were lowlights as Carlton, despite getting in the finals each year didn't win a finals match. Mike Fitzpatrick the Carlton captain during 1981 and 1982 retired in late 1983. The Carlton players appeared to have lost confidence and the will to win under Parkin who was replaced as Coach at end of 1985 by Robert Walls.

During 1985 Dick Pratt and I had secured five key interstate recruits, Kernahan, Bradley, Motley, Naly and Dorotich for Carlton. 1986 was a highlight as Walls successfully blended Carltons existing champions with these new recruits where we finished 3rd on the ladder, winning 15 games out of 22.

However after beating Hawthorn in the second semi-final, earning a grand final berth, Hawthorn beat us despite Carlton being 1986 grand final favourites. However in 1987 we turned the tables on Hawthorn by beating them in the 1987 grand final convincingly giving Carlton a Carlton a record 15th premiership and my first as president.

During 1987 we also completed the new corporate facility at Princes Park that would be named the John Elliott Stand. While Carlton were still celebrating our premiership win, the October 21st global stock market crash caused havoc in the financial markets.

1989 was big lowlight. At the start of 1989 we turned on a major celebration for our 125th anniversary where old players visited the club and we named our greatest team. Named as our greatest coach Ron Barassi's thank you speech was a shocker. Although grateful for being appointed number 1 coach he said, "I don't barrack for Carlton, I don't support Carlton, but thanks very much anyway". I couldn't believe it.

Our season mid-point performance of 2 wins out of 11 games was a disgrace, and losing to Brisbane Bears was our worst on-field performance since our centenary year in 1964. Something had to give and that was Robert Walls who was replaced during the 1989 season when Jezza was brought in as stop-gap coach.

My two major off-field highlights at Carlton during the 1980s, were my appointment as Carlton President in October 1983 and my role in implementing strategies to convert the VFL to a national code – the Australian Football League (AFL) in 1985.

Shortly after Ian Rice resigned as president of Carlton in October 1983, I was approached by Wes Lofts and Ian Collins to take over the presidency at a time my business life was very busy. Henry Jones had been taken over by Elder Smith Goldsbrough Mort to form Elders IXL and I was appointed CEO. Then followed the CUB takeover in late 1983 which created a much larger business. We had it better organised and I knew the expanded group was in a strong and financially sound position. In hindsight, I should have taken the role in 1979. Before accepting I told Lofts and Collins that I wanted to talk to all of the committee men independently.

I come to the view there was a great camaraderie at Carlton and that the club was used to success and expected it. Also there appeared to me a lot of opportunities that could be exploited to improve its finances, build up corporate support, and further increase seating, corporate supporter facilities and club memberships.

During my first two years as President, we introduced a range of positive changes including appointing new experienced board members, introducing the Presidents men supporter group and the Presidents lunches at home games, combining the management of the Football and Social Clubs and increasing the sponsorship base by using my Elders IXL and Fosters client networks. Implementing these changes established a sound base for Carlton to remain a major force in Aussie Rules.

When Carlton arranged a media conference in October 1983 to announce my appointment as President, I declared that Carlton supported playing all future grand finals at the MCG, the home of football, whereas the VFL wanted to play grand finals at their own ground, Waverley Park. I also emphasised Carlton's support for a national competition.

When I went to my first VFL Committee meeting as Carltons delegate I was staggered to learn how badly the meetings were managed and it became clear that each person present was only interested in how decisions affected their club. There was no overall strategy and direction for the VFL which had Dr Allen Aylett as President and Jack Hamilton as Secretary.

All the horse trading was done outside the meeting under "other business" and the leading clubs, Essendon, Richmond, Collingwood and Carlton were often left out of these discussions. At this time several clubs were in financial difficulty and were under investigation as to their insolvency. It became obvious the VFL under its then structure had lost its way. Something had to done!

In conjunction with Carltons General Manager Ian Collins, I developed a plan to resolve this problem by creating a break away competition where the four leading clubs, two new sides from SA and WA plus retaining Sydney Swans would create a national competition under an independent board of management.

Following various meetings with the presidents of Essendon,

Collingwood and Richmond who fully supported this overall plan for a national competition, meetings with other VFL presidents were held. While some were uncertain and sceptical, we eventually convened a meeting with Aylett and Hamilton to outline our detailed plan.

They then agreed to establish a sub-committee with John Kennedy as Chairman to assess and consider our range of recommendations. A major achievement was when the VFL agreed to appoint a four man independent part time commission and CEO to run the national competition. The new commission took office in 1985 and Ross Oakley (ex St Kilda player) became the first CEO of the AFL. He was also Chairman of the Commission. The rest is now history of how Aussie Rules survived and expanded over the last 30 years.

1990s

In 1990 Jezza certainly lifted the club spirit and we finished the season with a 11-11 result. We then kept him for another year but came to a view at end of 1990 he couldn't lead Carlton to success and did not renew his contract. Instead we brought back David Parkin as coach in 1991. In Parkin's first season we finished eleventh, the clubs worst placing in its history up till 1991. A big recruiting coup in 1992 was to secure Sydney's star mid fielder, Greg Williams. Parkin restructured his team around 5 champions, Kernahan, Bradley, Silvagni, WIilliams and Madden. Another future star was promoted from the reserves Anthony Koutoufides, normally known as 'Kouta'.

The 1992 season, with Williams making a significant contribution saw a big improvement in 1991, but even with an end of year 14-8 result, we didn't make the finals.

If 1992 was a lowlight, 1993 was both a lowlight and highlight as the 1993 flag was the one that got away.

In 1993, Carlton finished second on the ladder, behind Essendon. We played them at the MCG's first Friday night final in front of a huge crowd. Kernahan played a blinder, kicking seven goals and taking ten marks. Carlton won by two points. We then beat Adelaide and went into the Grand Final and suddenly we were hot favourites. Essendon then beat Adelaide to reach the grand final. Our confidence was high.

However Essendon's assistant coach, Neale Daniher's technical analysis on figuring out Justin Madden's ruck play was their secret weapon. They worked out a plan how to reduce Madden's range of plays at centre bounces, which in turn restricted Greg Williams's ability to control and drive the midfield. It took Carlton's coaching panel a full quarter to change centre bounce tactics, but Essendon protected their first quarter margin and run out winners to equal Carlton's record of fifteen flags. Our five champions, Kernahan, Willaims, Bradley, Silvagni and Madden – were all bitterly disappointed. So was I.

The 1994 season ended with Carlton in second place, but our 1994 finals performance was one of the most disappointing of my tenure as President. Geelong thrashed us at Waverley knocking Carlton out of the final series. A big lowlight.

Despite the 1993 and 1994 finals disappointments, Parkin was confident 1995 would be a good year. He was right. We won 20 games out of 22, a league record for the home and away season.

We won a place in the grand final by beating North Melbourne in the preliminary final where Silvagni, Kernahan and Williams were key players. We met Geelong the following week to win our 16th premiership flag. Carlton's five champions of the previous ten years were all in the best players. This was a team of champions that had become a champion team. I was delighted when I walked into the rooms and champagne was poured all over me. The joy and relief was enormous.

The years 1996 to 1998 were mediocre and it was evident Parkin was feeling the pressure of lack of finals success since 1995. We went into the 1999 season full of optimism after the good finish to 1998.

We finished sixth with a 12-10 record. After beating Brisbane and then West Coast in the early finals we met Essendon the premiership favourites in the qualifying final where the winner would meet North Melbourne in the grand final.

Carlton went in as underdogs but thanks to Silvagni, Bradley, Murphy and Fraser Brown's fierce tackle on Essendon's Dean Wallis preventing Wallis kicking a goal when Carlton were one point in front with seven seconds left, we won by a point. This win nearly cost me my life as big John Nicholls was sitting in front of me and when the siren sounded, he turned round and gave me the biggest bear hug I had ever had in my life. Fortunately after a while I could breathe again!

During 2000 Carlton won 13 games on end, but injuries prevented us getting to the grand final. As a result, Wayne Brittain was appointed senior coach for a three year term beginning in 2000. In 2001 the club had an inconsistent season finishing fifth on the ladder. Although we were defeated in the semi-finals, as we went into the 2002 season, Brittain still seemed to have the confidence of everybody at Carlton.

However primarily due to our poor on field performance in 2002, in part due to injury, Carlton supporters, quite rightly did not tolerate poor performance.

As a result the 2002 disaster unfolded where Wayne and myself lost our jobs as coach and president respectively. This was certainly not a highlight of my time with the Blues!

John Elliott

Born in Melbourne on October 3, 1941, John Dorman Elliott is an Australian businessman and a former federal president of the Liberal Party who was once touted as a possible prime minister of Australia.

John Elliott was educated at Carey Baptist Grammar School and the University of Melbourne where he gained an honours degree in Commerce and a Masters in Business Administration. In 1983 he became president of Carlton Football Club - a position he held for 20 years. During his time at the helm the Carlton football club won two premierships – in 1987 and 1995. John Elliott is a life member of the AFL.

Josh Frydenberg and his sister Lexi in Carlton Jumpers
Photo courtesy of the author, used with permission.

34

Carlton:
Much More Than a Football Club

Josh Frydenberg

My earliest memory of the Carlton Football Club was the 1979 Grand Final, the year we beat arch rivals, Collingwood, 11.16.82 to 11.11.77 in front of a bumper crowd of 113,545 people. They were the halcyon days for the Navy Blues when Mike Fitzpatrick dominated the ruck, Ken ('Bomber') Sheldon and Jimmy Buckley tore up the middle, Geoff Southby and the 'Flying Doormat' Bruce Doull were reliable as backs and Mark 'Sellers' Maclure could be counted on for a few goals up forward.

I was only eight years of age, but sometimes it seems like yesterday.

I will never forget the crowds roar 'Jesaulenko' as number 25, our captain-coach, leapt into the sky to grab another speccy. Every week Jezza's aerial dynamics would see him fly among the gods leaving many supporters to believe he was the closest we had to a club deity.

Out of all the great memories from that one day in September, a single image is seared in my memory and that of all Carlton fans. It was the special effort of our nuggetty back pocket player, Wayne 'Piggy' Harmes in chasing down his own poor kick in the last quarter, tapping it back in play to 'Bomber' Sheldon in the square who subsequently goaled. It was an historic moment. While Harmes' efforts saw him rewarded that day with the Norm Smith Medal for best on field, his heroics will be remembered for life by the Carlton faithful.

The arch rival Collingwood had been defeated and the victory was sweet. In the words of Carlton President, George Harris, post-match:

"There is only one thing better than knocking off the Magpies by 10 goals, it's pipping them by five points!"

The 1979 flag was the club's twelfth with premiership cups being added in 1981, 1982, 1985 and 1987. That is 16 in total since the club's establishment at the University Hotel on Lygon Street in 1864. Only Essendon has an equivalent amount of silverware in its cabinet, making Carlton arguably the most successful club in the VFL/AFL's 120 year history.

I have been a Carlton supporter all my life, except for a few months as a child when I was inexplicably drawn to Hawthorn before being lured back to Carlton with the promise of an Atari electronic games machine by my dad. I can honestly say there is a lot more that makes this club great than its exemplary on-field record: it is Carlton's egalitarian nature and its grassroots community spirit. Names like Barassi, Silvagni, Bortolotto, Marchesani and Jesaulenko fill the honour boards while giving a window to the multicultural diversity that permeates the club. In fact, if you looked at the country of birth of some on the players list, you would think you were at the United Nations. Robert Klomp was born in the Netherlands, Jesaulenko in Austria, Michael Sexton in Papua New Guinea and Setanta Ó hAilpín in Ireland to name just a few.

At Carlton you are judged by what you do, not who you are, and it is for that reason the club boasts such broad appeal. Prime ministers and captains of industry may have been the club's number one ticket holder, but there is little doubt the more than 20,000 club members are the heart and soul of Carlton.

Speaking of prime ministers, there are two in particular – Menzies and Fraser – that have had a long association with the club. Sir Robert and Malcolm Fraser were both number one ticket holders. Menzies loved his footy and would be a regular at the games. In 1952, the sports writer for the 'Argus' newspaper, Hugh Buggy, said of Menzies, "I was close to Mr Menzies in the 62,000 crowd that watched one of the roughest grand finals all time between Carlton and South Melbourne at Carlton Oval in 1945. Mr Menzies was then Leader of the Opposition and he was in the outer where rain patted steadily on his black homburg. He began tense and pale as Carlton battled against solid opposition for that first break that is so important in the grand final. It was a long time coming and R.G clenched and unclenched his hands, wiped his rain wet face with a handkerchief and swayed with the rocking crowd. He was quiet but obviously tensed up until a South player felled Carlton's Ken Hands with a vicious upper cut. Then we saw a new Mr Menzies. His face flushed crimson. He stamped his foot. All his reserve vanished. "That was atrocious" he yelled across the inclined plains of hats, "Absolutely atrocious. That man should be rubbed out for life." "You're quite right, Bob", sounded one solid Carlton supporter near him. "I agree with you for once, Bob. It was bloody murder. Come on the Blues. Fling yer weight into these mugs."

No matter where Menzies spoke he wasn't afraid to fly the Carlton flag. Once when he was speaking at the Collingwood Town Hall, deep in Labor territory, he told an already agitated audience, "I have two things to say: first, that the Liberals will win the next election, and second, that Carlton will win the Premiership." If there were a few votes on offer at the start of his speech, they certainly weren't there at the end!

But back to Hugh Buggy, he said of Menzies, "He makes no insincere pretence that he's interested in football in an academic way. He is an indefatigable supporter of Carlton and he doesn't give two hoots who knows it. He goes to the football to see the Blues win. For two hours he puts behind all the problems and pother of politics."

Later in Menzies' life, long after he left the Lodge, he was felled by a stroke. But even ill health would not deter him from missing his beloved Blues. Carlton built Menzies a special purpose ramp behind the goals at Princes Park so he could be driven up in his black Bentley and still watch the game with a bird's eye view. Rather than being frowned upon by the Blues supporters, when the Bentley went up the ramp, so did the cheers from the faithful. Menzies was a true Carlton man and the supporters knew it. I'm proud to say a copy of this iconic photo with the Prime Minister perched in his black Bentley watching the Blues defeat Footscray at Princes Park has pride of place in my Canberra office.

Like Menzies, Fraser was another longstanding Blues man. Famously, after the Grand Final win in 1981 Fraser played host to the team at the Lodge. All was going well until a few of the boys decided to pocket some of the fine cutlery, salt and pepper shakers and nutcrackers crested with the Coat of Arms. The heist caused quite a stir with the Prime Minister demanding the return of his silver a few days later when it was discovered the cutlery had gone missing. Wayne Harmes said, "I think he (Mr Fraser) knew when I shook hands with him when I was leaving that my top pocket was shaking like a cutlery cupboard." Indeed, in a hilarious video posted on YouTube, a former Carlton great, premiership player and member of the famed 'mosquito fleet' of small on ball players can be heard recounting the details of the great cutlery heist years later to club supporters.

Talking of memorable moments, it is worth mentioning that the 'Big Nick', John Nicholls, holds the club record of five best and fairest wins. There have been five Brownlow medallists, most recently Chris Judd in 2010; three Coleman medallists, with bad boy Brendan Fevola the last winner in 2009 with 86 'six pointers'. Craig Bradley, or 'Bradles' as he is affectionately known, is a club's games record holder with 375 and his best friend Stephen 'Sticks' Kernahan has the most games as captain with 226 and former Hawk David Parkin has the most games as coach with 325, three of which were premierships.

Interestingly but yet not surprisingly, many Carlton players, more than 200 in total, have over the years served in the armed forces. Tragically, 16 of these men have paid the ultimate price. In the Boer war, there were six Carlton sons, 87 in World War One of whom 11 never returned, and 132 in World War Two of whom five lost their lives. They were all brave patriots in uniform whose contribution to their nation forms an important chapter in Carlton's proud history.

So in many ways Carlton is much more than a football club. It's a place of passion and history, where there is great pride in wearing the navy blue jumper.

Unfortunately these days I can't get to the games as often as I wish, but when I do I find myself riding the bumps, getting frustrated by the umpires and celebrating the goals just as much as I did as an eight year old nearly four decades ago. I know I am not alone.

Recently with my parliamentary colleagues we convened a small Carlton supporters club hosting the Carlton President, coach and players for drinks and dinner in Canberra. They were fun nights where a love of our club and the game transcended the political divide, as it should and as it does. Sport is the great equaliser bringing together people from all walks of life.

The final word goes to my father Harry who was the one who first introduced me to Carlton as a boy. My dad was born in Carlton in 1942 and attended the Princes Hill Primary School in North Carlton. He remembers vividly how the club used to give the teachers free junior memberships that were distributed to the well behaved students for each weekend game. For those weeks my dad didn't get a teachers award, he would enter the ground at three quarter time when the gates were open to all and sundry. These experiences instilled in him a love of the Carlton Football Club which he has passed on to me.

Some of my fondest memories as a kid are of my dad taking my sister and I to our regular seats at a Saturday afternoon game at Princes Park just below the broadcast box. After what was invariably another win, we would sing the Carlton theme song all the way home, only stopping for our religious ritual, a hot jam donut. Those days and those burnt lips I will never forget.

Now a father myself, I have a responsibility to pass on that love of the Navy Blues to my little daughter. My only hope is that Gemma sees as much on field success as I did and that she appreciates it is the culture, values and history that makes the Carlton Football Club truly great.

Josh Frydenberg

Josh Frydenberg was born in Melbourne on July 17, 1971. He is the Federal Liberal Member for Kooyong and the Minister for Resources, Energy and Northern Australia. Prior to his current position in Cabinet, he was Assistant Treasurer and before that Parliamentary Secretary to the Prime Minister, responsible for deregulation. Josh was first elected to the Australian House of Representatives at the 2010 federal election and re-elected in 2013. He is the seventh person since Federation to hold the seat of Kooyong. Josh has degrees from Monash, Oxford and Harvard universities and is a former Director of Global Banking at Deutsche Bank. He is also a keen tennis player having twice represented Australia at the World University Games in the United Kingdom in 1991 and the United States in 1993.

Terry Bright, Geelong's only consistent goalkicker during the 1980s, Scanlens 1982.

Photo courtesy of the author

"Give me a child until he is 7"
The 1989 Grand Final: Geelong vs Hawthorn

Anthony Cappello

As Aristotle once wrote: "Give me a child until he is 7 and I will show you the man". I was seven years old when my uncle Joe Inturrisi introduced me to Kardinia Park and my beloved Cats. From that young age of seven, I watched, listened and read almost every game Geelong played. From the gravel hill on the city end of Kardinia Park. It was here I watched the likes of Terry Bright, the long fullback kicks of Gary Malarkey, the red haired champs of Robert Neal and John Mossop and who would forget Leo King, who missed a sitter from the forward flank one Saturday afternoon. It was the same blind flank that Gary Ablett lined up for a shot at goal. It was the Saturday afternoon and the night before Star Wars had aired on TV for the first time. As he lined up, there was an eerie silence at Kardinia Park, until someone yelled out at the right moment: "use the force, Gary, use the force – trust your feelings". Of course, I don't remember if he scored the goal.

I remember those years that we just missed out (1980, 1981) thanks to Collingwood. The VFL reserves was telecast live on TV, then the senior teams would come out for the Preliminary Final, only to have the transmission cut just before the bounce. The 80s were a disaster for Geelong, 6th and 9th seemed to be our spots. I remember the long conversations with my uncle on the way back to Melbourne from Geelong trying to work out a suitable forward combination for the Geelong team. My uncle and especially my cousins recalled that it was only me talking all the way home from Geelong. But all I could remember were the disasters in that forward line, Terry Bright could never kick more than four goals a game, Leo King missed sitters and Mark Jacko Jackson was too busy doing cart wheels.

My father, who started to become a believer in the Geelong Cats thanks to the daily devotion of his son, had come to the conclusion that Geelong would never win a flag. Why? Well according to my father, Geelong were the outside team (outside of Melbourne) in the VFL and the powers to be, would never allow the flag to leave the city of Melbourne. He had a winning argument, confirmed by the terrible umpiring decisions. My father's winning argument was seriously challenged when Gary Ablett Snr and Malcolm Blight came to Geelong and managed to reach the final and that was in 1989.

In my life, I had never witnessed Geelong in a Grand Final, this belonged to those Melbourne teams. In the first final of 1989, Geelong was slaughtered by the Bombers, but then Geelong went onto thrash Melbourne and Essendon. I was in disbelief, Geelong was actually in a Grand Final. There was no Collingwood to stop us, as they did in 1980 and 1981. Geelong was in the Grand Final with the team which was to become the nemesis of Geelong – Hawthorn.

In 1989 I was a third year apprentice with the last Australian owned lift company, Edminston and O'Neill. Based in a little laneway in North Melbourne, they serviced many smaller and medium sized lifts, mainly 2-8 floor lifts. The company was owned by a devout Christian and most of his employees were recruited within his inner Christian circles. How, I, as a nominal Catholic managed to score an apprenticeship is still a mystery to me. The point of this long background, was that I had to convince my devout Christian tradesman that we had to service the non-existent lift in Flinders Lane, around lunchtime. The plan was that I would then try to make my way to the Grand Final Parade. Unfortunately, as luck would have it, some Collingwood supporter managed to get himself stuck in a lift at RMIT and we had to free him. In all, I missed out on the Grand Final Parade, but to my surprised my father had managed to go with my youngest sister, boasting at the dinner table that he managed to shake hands with Gary Ablett snr.

Grand Final day arrived and at 10am, at my parents Reservoir home, where I still lived, there was a knock on the door. A physically challenged turd-looking man in an Adidas tracksuit, which was too small for his under exercised body, asked for Anthony Cappello. I answered the door and replied that I was Anthony Cappello. He then handed me an envelope and then ran or rolled back to his Volvo.

Could these be Grand Final tickets? Did I have a Fairy Godmother, dressed like a turd who drives a Volvo? I opened the envelope and to my horror it was a summons to appear in court. What a way to celebrate Grand Final day. As an 18 year old with a licence, I managed to run my car off the road into someone's front garden in Bulleen. At the time, I was relieved that I had done no damage to the house or my car. I had to pay $180 for a tow truck and then apologised to the owners who were thankful that I didn't join them for dinner with my Mazda. What I didn't expect was a later claim for the whole re-landscape of their entire front garden as a result of my expected visit. When I denied I had done really that much damaged, I never heard from them again, until the turd with the Volvo turned up and handed me a summons.

With my world in chaos – and over and over again in my life when my world be in chaos – I would be distracted by my beloved Geelong Football Club. But the summons could wait as the siren sounded, the Grand Final with, yes; Geelong, had commenced.

My recollection of the first quarter was not the carnage being done to the Hawthorn Football Club players, Brereton, Dipper, etc., but the carnage being done to the Geelong Football Club on the scoreboard. I had started in the same room as my father, but as the goals went in, his theory of the conspiracy sounded out, as if he was a unionist at a picket line. I don't remember the words, just the annoying sound of an angry man. Now I had moved in the lounge room, that Italians tend to use as a museum, no one ever goes in there, unless you a long-time friend from Italy, then you have the honour of entering the lounge room.

The first quarter was over, Geelong was behind by 40 points. I was devastated, heart broken and in agony. My youngest sister attempted to enter the lounge to offer me a coffee, but after poking her head into the room she decided not to enter.

The rest of the game we were on catch up, and that final quarter saw me on my knees begging for a miracle. If Mecca was North then my prayers went unanswered. The miracle never came and Geelong had lost the most remarkable Grand Final by a goal. Gary Ablett senior received the Norm Smith, but it was a small consolation. That Holy Grail alluded me, and I went to bed that night with the chaos of my life surrounding me. What if, and different scenarios played out in my mind, the emptiness was overwhelming and the morning took forever to come. I didn't enter a deep sleep, I just couldn't sleep.

Of course, I endured three more Grand Finals with the same result. But this all changed in 2007. The Channel Ten pre-game promo, brought back the pain of 1989, with the song, Forever Young, as it introduced the Grand Final. Here the stern faces of those Geelong players who missed out in 1989, 1992, 1994, and 1995 was inserted into a painful montage. Could this team in 2007 make it all better? As the montage claimed, their tears (and mine) could live on or be resurrected in the team of 2007.

Geelong thrashed Port Adelaide that day, in fact by a mere 119 points. The Holy Grail had been achieved, but that night in 2007, after the game, all I wanted to do was go to bed. Once in bed, I fell into a deep sleep. It was here that a lifetime of memories came flooding back, my childhood, those losses, those memories, of me and my uncle at Kardinia Park, the forward line dliemmas and a smile that my father and his conspiracy theory was finally proven wrong!

Dr Anthony Cappello

Anthony Cappello was born and bred in the Melbourne suburb of Preston, where he played three games of Aussie Rules football for Marist Brothers Preston during 1983 season. The son of Italian immigrant parents, he worked as a Lift Mechanic for Edminston and O'Neill Lift Services before attending Yarra Theological Union where he completed a Bachelor of Theology. This was followed by an MA and a PhD at Victoria University. Dr Cappello is the founder and a director of Connor Court Publishing – the publishers of this book.

36

The Drawn VFL Grand Final of 1977

Andrew Ireland

I've never felt so numb than I did sitting on the MCG at about 5.30pm on Saturday 24 September 1977. I didn't know what to feel or what to do as an extraordinary range of emotions flooded across the hallowed turf.

A stadium that only minutes earlier had been packed with 108,224 screaming fans may as well have been empty for all I knew or cared after the VFL grand final had finished in a draw.

Like 19 Collingwood teammates and 20 North Melbourne opponents I was overcome by a feeling of emptiness and the unanswerable question of "what happens now?" as an eerie silence hung over the magnificent stadium on one of the great days on the Australian sporting calendar.

It was supposed to be a turning point in Collingwood Football Club history, and the highlight of my career. The day when arguably Australia's most famous club killed off the dreaded 'Colliewobbles' and a no-frills Magpies half back flanker lived out a life time dream.

Four times since their last flag in 1958 Collingwood had played in the grand final. And four times they had lost. Not again. Surely not, I thought. And definitely not when we led an out-of-sorts North Melbourne by 27 points at three-quarter time.

But instead of the glorious victory that beckoned we were left with the most hollow feeling imaginable. A feeling that came with the inconclusiveness of a drawn grand final, and got immeasurably worse seven days later when Collingwood lost the replay by 27 points.

It was Collingwood 9-12 (66) to North 4-15 (39) at three-quarter time in the first grand final of '77, after North had been held goalless in the second and third quarters. How they were able to walk away from the biggest game of the year with their premiership dream still alive was a phenomenal effort.

But this was no ordinary North side. They'd been premiers for the first time in club history in 1975 and were playing in their fourth consecutive grand final, having lost to Richmond in '74 and Hawthorn in '76. And they were not about to surrender without the fight of a lifetime.

Even before the grand final it had been a golden year for Collingwood. Having finished wooden-spooners under Murray Weidemann in 1976 with a miserable 6-16 win/loss record, we'd recruited four-time premiership coach Tommy Hafey from Richmond to take charge of a rebuild. Max Richardson began what would be a one-year stint as captain, replacing Des Tuddenham.

It had been a remarkable turnaround. We'd gone 18-4 through the home-and-away season, and had an aggregate losing margin of 46 points. Three times we'd been beaten by less than 10 points.

In Round 4 we beat Richmond by 26 points in front of 92,436 people at the MCG. It was Tommy's first game coaching against his former club and an early forerunner for what would later become a regular AFL showcase event on Anzac Day. Even then I had a feeling that special things would follow for a Collingwood side playing with a real unity and purpose.

But I nearly wasn't part of it. In Round 8 against St. Kilda at Victoria Park I smashed my arm. Having tackled the Saints' Trevor Barker I turned him around and into the path of my rampaging Collingwood teammate Kevin Worthington.

In his efforts to clean up the Saints pin-up boy, 'Wortho' succeeded only in putting me in hospital via a collision which broke my arm above the elbow. The bone shot up into my shoulder and my arm was literally 15cm shorter than normal.

I was carried off on a stretcher and it was fair to sign my prospects didn't look bright.

The experts decided not to operate and instead they reset my arm manually. For many weeks I slept sitting upright in a bean bag on my bed in the hope that gravity would help it heal.

I did my rehabilitation in the new Bolte Wing of St. Vincent's Hospital, which was the popular destination for car accident victims. In comparison to patients who had lost limbs and even worse I was fine, but a grand final seemed a long, long way off.

Eventually it did, and after one game in the Reserves I returned in Round 21 to a senior side that had sat on top of the ladder since Round 6 and was set for one almighty assault on the finals.

We finished one game clear of defending premiers Hawthorn (17-5) and two games ahead of North (16-6), with Richmond (14-1-7) and South Melbourne (13-1-8) making up the final five. Collingwood enjoyed a week off in week one of the finals as Richmond eliminated South by 34 points, and Hawthorn beat North by 38.

The following week North bounced back to beat Richmond by 47 points, and Collingwood came from 17 points down at quarter-time to beat Hawthorn by two. Ronnie Wearmouth had 31 possessions, the second-highest tally in his 186-game career, and Phil Carmen and Peter Moore kicked four goals.

But in a defining moment in Collingwood history Carman was reported for striking Hawthorn's Michael Tuck with a forearm and suspended for two matches. He would miss not one grand final but two in a body blow which ultimately we could not overcome.

Tommy was as filthy as I ever saw him. Carman had kicked 41 goals that year, behind only Peter Moore (76) and Graeme Anderson (46) in our side, and was the best player in the game at the time. His absence had a two-fold effect. Not only did we miss his brilliance but it meant we had to switch Ross 'Twiggy' Dunne from a half forward role in which he was nearly unstoppable to a less suitable role at centre half forward. No doubt if Carman had played in the grand final we would have won.

In the preliminary final, as the Pies enjoyed another week off, North held Hawthorn to five goals and won by 67 points. Barry Cable collected 38 possessions, second-highest in his decorated career, and kicked three goals.

In the traditional Monday night opening to grand final week my Collingwood teammate Billy Picken finished third in the Brownlow Medal behind South's Graham Teasdale and Richmond's Kevin Bartlett. Len

Thompson, who would later win the Collingwood B&F, was equal fourth in the medal with Hawthorn's Leigh Matthews and Carlton's Bruce Doull.

I was a 24-year-old still living at home with my parents at the time as I prepared for my 44th VFL game and my first grand final. Working full-time at the club, I'd spent a lot of time during the week helping friends get grand final tickets.

It was a frantic time and an historic time in football history. It was the first grand final televised live, and from memory it was the first year of color television. For the first time, too, we had the now traditional grand final parade through the streets of Melbourne on the Friday before the game, and for the first time there would be pre-game entertainment at the grand final. I can still remember hearing Barry Crocker belting out 'The Incredible Dream' from deep in the MCG rooms prior to the first bounce.

My preparation wasn't exactly faultless. On the Thursday night at training in twinged my hamstring. It wasn't too bad and we agreed I'd play with a little local anaesthetic. After all, I only had one game to get through. Little did we know!

At selection Tommy made only one change to the semi-final side, including Shane Bond to replace the suspended Carmen.

The Collingwood side was:

B: Robert Hyde (dvc), Kevin Worthington, Doug Gott
HB: Andrew Ireland, Billy Picken, Phil Manassa
C: Ricky Barham, Stan Magro, Wayne Gordon
HF: Wayne Richardson, Ross Dunne, Graeme Anderson
F: Peter Moore, Rene Kink, Ray Shaw
R: Len Thompson (vc), Max Richardson (c), Ronnie Wearmouth
Res: Gerald Betts, Shane Bond
Coach: Tom Hafey

North Melbourne, led by David Dench in the absence of injured captain Keith Greig, went in unchanged from the preliminary final.

The North side was:

B: Ross Henshaw, David Dench (a/c), Frank Gumbleton
HB: Gary Cowton, Darryl Sutton, Ken Montgomery
C: Stan Alves, Xavier Tanner, Wayne Schimmelbusch (a/vc)
HF: Steven Icke, Malcolm Blight, Arnold Breidis
F: Brent Crosswell, Phil Baker, John Cassin

R: Peter Keenan, John Byrne, Barry Cable
Res: Stephen McCann, Bill Nettlefold
Coach: Ron Barassi

It was a fluctuating affair. North led 4-4 to 1-5 at quarter-time and 4-10 to 4-8 at halftime. Collingwood kicked 5-4 to 0-5 in the third quarter to take control as the Kangaroos kicked 13 consecutive behinds from the 24-minute mark of the first quarter. Arnold Breidis finished with seven behinds without a major score.

But North kicked the first five goals of the final term after Darryl Sutton, swung to full forward by coach Ron Barassi in what proved a three-quarter time master stroke, had kicked the first. Phil Baker kicked two goals in a row late in the game to take his tally for the day to six and all of a sudden the Roos were in front.

But with 40 seconds to play Dunne took a terrific pack mark 20m from goal straight in front. A very reliable torpedo kick, he stuck with what he knew best and found the goals under enormous pressure to tie the scores.

Then came a passage of play I'll never forget. I'd played on Malcolm Blight throughout the day and had done OK, but I could have made an absolute goose of myself in what proved to be the last marking contest of the game.

I'm not sure what came over me, but with three North players around me as the ball was kicked into the North scoring zone I decided rather than punch it away, as I should have done, I went for the mark. If I'd dropped it they would almost certainly have scored to win the game, but luckily it stuck and a mongrel kick out to Bond on the wing was enough for time to run out.

The final score was Collingwood 10-16 (76) to North 9-22 (76).

Ken Montgomery led the possession count for North with 26 while Wayne Richardson did likewise for Collingwood with 24. Peter Moore kicked four goals.

It was the second drawn VFL grand final after Essendon suffered a similarly costly attack of the kicking woes in 1948. That game finished Melbourne 10-9 (69) to Essendon 7-27 (69) before Melbourne won the replay by 39 points.

As we trudged off the ground we had more questions than answers.

What do we do next? How do go from utter devastation to get ready to do it all again?

The first commitment after the normal warm-down was the pre-planned Grand Final Dinner at the Windsor Hotel. It was as flat a night as you can imagine. We'd been 27 points up at three-quarter time and failed to get home.

I did what most players did on a Saturday night in the 1970's ... I had a few drinks. It was the norm. What wasn't so normal was the harassment my parents went through at home, answering countless calls from people looking to avoid an overnight sleep out and get tickets for the replay.

As you are prone to do after a drawn game, especially a drawn grand final, I thought back over all the one-on-one contests and pondered what I could have done differently.

In particular I remembered a contest in the fourth quarter when Picken at centre half back had tried to pass the ball to me up on the wing. His kick fell short and rolled out to the members' wing, sending me on a long chase with North's Wayne Schimmelbusch.

"Schimma" was first to the ball and tumbled it forward. From the ensuing scrimmage in the goal mouth it was punched through for a behind. "What if?" I thought.

For more than 20 years that same image kept reappearing in my head. Over and over again. I wouldn't call it a nightmare, but it wasn't a pleasant memory. And it wasn't until the Brisbane Lions beat Essendon in the 2001 grand final and I'd tasted that unforgettable success as a CEO that it stopped. Never again did I have that recurring dream.

The job of getting the players up for the grand final replay fell to Tommy. It was business as usual.

A normal Hafey week back then, when all games were played at 2pm on Saturday, was Sunday recovery, Monday running, Tuesday a solid two hours, Wednesday a light run and Thursday about ninety minutes. Friday off. So that's what we did in grand final replay week.

I was a big Tommy fan, and it didn't escape me that when we didn't train as hard as normal throughout the year we were beaten so I had no issues. If we didn't train as hard as we did we may not have reached the grand final. And we'd had two weeks off during the finals while North had played every week.

Still, with the benefit of hindsight and the huge changes to modern preparation techniques that were to follow, I'm not so convinced that perhaps a lighter training load might not have been a better option.

It didn't matter to Doug Gott, who had cracked his knee cap in the first grand final. A Victorian cricketer who, like me had attended Northcote High School and played at Ivanhoe Amateurs, he never played again. He finished with 97 career games.

Chris Perry, who hadn't played since Round 18 due to injury, was recalled for the replay in the only change to the Collingwood side. North again went in with the same 20.

In front of 98,366 the replay didn't live up to the same heights. With Breidis kicking five goals after shaking off his kicking woes of a week earlier, North led throughout. They were six goals up before a 10-minute Magpies burst cut the margin to 11 points at halftime.

The Kangaroos, though, regained the ascendancy in a third quarter which is best remembered for a remarkable Phil Manassa goal in which he left Blight in his wake, bouncing the ball four times running from half back.

Peter Moore kicked five goals while Manassa kicked three goals and had a team-high 21 possessions. John Byrne (29) and Breidis (28) led the possession count for North.

Moore also ensured that grand final runners-up medals were awarded for the first and last time in 1977. He was so disappointed by the result he hurled his medal into the crowd. It was a heavy thing and could have nearly killed someone if it hit them in the head.

Thirty-three years on a third VFL/AFL grand final was drawn when St. Kilda and Collingwood finished level in 2010. And on that occasion the Pies won the replay by a thumping 56 points.

Coincidentally, 24 hours after Collingwood and North Melbourne played an epic draw in '77 the first drawn rugby league grand final in Australia was played between St. George and Parramatta. They finished 9-9 after extra time. Seven days later St. George won the replay 22-0.

In '78, too, the rugby league grand final was drawn between Manly and Cronulla at 11-11. This time there was no extra time and Manly won the replay on the following Tuesday 16-0.

The NRL very nearly had a third draw in 2015 when the grand final between Brisbane and North Queensland was level at the end of normal time before North Queensland took it in golden point. A field goal from Johnathan Thurston decided the premiership.

This prompted widespread debate on what is the best method. Having played in a draw and three losses I can tell you neither is especially palatable, but I could never come at a golden point outcome in the AFL. Imagine a rushed behind deciding a flag. No thanks.

Perhaps I could be convinced to play extra time, as is the AFL policy in all lead-up finals, but if scores are still level I'm all for a replay. It's a unique part of our unique game.

Andrew Ireland

Andrew Ireland has enjoyed a phenomenal career in the VFL/AFL over more than 40 years as a player and administrator, and has been among the game's most influential and successful figures in the development markets of Queensland and New South Wales. He played 110 games including four grand finals for Collingwood from 1975-80 before cutting short his playing career and heading north to move into administration. He served as State Director of Coaching with the then Queensland Australian Football League (1981-86) and later was QAFL General Manager (1986-90).

He returned to the elite competition in 1990, taking over as Brisbane Bears Chief Executive and driving the club's pivotal relocation from Carrara on the Gold Coast to the Gabba in Brisbane in 1993. He also played a crucial role in the Bears' historic 1996 merger with foundation VFL club Fitzroy to form the Brisbane Lions, and was Lions CEO until 2001 when the club won an historic AFL premiership. Thereafter he was lured south to join the Sydney Swans, serving as the club's General Manager-Football (2002-09), Chief Executive (2010-2014) and CEO/Managing Director (2015-Current). Under his leadership the Swans won the premiership in 2005 and 2012. He was awarded AFL Life Membership in 2006.

37

An Inspirational Journey with No. 37

Michael O'Loughlin

When I look back on the 17 or so years I have known Adam Goodes – there is no shortage of heartfelt moments and memories we have shared – good and bad – that I could recount. We have been team mates, we are relatives, we are best mates and he is the godfather of my three children. On field and off field, we have shared an unbelievable journey.

Rather than moments, I look at the journey in its entirety. I look back at a 17-year-old aboriginal kid who walked through the doors at the SCG – who had no idea what he was stepping into – and his rise to become one of the most significant sportsmen, and leaders of recent times. For me to witness that journey, and more significantly, be part of it, has been a joy. An inspiration. When you look at the journey, it just stirs so many emotions.

Our journey started with a phone call to Adam after his name was called at pick 43 in the 1997 national draft. When his name was read out, my mum said 'that is your relative'. 'Really?', I asked. She proceeded to tell me the story of his mother Lisa and how we are connected. I rang to welcome him to club and tell him that I looked forward to meeting him. We probably didn't meet for another few weeks but once we did I took it upon myself to look after him. He was always pretty smart but I just made sure he was doing the right things with his training and eating. And to just to make sure he had someone he could chat to. There was no magic moment where we became instant mates for life – but the journey started and we grew together from there.

There are so many amazing footy moments that we have shared since that day. Winning finals, winning premierships, winning Brownlows and playing in milestones and record breaking games. We have been so lucky in our careers to share so many brilliant moments.

One of the most memorable moments for me was not playing alongside Adam, but watching him from the stands. The 2012 Grand Final was – and I keep using this word, one of the most memorable moments for me was not playing alongside Adam, but watching him from the stands. The 2012 Grand Final was – and I keep using this word, and will many times again – inspirational. While Adam had built a reputation for his speed, power and skill, it was what he did on one leg that day after tearing his medial ligament in the first quarter, that will stick with me forever. When you are in a big game, a tight game, on one leg, you have to dig deep and find something. It doesn't always go to plan, but he found a way that day to make a massive impact. That goal in last quarter – you can't teach that stuff. That was just pure class. It was incredible. That performance to me, as someone sitting in the stands, was as emotional as any I ever shared playing alongside Adam. There were plenty of tears that day. To me, it was perhaps Adam's most significant performance on the field in his distinguished career.

Six months down the track, back on the MCG, he would add another significant moment when he called out racism in the stands during the final quarter of the Indigenous Round game against Collingwood. I was commentating in the box for channel seven that night and it was very hard to talk about. I didn't know what was said, what had happened.

After the game, Adam was visibly upset and I spoke to him and the most disappointing thing for him was that she was so young. If it was some bloke who was drunk, he probably wouldn't have cared as much, but he just really felt for the young lady. He was genuinely upset that she was yelling out and didn't understand. While everyone wanted to have their say on it, I look on that incident and it strikes me that it took some serious balls to do what he did. To call out that casual racism that is just so prevalent in our society. Clearly, racism is around when a young girl can say what she said and not understand. She learned that from someone.

He did the right thing that night. He re-started a conversation we needed to have about racism, something that Nicky Winmar had done 20 years earlier when he lifted his guernsey and pointed proudly to his skin. He was articulate, and too any people forget how compassionate he was to that girl. He didn't blame her, he just wanted her – and as a result many, many more Australians – to understand how it hurts.

I use the word 'proud' a lot when talking about Adam. When he was named Australian of the year at the start of 2014 – pride, again. What an honour. I couldn't contain my excitement for him. I called him as soon it was announced and let him know just how proud I was. The way he handled himself during that time was amazing. As a kid, he didn't have the courage to stand up for who he was. It's hard. But footy gave him the confidence and gave him the platform where he knew he could be an important role model for all people. When you have the courage to stand up for what you are passionate about, inevitably – unfortunately – people will try and cut you down.

For me – to see him go through what he did in the latter part of his career – it's really hard to watch and listen. Harder for Adam – obviously – but for me it has been terrible. The booing. The negative energy directed at Adam, most significantly in his final year, was heartbreaking. Disgusting.

Watching the Swans round 17 game against West Coast in Perth on TV was probably the most emotional I've ever been with my kids, when my son James asked – 'why are those people booing uncle (Adam)?' It was really hard to explain. 'Has he done something wrong?' he asked.

That is when I paused the TV and explained that there are people out there who want to get under your skin. He responded by saying, 'that isn't fair'. I was so angry. It was first time I'd wanted to turn off a Swans game. I spoke to James about jealously, a little about racism and how do you react to that. When people do the wrong thing you need to call them out. It was a really difficult conversation to have with a seven year old.

I spoke to Adam after that game and when he returned to Sydney. It was probably the toughest week I've had during our jounrey. I know he needed space to do what he needed to do. He need to get away, and that meant I couldn't be there to wrap my arms around him. It was hard. As he took the time away he needed, I went to the SCG for the Swans and Adelaide game. It was incredibly emotional for me to see that support for Adam. The Swans people were just incredible and I know, although he only saw half of the game, that he felt it too. That support helped bring him back to the game. No doubt.

Would the 17 year old kid who walked through the SCG doors be able to handle what he went through in 2015? No. But seeing his transition into a strong, proud, black, passionate leader has been inspiring.

Michael O'Loughlin

Michael O'Loughlin played 303 matches with the Swans, kicking 521 goals. He is a member of both the Swans and the Australian Football Hall of Fame. He is currently head coach of the QBE Sydney Swans Academy and is the co-founder of the GO Foundation, which provides educational scholarships for Indigenous children, along with former teammate, friend and relative Adam Goodes.

Adam Goodes, Sydney
Courtesy News Ltd

Epilogue

The Highs and Lows of Aussie Rules Football Weather

Weatherman Dick

The Grand Final of 2015 was notable from at least two standpoints. Firstly Hawthorn, by defeating the West Coast Eagles, managed that rare achievement of winning three consecutive Premierships, the first side to do so since the magic run of Brisbane during 2001, 2002 and 2003.

Secondly, this was the hottest Grand Final ever, with the mercury climbing to 31.3 C. This beat the old record of 30.7C, set on 26 September 1987. On that day, Carlton had a solid victory against Hawthorn, with the final score-line reading 15.14 (104) to 9.17 (71).

At the other end of the temperature scale was the 1958 Grand Final when heavy rain during the match slowed the pacy Melbourne Demons down and the gritty Collingwood side got up for one of the biggest upsets of all time. Melbourne were hot favourites having smashed the Magpies by 45 points in the second semi final and most assumed that the Demons had the game pretty well sewn up.

Some tough tactics by the Magpies captain Murray Weideman, playing at centre half forward, and Barry "Hooker" Harrison, the ruck-rover, helped Collingwood defeat Melbourne, 12.10 (82) to 9.10 (64). On this day, the 20th September 1958, the temperature only managed to reach a winter-like maximum of 11.3C, making this the coldest Aussie Rules Grand Final Day on record.

Other aspects of the weather, as well as temperature, have played a crucial part in key football matches of the past – with some rather strange consequences.

In the extraordinary preliminary final of 1921 between Carlton and

Richmond, the match was delayed after a massive hailstorm carpeted the MCG in ice. A contemporary newspaper report noted that: *'The hailstones averaged the size of pigeon-eggs, and some were as big as a fist, jagged pieces of ice that were a menace to those unsheltered on the banks. The field was a mound of crystal, a lake of crushed ice, white as snow".* For the record, Richmond won the game that day, defeating the Blues 67 points to 59.

The 1927 Grand Final was more of a regatta than a footy match with torrential rain falling throughout the game, turning the field into a quagmire. Craftily coached by the legendary Jock McHale, the Collingwood side played superior wet weather football and beat Richmond 2.13 (25) to 1.7 (13), in what turned out to be the lowest aggregate score for any Grand Final.

The Australian Rules Football Carnival of July 1950 was a much-anticipated event with the participating States fielding their strongest sides to battle for the prestigious title of national champion team.

For the first time an interstate Aussie Rules carnival was held in Brisbane, in an attempt to promote the game in Queensland. Normally July is one of the drier months of the year in Brisbane, but July 1950 turned out to be the third wettest July on record, with a total of 218 mm falling for the month, compared to the long-term average of 51 mm. This resulted in the playing surface at the Brisbane Exhibition Ground degenerating into an absolute bog.

Ground conditions were utterly appalling. Indeed the mud was so bad that many competing players suffered from a rash and throughout the carnival penicillin ointment was widely used.

South Australia had a particularly strong side, including John Marriott, Jack Oatey, Dick Russell, Brian Burke and Ray Whitaker. Another notable player was Eddie Tilley, one time captain of Sturt, who was both a great player and a tough one, entirely capable of handing out some rough justice if required. Tilley was set to retire after the Carnival with the game between South Australia and Victoria scheduled to be his last.

Although the legendary Jack Dyer of Richmond – widely known as "Captain Blood" – was no longer playing football, he attended the Carnival as a journalist. Renowned for creating mischief on and off the field, Dyer approached Tilley before the match, urging him to go out in a blaze of glory. Dyer nominated four Victorian players that were "weakies" who could be put off their game by some tough play. He persuaded Tilley to take them on.

Unknown to Tilley, the players nominated were possibly the meanest quartet in the entire VFL - Ted Jarrard, Don ("Mopsy") Fraser, Charlie Sutton, and Gordon Hocking. Fraser in particular was a brilliant player, but possessed a volcanic temper that had seen him suspended for an incredible 86 matches of football.

Dyer described what happened in the first quarter: "Crash. Down went Jarrard in the mud. Tilley caught him a beauty and must have been thinking how easy it all was. He didn't for long. Ted dragged himself from that foot of mud. His eyes were blazing and you could see the whites of the eyes of Mopsy, Sutton and Hocking. They descended on the luckless Tilley in a pack. They drove his body two feet into the mud. They went berserk". In fact, Frank ("Checker") Hughes, the Victorian coach, was screaming at the bleeding Jarrard to get off the ground because he was scared of him getting tetanus!

Following a rough, bloody, muddy match, Victoria emerged the winners, beating South Australia 68 points to 39. After the game Dyer ducked for cover but Tilley found him. "Aw Jack, what have you done to me? That was a nice bunch of weakies you set me on to!"

As well as heat and rain, there have also been numerous occasions where the wind has influenced an Aussie Rules football match. Again one of the most humorous accounts is by Jack Dyer in his best-selling book "Captain Blood", published in 1965.

In a game between North Melbourne and Carlton in early 1940 a westerly gale was blowing down Princes Park before the start of a match when the two captains (Dally O'Brien for North, who was notoriously hard of hearing, and Carlton's hardman Bob Chitty) came to the centre for the coin toss. To win this would prove a tremendous advantage.

Dyer recalled: "O'Brien tossed the coin and Chitty opened his mouth, pretending to call. The coin fell heads, Chitty had a good look and O'Brien cocked an ear and asked "What did you call Chit?" "Heads", roared Chitty and signalled his side to kick with the gale. They kicked six goals in no time and won easily.

Weather in its many forms has played a key role in the history of our great game.

It can still cause issues that are taken into account by the coaches, players and administrators before and during each match. Wet weather drills may be considered by the coach, player cooling prepared for hot days and special tactics used for windy conditions.

Like much else in life, the weather itself is out of our control. The reality is that it can bring out the best and the worst in footballers, and their coaches. As Bill Bowerman, co-founder of Nike said: "There's no such thing as bad weather, just soft people!"

> **Weatherman Dick** is the nom de plume of a well-known Australian meteorologist who has a great interest in both weather and Aussie Rules football. Dick is a Swans tragic and has been a member of the club since 1993.

Jock McHale, brilliant coaching in the "Downpour" Grand Final in 1927 brought Collingwood across the line for a 12-point win in atrocious conditions. In a record low grand final score Collingwood 2.13(25) defeated Richmond 1.7(13)

Image: Wikipedia Commons

www.ingramcontent.com/pod-product-compliance
Ingram Content Group UK Ltd.
Pitfield, Milton Keynes, MK11 3LW, UK
UKHW021324180426
11947UKWH00017B/1428